FROZEN IN TIME

FROZEN

IN TIME

A Minnesota North Stars History

ADAM RAIDER

University of Nebraska Press | Lincoln

The University of Nebraska Press is part of a land-grant
institution with campuses and programs on the past,
present, and future homelands of the Pawnee, Ponca,
Otoe-Missouria, Omaha, Dakota, Lakota, Kaw, Chey-
enne, and Arapaho Peoples, as well as those of the relocated Ho-Chunk, Sac and Fox, and Iowa Peoples.

First Nebraska paperback printing: 2023

Library of Congress Cataloging-in-Publication Data
Raider, Adam.
Frozen in time: a Minnesota North Stars history /
Adam Raider.
pages   cm
Includes bibliographical references.
ISBN 978-0-8032-4998-1 (hardcover: alk. paper)
ISBN 978-1-4962-3754-5 (paperback)
ISBN 978-0-8032-8639-9 (epub)
ISBN 978-0-8032-8640-5 (mobi)
ISBN 978-0-8032-8641-2 (pdf)
1. Minnesota North Stars (Hockey team)—
History. I. Title.
GV848.M56R35 2014
796.962'6409776579—dc23
2014020827

Set in Lyon Text by L. Auten.

For Amy and Evelyn, *the best line-mates a guy could have.*

CONTENTS

ILLUSTRATIONS

PREFACE

In 2010 a friend gave me his extra ticket to the Winter Classic at Fenway Park. The Boston Bruins were hosting the Philadelphia Flyers, but I didn't much care who was playing. To me the Winter Classic is a celebration of hockey that transcends team affiliation. That's why, in a stadium of thirty-eight thousand spectators, I was one of the few not wearing any Bruins or Flyers paraphernalia. Instead I wore a vintage Dave Gagner North Stars jersey. It's green and gold and bright enough to burn your retinas. All skiers and mountain climbers should wear North Stars jerseys so they can be found by rescue teams after avalanches.

I had just passed through the turnstiles on Yawkey Way when I heard someone call out in a Boston accent as thick as the sludge at the bottom of the Charles River, "NAWTH STAAHHS!"

I turned to see a Bruins fan walking in my direction and smiling from ear to ear.

"Awesome jersey, bro!"

And it was like that all afternoon. People actually stopped to take my picture. I felt like a celebrity, but without the entourage, Botox forehead, or disposable income. The pure, almost childlike joy that this jersey inspired in others reminded me that hockey fans, perhaps more than fans of any other sport, have a wonderful appreciation for the history of the game.

I'm honored that you've chosen to join me on this journey into hockey's colorful past and pleased that I finally have an opportunity (in print!) to thank everyone who helped make it possible.

I'll start with Rob Taylor and all my new friends at the University of Nebraska Press, who agreed that there's always room on the shelf for one more book about a defunct hockey team.

It was my good friend and occasional writing partner, Russ Cohen, who first suggested that I approach this particular publisher. After years of employing selective auditory attention in our conversations, I'm so glad that I finally took Russ's advice about something.

My agent, Laurie Hawkins, championed this project far longer than any sane person should have. Her steadfast advocacy should (but probably won't) teach me the virtue of patience.

I am eternally grateful to the players, coaches, journalists, broadcasters, fans, and others who graciously gave of their time in interviews. This work is greatly enriched by their insights and anecdotes.

A debt of gratitude is owed the Dallas Stars organization for providing me with access to a mountain of research material as well as photos from the team archives.

Additional images were provided by the Terrence Fogarty Studio, the Oshawa Generals, the University of Minnesota–Duluth, and USA Hockey.

Thanks also to my Buffalo connection, Eric Reich and Dave Ricci, for their editorial support, and to Bob and Julie Dill for the same.

Closer to home, I'm grateful for the love and encouragement I've received from my family, especially my wife, Amy, and my daughter, Evelyn, who didn't always understand why Daddy had to lock himself away in his office on nights and weekends but greeted me with hugs whenever I emerged.

FROZEN IN TIME

~~STEALING~~ BORROWING CANADA'S GAME

It was nearly 1:30 a.m. on June 19, 1999, when Dallas Stars winger Brett Hull shoveled the puck past Buffalo Sabres goalie Dominik Hasek, ending one of the longest playoff games in the history of the National Hockey League and earning the Stars their first Stanley Cup.

Up in the Twin Cities, devotees of the erstwhile Minnesota North Stars could be forgiven for not dancing in the streets. The team's controversial flight from Bloomington six years earlier remained a sore subject, but for those who still carried a torch for the North Stars, Hull's goal was cause for a decidedly muted celebration.

"Secretly," confessed one closet loyalist, "I was thrilled to see Dallas win the Stanley Cup because I still had feelings for some of the former North Star players. Some of my friends might have hanged me if they knew I was cheering for the Dallas Stars, so I watched the games alone. Although they left town, in my jealous heart the Stars were still *our* team."

Jealousy. One can't have jealousy without passion, and Minnesotans have always been passionate about hockey. On a landscape dotted with frozen ponds and lakes, it's no wonder that they were among the first Americans to embrace the sport. In fact, Minnesota is believed to be the site of the first organized hockey game played in the United States.

Hockey was really an outgrowth of ice polo, once a popular activity and the main winter sport in St. Paul. It was a game played outside with teams of six or seven players using short, curved sticks to whack a ball into a cage slightly smaller than today's soccer goals.

Ed Murphy, a young American athlete who had watched ice hockey in Canada and preferred it to ice polo, is credited for helping import the Canadian pastime to St. Paul in 1894.

On February 18, 1895, the University of Minnesota hockey team, comprising former football and ice polo players, squared off against a veteran squad from Winnipeg known as the Victorias. The visitors went on to beat the collegians, 11–3. It was a rough start for Minnesota in sanctioned competition, but the game was, by most accounts, well played and well attended.

Within a few years grade-school kids throughout the area were playing hockey, while adults took up the game at new public rinks. As the curtain closed on the nineteenth century, organized leagues began operating in other densely populated urban areas in the Midwest and the Northeast. Cities like Chicago, Detroit, Pittsburgh, Boston, Philadelphia, and New York gradually adopted Canada's game, but the craze began in Minnesota.

BUCKS AND PUCKS

It wasn't long before the most skilled skaters were playing for pay in professional circuits like the National Hockey Association, a union of Canadian-based clubs that was later reorganized into the National Hockey League. Although it once had as many as ten members, the NHL shrank to six teams in 1942 and would stay that way for the next twenty-five years.

Historians tend to have a highly romanticized view of hockey's Original Six era. After all, it was the age of Gordie Howe and Maurice (The Rocket) Richard, when sticks were still made of wood and the best seat in the house cost only five dollars. But it was also a time of competitive imbalance when league rules gave teams the territorial rights to every amateur player within a fifty-mile radius. That was great for teams located in or near Canada but lousy for everybody else. The small number of teams also severely limited player movement, making it even easier for the Montreal Canadiens, the Detroit Red Wings, and the Toronto Maple Leafs to perpetuate their dynasties. Between them those three clubs accounted for *twenty-four championships in twenty-five seasons.* Something had to change.

Over the years there was talk among league execs that the six-team NHL needed to expand in order to grow its business. Not everyone agreed.

Chicago Blackhawks owner Arthur Wirtz feared expansion would dilute the talent pool or destabilize the league. His partner, James Norris, predicted that expansion wouldn't earn the owners a nickel. "So the new guys cough up two million dollars for a franchise and players," he said. "How much will we see of that after taxes?"

A majority of owners came to recognize, however, that minor league hockey had enjoyed substantial growth in postwar America, proving that demand for their product existed outside those Original Six strongholds.

"We need a broader North American image," league president Clarence Campbell said. "Look at the map of the continent, and you see the NHL is a not very extensive group. We're in a small area. Hockey needs a broader base."

And with it, he hoped, a lucrative national television contract, as well as advertising and promotional tie-ins.

In the 1950s and early 1960s, the NHL flirted with expansion, entertaining applications from prospective ownership groups from all over the United States and Canada. But they were usually rejected because the league anticipated excessive travel costs or cited insufficient capital on the part of would-be franchise owners. So the status quo reigned until March 1965, when Campbell officially announced the NHL's plan to double in size from six to twelve teams beginning with the 1967–68 season.

A flood of applications poured in, with the NHL's Board of Governors facing the daunting task of deciding which markets could best support pro hockey. Groups from Baltimore, Buffalo, Cleveland, Philadelphia, San Francisco, and Vancouver were among the many eager suitors.

One market given very careful consideration was Minneapolis–St. Paul. The league respected Minnesota's rich tradition of amateur hockey and, perhaps more importantly, viewed the region as having achieved "big league" status thanks to the success of baseball's Twins and the NFL's Vikings. The state had also produced some of the few American-born NHL players up to that point. The city of Eveleth alone hatched goalies Frank (Mister Zero) Brimsek, Mike Karakas, and Sam LoPresti as well as defenseman John Mariucci.

Walter Bush Jr., a lawyer who once helped bring pro hockey to Minneapolis in the form of the Central Professional Hockey League's Minneapolis Bruins, lent instant credibility to one of two Minnesota expansion bids. He was joined by Bob McNulty, the construction mogul who would later develop Detroit's Joe Louis Arena, and Gordon Ritz, a television executive and former assistant publisher of *Sports Illustrated*.

Bush's credentials were impeccable and his passion for hockey undeniable. He had played the game at the Breck School in his native Minneapolis and at Dartmouth, and later, while working toward his law degree at the University of Minnesota, he helped organize the United States Central Hockey League, which eventually dropped the "Central" to become the USHL. He had also been involved with the U.S. National Team and the U.S. Olympic Team. In short, few men had done as much to promote and grow hockey in Minnesota and throughout the nation as Bush, and bringing the NHL to the Twin Cities area was simply part of a natural progression.

Following the model first laid out by the Vikings, Bush and company were careful to build an ownership group that represented the cities of Minneapolis and St. Paul equally: Bush, Ritz, McNulty, and Wheelock Whitney from Minneapolis and John Driscoll, Harry McNeely, John (Smokey) Ordway, and Bob Ridder from St. Paul (the "Minnesota Eight" eventually grew by one with the addition of St. Paul's Bill Rasmussen). Most of the investors had played hockey in college and graduated from

Ivy League schools. Their position was strengthened when a rival bid from a group headed by St. Paul attorney Joseph Maun dropped out.

The next two years were filled with much deliberation as applicant cities fell in and out of favor for one reason or another. Finally, on February 9, 1966, the NHL announced its six newest members: Los Angeles, San Francisco-Oakland, Philadelphia, Pittsburgh, St. Louis, and Minneapolis-St. Paul. Baltimore was named an alternate in case any newcomer dropped out or could not fulfill its obligations. Each new team would pay a $2 million expansion fee to be divided equally among the six existing teams.

The Twin Cites owned the smallest television market of the bunch. But the NHL didn't seem to mind . . . not as long as that $2 million check cleared.

The next order of business was finding a place for the new team to play. At the time the largest arena in the area was St. Paul Auditorium, but it seated only 8,500—well short of the 12,500 minimum capacity mandated by the league. Building a bigger, state-of-the-art facility was the only option. Talks began with the Metropolitan Sports Commission—overseers of the old Metropolitan Stadium—to get an arena built in Bloomington, a suburb between Minneapolis and St. Paul, because it was already home to the Twins and Vikings.

Initially, civic officials were cool to the plan. "I was flatly told, 'No, we're not building a new arena,'" Walter Bush recalled. "So we worked out a deal with the commission where we could build the arena on their land, turn it over to them, and then take back a thirty-year lease. Then, every time we had an event at the arena, we'd take a mythical 10 percent off for rent and keep track of it on a separate piece of paper. When the imaginary rent finally equaled what we paid for the building, then we started paying real money. It worked quite well."

The commission finally agreed to construction of the building, which would later be called Metropolitan Sports Center, or Met Center for short.

When a season ticket drive began, two groups of businessmen—one from St. Paul and one from Minneapolis—held a contest to see which city could sell the most tickets. Before it was over, six thousand were sold (nobody seems to remember who won the contest).

Bush and company let fans help decide what the team should be called. Among the suggested names were Blades, Norsemen, Lumberjacks, Mallards, Muskies, Puckaroos, and Voyageurs. But none of those rolled off the tongue like North Stars, the winning moniker derived from the state's motto, "L'Etoile du Nord," or "The Star of the North."

2

FIGHTING FOR RESPECT (1967–1978)

Expansion was the biggest thing ever to happen to the NHL, so in order for this brave initiative to be successful, the process by which new teams were stocked with players had to be reasonably equitable.

The plan approved by owners, but generally bemoaned by their general managers, called for an expansion draft to be held in the summer of 1967 in which existing teams were required to protect one goalie and eleven other players, exposing the rest to be claimed by the new clubs until each had a complete twenty-man roster.

The task of building the North Stars would not be easy, but Walter Bush was confident that he had someone who was up to the task. Tabbed to serve in the dual role of general manager and coach was Wren (The Bird) Blair, the former director of player personnel for the Boston Bruins noted for having once signed a fourteen-year-old prodigy out of Parry Sound, Ontario, named Bobby Orr. Previously, Blair ran Bush's Central Professional Hockey League (CPHL) team in Minneapolis.

Colleagues warned Blair to stay away from the expansion teams. "Why wouldn't you stay with the Bruins?" Boston GM Hap Emms needled Blair. "You're going to get fired—all the guys who take these jobs are going to get fired."

But Bird was enamored with the romantic idea of being the very first manager in the history of the North Stars, and he believed that among all the new teams, he stood the best chance of success with Minnesota. He knew that ownership would give him the control he needed to build the North Stars properly.

He also knew that at the expansion draft in Montreal, the North Stars would be picking from the flotsam and jetsam discarded by other teams. Almost without exception these were the locker-room malcontents, underachievers, career minor leaguers, washed-up has-beens, and fringe talents deemed expendable by the Original Six.

"We went into that draft and picked what we thought were the best players available," said Blair. "Then I took my scouts up to my hotel suite and tossed our player list on the coffee table. 'Now gentlemen,' I said, 'our first order of business is to get rid of these players as fast as we can.'"

Bird jettisoned as much dead weight as he could, but his roster was by no means devoid of talent. A few of the better acquisitions included Cesare Maniago, a tall and gangly goaltender cast off by the Rangers; Dave Balon, a two-way forward left unprotected by the Canadiens; and Bill Goldsworthy, a tough but skilled forward with roots in the Bruins system. Elmer (Moose) Vasko, a rugged defenseman who had played his whole career with Chicago, was coaxed out of retirement to give the young Minnesota squad a veteran presence on the blue line.

HE WORE THE NORTH STAR: DAVE BALON

That he could be used in almost any game situation is a major reason why Dave Balon was chosen fourteenth overall by the North Stars in the 1967 Expansion Draft.

Balon was a coach's dream: willing to venture into the dirty areas of the ice to battle for the puck and skilled enough to send over the boards for a power play. In his first and only season as a North Star, Balon posted what were then career highs in assists (32) and points (47) and was selected to play in his third NHL All-Star Game.

In June 1968 Wren Blair traded Balon back to his original team, the Rangers, in a three-for-one deal intended to boost the North Stars' depth. None of the new players came close to matching the success Balon would enjoy in New York.

Late in his career, Balon began to feel the effects of multiple sclerosis, a degenerative disease that attacks the central nervous system. He battled MS bravely for nearly thirty years until finally succumbing to the disease on May 29, 2007. He was sixty-eight.

"The first year that we were there," Maniago recalled, "the majority of us were in the same boat. We were basically castoffs riding the fence with the Original Six teams, and we pulled together because of that. Talk about team unity—it was there. No one wanted to disappoint each other. We were all there to pull our own load, and we molded into a pretty good team."

FACE-OFF

Construction crews were still installing seats at Met Center on the day of the North Stars' October 21 home opener. Nearly thirteen thousand fans were on hand along with Clarence Campbell to witness the team's first-ever game in Bloomington as it hosted Oakland. Bill Goldsworthy opened the scoring, and the North Stars skated to a 3–1 victory, the first in franchise history.

The North Stars, like their Western Division brethren from St. Louis, Philadelphia, or California, were considered huge underdogs in any contest against an Eastern Division foe. To garner even a tie against an Original Six team was considered a victory unto itself.

A few weeks later, a standing-room-only crowd of 15,128, at the time the largest ever to watch a hockey game in Minnesota, packed Met Center as the North Stars faced the defending Stanley Cup champion Maple Leafs.

Wren Blair's gang came out firing in the first period, outshooting Toronto 19–6. Leafs goalie Bruce Gamble held off the Minnesota surge until late in the first, when North Stars defenseman and team captain Bob Woytowich took a pass from left wing Ted Taylor and hammered the puck into the Toronto net. The Leafs countered on a long slap shot by Ron Ellis that eluded Maniago with only one second left in the period.

Minnesota's miserly defense held Toronto to only three shots in the second period, and the North Stars took the lead for good on a goal by left wing Andre Boudrias with just over two minutes remaining. Neither team scored in the third session, and Minnesota, which held the defending champs to just fourteen shots, had a 2–1 win.

In their debut campaign the North Stars went on to earn victories against all of the Original Six teams, except the Rangers.

THE FIREPLUG

Leo Boivin wasn't a mountain of muscle like Scott Stevens or Tim Horton—he stood about five feet eight and weighed no more than 185 pounds—but that low center of gravity helped make him one of the most devastating hitters of his era. In fact, Horton once commented that "Fireplug" was one of the toughest defensemen to beat in the league. A former captain of the Bruins who also played for the Red Wings and the Penguins, Boivin was traded by Pittsburgh to the North Stars in January 1969 and spent the final year and a half of his Hall of Fame career doing what he did best: breaking up rushes with his trademark hip checks, then skating away with the puck.

AN EARLY TRAGEDY

Bill Masterton was a Winnipeg native and former All-American at the University of Denver whose dreams of NHL stardom were rekindled by the Great Expansion.

After college Masterton signed with the Montreal Canadiens but was immediately assigned to the minor leagues. After finishing sixth in American Hockey League (AHL) scoring with the Cleveland Barons in 1962–63, he went into semiretirement and took a regular job in contract administration at Honeywell because he knew he had no shot at cracking the loaded Habs roster.

He returned to hockey and bounced around the USHL for a couple of seasons, including a stint with the St. Paul Steers, before joining the U.S. National Team.

That's where the six-feet, 186-pound forward first caught the eye of Wren Blair, who liked Masterton's style and encouraged him to reconsider a career in pro hockey. Masterton agreed to give it another shot, and Blair purchased Bill's rights from the Canadiens.

1. Bill Masterton. Graphic Artists/ Hockey Hall of Fame

Remembered as quiet and gentlemanly, Masterton scored the first goal in the regular season history of the North Stars, on October 11, 1967, at St. Louis in a 2–2 tie with the Blues. Sadly, his name is a notable one in the annals of hockey for a different reason.

Three months later, on the night of January 13, 1968, the first-place North Stars hosted the Seals at Met Center. Less than five minutes into the game, Masterton skated toward the Oakland goal with linemate Wayne Connelly. Just as he slid a pass to Connelly, Masterton was checked cleanly by Oakland's Ron Harris and then collided with Seals defenseman Larry Cahan. Masterton bounced off Cahan and was sent hurling backward, striking his head on the ice with such violent force that blood gushed from his nose and ears.

Unconscious, he was rushed to Fairview-Southdale Hospital in Edina, where doctors determined that he had suffered a massive internal brain injury. The situation was grave. Physicians were powerless to do much, realizing that no surgical procedure could repair an injury that serious.

When team doctor Frank Sidell met with Wren Blair later that night, he advised Blair to find another center as soon as possible because he didn't think Masterton would make it.

While Masterton spent the rest of the night on life support, Blair kept tabs on the situation through Bob Reid, Met Center's building manager. Reid stayed at the hospital through the night and into the next day, while the team left for Boston to begin a two-game road trip.

A blinding snowstorm complicated the team's travel arrangements, and it took several flights for all the players to reach their destination. In fact, it was more than halfway through the second period before the entire team made it to Boston Garden. Tired and emotionally drained, the North Stars were too distracted to put up much of a fight against the Bruins, who rolled to an easy 9–2 win.

Blair checked in with Bob Reid for another update on Masterton's condition. Although there was nothing new to report, Reid told Blair to address the team after the game and prepare them for the worst: doctors planned to remove life support sometime during the night.

Bird stayed up in his hotel suite with assistant GM John Mariucci and spent several nerve-wracking hours waiting for the fateful call. At about 4:00 a.m., roughly twenty-seven hours after the accident in Bloomington, the telephone rang. Masterton was gone, leaving behind a wife and two children. He was twenty-nine.

At daybreak, Blair and Mariucci went room by room to deliver the news personally to each member of the team. "Most players broke down," Blair recalled in his autobiography, *The Bird*. "Most of these young men had never experienced a death in their own families, and yet here they were facing the loss of a teammate."

"I've lost a person I valued as a friend as well as one of the finest players in our organization," Walter Bush told the *St. Paul Dispatch*. "Bill certainly exemplified the type of person I would want my children to become."

Masterton's was the first injury-related fatality in the history of the NHL, and it led to wider use of helmets throughout the league.

DID YOU KNOW?

Bill Masterton was believed to be the second player in the history of professional hockey to die as a result of injuries suffered during a game. In 1907 Owen (Bud) McCord died after being injured during a Federal Amateur Hockey League game at Cornwall, Ontario.

Back then the vast majority of skaters still played without protective headgear, and many goalies operated without masks. These were optional devices that most players considered a nuisance. Winger Bobby Rousseau, for one, complained that while wearing a helmet, he had a hard time sensing when other players were approaching from behind. Owners didn't like helmets because they thought fans wouldn't be able to recognize players on the ice.

But bravado was the biggest culprit. Too many players equated helmets with weakness. Blackhawks star Bobby Hull, whose free-flowing blond hair made him immediately identifiable from the uppermost balcony seats of Chicago Stadium, confessed: "We should all be wearing them, except we're just too damn vain."

Andre Boudrias was the only member of the North Stars to wear a helmet before the incident, although Dave Balon, Masterton's former linemate, was one of the first to don headgear afterward.

Though Clarence Campbell conceded that only "the inordinate skill of the players" had prevented previous fatalities in a game rife with built-in hazards, he said there were no immediate plans to make helmets mandatory. "I never believed in helmets and I still don't," Blues GM Lynn Patrick sniffed. "The game's been played without them, and no one ever got killed before."

Canadiens GM Sam Pollock agreed. Pointing to a newspaper headline that told of Masterton's death being only the league's first, Pollock asked simply, "Need helmets? There's your answer."

2. Cesare Maniago follows the play as Chicago's Bobby Hull gives chase. Courtesy of the Dallas Stars

The twenty-first annual NHL All-Star Game was played at Maple Leaf Gardens in Toronto the day after Masterton's death. A one-minute moment of silence was observed before the game.

The North Stars later retired Masterton's number, 19, and established the Bill Masterton Memorial Cup, a club award to be presented annually to the team's most valuable player. Cesare Maniago, who posted six shutouts during that inaugural season, was the first recipient of the award.

And after the season, the NHL Writers' Association created an award of its own in Masterton's honor: the Bill Masterton Memorial Award, to be given to the player who best fits the description "unsung hero," though in later years it was given to players who best exemplified the qualities of perseverance and dedication to hockey.

"Bill's wife, Carol, was a wonderful lady who never blamed hockey for what happened," said Bush. "It was just a freak thing. I know he would've been very valuable to us. It ended up that we put some scholarship money aside for their two kids."

But Ron Harris, whose routine hit on Masterton set this awful chain of events in motion, never fully forgave himself for what happened that night in Bloomington. "It bothers you the rest of your life," he told an interviewer in 2003. "It wasn't dirty, and it wasn't meant to happen that way. Still, it's very hard because I made the play. It's always in the back of my mind."

Masterton's funeral was planned for the afternoon of January 18. But since the North Stars were scheduled to host the Flyers that night, Wren Blair telephoned Clarence Campbell and asked to have the game postponed. After all, Blair reasoned, his players couldn't be expected to take the ice only hours after burying a teammate.

The league president refused, saying it would be "impossible" to reschedule the match.

So at the funeral, the North Stars players and their wives sat on one side of the church, and the entire Flyers team sat on the other. They met that night as planned, and Philadelphia won, 4–2.

Players were still in a state of shock. But Blair, that tireless motivator, was determined to put the tragedy behind them. He challenged his men to overcome their grief to focus on their jobs. He juggled lines often and ran the club like a taskmaster when he had to. Veterans who slacked off were benched. He tried to reestablish a sense of normalcy, at least as normal as things could be under the Blair regime.

For all the bombast and spectacle that accompanied Bird, this might have been his finest hour as a coach and leader. By late January the North Stars had emerged from their funk to compete strongly.

Blair proved he was a slick dealer that season too, landing center Milan Marcetta and left wing J. P. Parise from AHL Rochester for a package of veterans and prospects. The young Marcetta would prove his worth in the playoffs with seven goals, while Parise finished with eleven goals and twenty-seven points in forty-three games.

Wayne Connelly, Dave Balon, Andre Boudrias, Ray Cullen, and Mike McMahon all had productive seasons. They each had something to prove, both to themselves and to the teams from which they came. Connelly, who led the team with thirty-five goals and fifty-six points, had been left unprotected by the Bruins, while Cullen, an accurate shooter who finished second on the North Stars with twenty-eight goals and fifty-three points, was plucked from the Red Wings. McMahon, a good puck-handling defenseman, had been a rookie flop on Broadway four seasons earlier but would lead all blueliners with fourteen goals and forty-seven points.

On the whole North Stars players enjoyed Minnesota, and the cold climate helped keep them in the mood to play hockey. Boudrias, who had played minor hockey in warm weather cities and found the experience altogether strange, found the icy air especially refreshing, while Andre Pronovost, a rookie called up from the North Stars' Central Hockey League affiliate in Memphis, complained that in Tennessee, his wife never had an opportunity to wear her mink coat.

3. Wayne Connelly. Graphic Artists/ Hockey Hall of Fame

Fans were enthusiastic too, though it may have taken a little calculated prodding from Blair to get them going. He once half-jokingly complained in the local papers about how quiet they seemed during games, describing them as a bunch of "phlegmatic Swedes." Their temperament changed one night during a December game against the visiting Penguins. When the crowd littered the ice with programs and newspaper as a protest of referee Bill Friday's officiating, they were also showing Blair that they knew how to get rowdy.

The team won only five of its last twenty-two games to finish fourth in the West Division, just two points ahead of fifth-place Pittsburgh. But that was good enough to qualify for an unexpected postseason berth and a first-round meeting with Terry Sawchuk and the Los Angeles Kings. It was a hard-fought, seven-game affair that saw Minnesota rally from 2-0 and 3-2 series deficits. Game Six was won on an overtime goal from Marcetta, while Game Seven was sealed in a 9–4 rout at the Forum.

Averaging a point per game, Bill Goldsworthy was on fire, and Cesare Maniago was playing as well as any goalie in the league. Of all the new teams, the North Stars stood as good a chance as any of making it to the finals.

Next they met St. Louis in the semis. Like the North Stars, the Blues were a well-run, well-constructed outfit. They were coached by Scotty Bowman and built around All-Star goalie Glenn Hall. They also had older, experienced players like Doug Harvey and Dickie Moore, both of whom had once been stars with the Canadiens.

Frustrations ran high since the North Stars, never figuring they would be a playoff team, booked Met Center during the playoffs for the Ice Capades. As a result they had only two home games in the series. One of those was Game Six, a 5–1 Minnesota win.

Three games of the series had already been decided in overtime, with Minnesota losing a pair. Game Seven was scoreless until the closing minutes of regulation, when Minnesota center Walt McKechnie fired a thirty-five-feet wrister that beat a screened Hall with just over three minutes left to play. The Blues' Dickie Moore tied the game thirty-one seconds later to force overtime.

REMEMBERING DICK DILLMAN

The third employee ever hired by the North Stars, Dick Dillman remained with the team as its public relations director until his death in 1988 at age fifty-eight.

As the primary liaison between the team and the media, Dillman was one of those behind-the-scenes types essential to the smooth running of any professional sports franchise. It was Dillman's job to establish relationships with the local beat writers, drum up publicity for the team, and occasionally try to put a positive spin on a story that might be unflattering to the club or its personnel. He wrote press releases, edited the team's annual yearbook, scheduled interviews and public appearances for the players, and managed to do it all without treating reporters like something he'd found under a rock.

In recognition of Dillman's hard work, professionalism, and accommodating manner, the Professional Hockey Writers' Association established the Dick Dillman Award, which is given annually to the team judged to be the best in media relations by members of the PHWA.

Dillman's love of hockey and skills as a writer rubbed off on his daughter, Lisa, who became a sportswriter for the *Los Angeles Times*, eventually adding the Kings beat to her resume.

In the first extra session, Wayne Connelly skated in alone toward Hall but was pulled down from behind by St. Louis defenseman Jimmy Roberts (not to be confused with Jim Roberts, a left wing who played three seasons for Minnesota in the 1970s). The home crowd expected the visiting North Stars to be awarded a penalty shot, but referee Art Skov allowed play to continue.

The deadlock was broken in the second overtime, when Ron Schock beat Maniago on a breakaway, bringing the North Stars' inaugural season to a heartbreaking end.

If there was a silver lining to be found, it was that the North Stars led all new teams in average attendance with 11,762, proving that hockey was no longer just a game for Minnesota's high schoolers and collegians. Al Shaver, the team's longtime radio play-by-play man, fondly remembered it as "one hell of a year."

"When the team came back from St. Louis on Braniff Airlines," he said, "they had to move the plane over to one side of the airport because there were thousands of people out there to welcome the North Stars back. That series is what made pro hockey in Minnesota."

AROUND THE LEAGUE: 1968–1969

The NHL moves to a seventy-six-game schedule. The Amateur Draft is expanded to cover any amateur player of qualifying age throughout the world. Boston's Phil Esposito becomes the first player to top the 100-point mark with 126.

THE SOPHOMORE SLUMP

Wren Blair had never intended to coach for more than one season, so in November 1968 he handed the reins over to John Muckler, at that time the coach and GM of the North Stars' minor league affiliate in Memphis.

The North Stars started well under Muckler, winning three of four. But after that they won only three of their next thirty games. By January Blair was back behind the bench, and Muckler was out of a job.

Bill Goldsworthy's development was taking longer than expected. Playing well the previous postseason gave him confidence that had been lacking, but it also made him cocky. When the lucky bounces stopped coming and his scoring trailed off, Goldy became frustrated, and his effort waned. The talented but erratic North Star was sent to the minors for a spell. He returned to Minnesota after only six games but continued to struggle.

The 1968–69 season also saw the arrival of wingers Claude Larose and Danny Grant from Montreal. The two played on the same line and complemented each other well. Larose produced sixty-two points on twenty-five goals and thirty-seven assists, many of the latter coming on feeds to Grant, who scored thirty-four goals and sixty-five points. That set an all-time rookie record, breaking the mark of sixty-two set by Toronto's Gus Bodnar in 1943–44. He went on to win the Calder Trophy as the top rookie, becoming the first player from an expansion team to win one of the league's major regular-season awards.

Deals between the North Stars and the Canadiens were becoming routine.

"When we came into the league," Blair told Gary Ronberg in *The Ice Men*, "I wasn't afraid to crawl into [Montreal GM] Sam Pollock's office on my hands and knees. Sam has more players than anybody else. I wasn't proud. I begged for players. I made this deal and that deal—all kinds of deals. I asked for favors and did favors. But let's face it—I'm in a den of thieves. Every club in this league is out to do one thing: win. Every manager in this league is under a great deal of pressure to win, and if he's not, he's liable to cut a few throats in order to. I've had my throat cut a few times, but I've cut a few myself."

Blair probably wanted to cut some throats after the North Stars finished tied with Pittsburgh with fifty-one points, the worst in the NHL.

GOLDY, GUMPER, AND GIBBS'S BIG NIGHT

The North Stars won a coin flip with the Penguins to secure the top draft pick in the 1969 draft, which they used to take Dick Redmond, considered the best attacking defenseman to come out of the Canadian juniors since Bobby Orr. Redmond, however, never really caught on with the North Stars, appearing in just sixteen games over the next two seasons before being traded to the Seals.

In the third round the North Stars selected goaltender Gilles Gilbert from London of the Ontario Hockey Association (OHA). Gilbert would eventually achieve some notoriety in Boston but began his career as a backup behind Cesare Maniago.

MILESTONE: NOVEMBER 8, 1969
Bill Goldsworthy scores his first career NHL hat trick in a 5–2 win over the visiting St. Louis Blues.

The 1969–70 season marked Bill Goldsworthy's breakout campaign. An emerging star, he came to training camp in the best shape of his life and began living up to the high expectations many had for him since the expansion draft. He produced thirty-six goals, with every one punctuated by the on-ice jig that became his trademark, "The Goldy Shuffle." He played on a line that featured J. P. Parise on the left wing and Tommy Williams at center. The trio brought excitement to Met Center and finished 1-2-3 in team scoring.

For the rest of the team, however, this was a roller-coaster season. After a December 6 win over Montreal, the North Stars went more than a month before winning their next game. Desperate for a solution, Wren Blair stepped aside as coach—again—and asked center Charlie Burns to move from the ice to the bench. The change in duties was envisioned as a temporary move, and Burns was given the title of assistant coach, although his tenure lasted longer than anyone expected.

The experiment was a failure, and the North Stars continued to sputter, slipping helplessly into a twenty-game winless streak. Maniago looked lost in goal, and if Blair didn't find him some help soon, another season would be down the tubes.

So Blair coaxed former Canadiens goalie Lorne (Gump) Worsley out of semiretirement to split duties with Maniago. Gump's rights were transferred to Minnesota for cash.

This was long before teams began using goalie coaches or "consultants," and Maniago, his confidence nearly shot, immediately sought advice from the veteran Worsley. "He was a godsend to us," said Maniago. "I knew I was doing something wrong, but there was nobody around who knew what it was. I'd been busting my rear end for two weeks, and I couldn't work any harder. Sure enough, Gump came. He watched me in practice and told me to come out a bit, open up the legs, and bend the knees. That was it—that's all it took."

When the North Stars took the ice against the Maple Leafs in a Sunday afternoon game on March 1, there was a plump new face on the Minnesota bench. Gump, suiting up in the green and gold for the first time, lifted the spirits of the team just by being there. Maniago stopped forty-one shots and the new-look North Stars rolled to an 8–0 win.

HATS OFF FOR COLLINS

Bill Collins scored the first two hat tricks of his NHL career in the same week, against the same team. The right winger struck three times in Minnesota's 8–0 win over the Maple Leafs on March 1, 1970, then did it again six days later when the North Stars beat the Leafs 8–3 at Toronto.

Worsley was in goal a few days later in a 2–2 tie against Philadelphia and back in the nets again at week's end in helping the Stars to an 8–3 win in Toronto. The following weekend Gump posted back-to-back victories at home against Pittsburgh and against the Rangers in New York, where he had spent his first ten seasons. It was Minnesota's first-ever win at Madison Square Garden.

The North Stars continued to play well throughout March, but it was not clear if their late surge would be enough to secure a playoff spot. Needing a win to make the playoffs, the team spent the final weekend of the regular season in Pennsylvania for back-to-back games against Philadelphia and Pittsburgh.

The Saturday afternoon match against the Flyers remained scoreless into the third period, with Worsley and Philly's Bernie Parent brilliantly matching each other save for save. With just over twelve minutes remaining, Tommy Williams won a face-off for Minnesota at center ice. Defenseman Barry Gibbs, who was nearly eighty feet from the opposing goal, got the puck and shot it deep into the Flyers' zone. He never imagined it would go in, yet somehow the puck eluded Parent and ended up in the net. It was a fluke goal scored on a routine play, but that fluke turned out to be the biggest goal of Gibbs's career because Minnesota held on for the 1–0 win, assured itself a playoff spot, and simultaneously eliminated the Flyers from postseason contention.

The North Stars wrapped up the regular season with a 5–1 win over the Penguins, earning themselves a first round meeting with St. Louis. The Blues prevailed in six games, however, and then went on to beat Pittsburgh to advance to the Stanley Cup Finals for the third straight year.

HEIGHTENED EXPECTATIONS

At the dawn of the new decade, the consensus throughout hockey was that the North Stars were among the best of the six expansion teams, though certainly not yet on par with established clubs like Chicago, which became a divisional rival when the league realigned in 1970.

AROUND THE LEAGUE: 1970–1971

Two new teams join the NHL: the Buffalo Sabres and the Vancouver Canucks. The Oakland Seals are renamed the California Golden Seals prior to the start of the season. Clubs now play a seventy-eight-game schedule. Boston's Bobby Orr sets NHL records for most assists (102) and points (139) in a season by a defenseman.

Charlie Burns could not continue as a player-coach, and an increasingly stressed Wren Blair knew that his head wasn't big enough to wear the hats of both coach and GM. Suffering from high blood pressure and too many sleepless nights, he decided to divide the posts permanently. "If I'd kept it up," Blair later admitted, "the job would've killed me."

In hockey circles Jackie Gordon was considered the best coach outside the NHL when the North Stars brought him aboard in 1970. Round-faced and laconic, Gordon had spent many years with AHL Cleveland as a player, coach, and general manager and had a hand in four Calder Cup championships. He changed the North Stars' style by emphasizing defense. Forwards had to do a lot more checking, which meant that while they weren't getting many scoring chances, the opposition wasn't, either.

MILESTONE: MARCH 30, 1971

Murray Oliver scores the two hundredth goal of his NHL career in a 2–1 loss against the visiting Vancouver Canucks.

Another important development for the North Stars was the arrival of Ted Harris from Montreal. Assuming the role of captain, the steady if unspectacular blueliner shored up a vital weakness on defense and would represent the North Stars at the 1971 and 1972 All-Stars Games. Perhaps more importantly, Harris had playoff experience, having won four Stanley Cups with the Canadiens.

Another ex-Montrealer, right wing Bobby Rousseau, came over in a trade for Claude Larose.

But in late November 1970, tragedy struck the North Stars again.

Early one morning Blair received a frantic telephone call from Tommy Williams, begging him to get over to his house as soon as possible. All Blair knew for sure was that Williams' wife, Emmie, had been found dead in their garage.

Blair got dressed and raced over to Williams's house. He arrived to find police cars and fire engines parked along the street with their lights flashing. Neighbors stood outside, staring. Tommy was inside with his kids.

Distraught, Williams explained to Blair about how the couple had been out late the night before. Then there was an argument. When they got home, Tommy went to bed, but Emmie never followed. Later that night Tommy woke up and searched the entire house for his wife before opening the door to the garage. Hit by a wave of carbon monoxide fumes, he spotted Emmie in the car, its engine still running.

No one knew for sure whether Emmie's death had been a suicide or just a terrible accident. Police suspected the latter.

Bird was terribly fond of Williams—he had signed the center to his first pro contract while working for the Bruins organization—and offered what little comfort he could.

The funeral was held a few days later, and three or four days afterward Williams returned to the team. But Emmie's death still haunted him, and he began to drink very heavily. Over the next few months his play deteriorated, and he was eventually taken out of the lineup.

"Maybe Minnesota is the worst place for Tommy to try and turn his life around," Blair told Jack Gordon. "This is his home state, and all his memories are here."

In February 1971 the North Stars traded Williams to Oakland for center Ted Hampson. Blair hated having to make the deal but believed it was for the best.

The same day of the Williams trade, Minnesota picked up veteran defenseman Doug Mohns and rookie forward Terry Caffery from the Blackhawks for Danny O'Shea. On paper the North Stars were a much-improved club and finished fourth during the regular season, only a point behind third-place Philadelphia.

Minnesota drew St. Louis again in the opening round of the playoffs. The Blues had ousted the North Stars in their two previous postseason meetings. But the third time was a charm, with Minnesota prevailing in six games.

No one really gave the North Stars much of a chance against the Canadiens in the semifinals, especially after Henri Richard and his pals embarrassed the Minnesotans, 7–2, in Game One. But the North Stars answered with a 6–3 victory in Game Two, the first win by an expansion team over an Original Six team in the playoffs.

The series was tied two games apiece when the Habs, back on their home ice in Game Five, issued the North Stars a 6–1 beating and returned to Minnesota with hopes of finishing off the upstarts.

Game Six, played on April 29, 1971, was one of the most memorable of the expansion era. Montreal's Rejean Houle snapped a 2–2 tie late in the second period when he banged home a rebound of Henri Richard's shot. The Canadiens carried a 3–2 lead into the closing minutes of the third period when Blair pulled Maniago for an extra attacker. As the final seconds ticked off, Ted Hampson carried the puck across the Montreal blue line.

The tiny center dished the puck to Jude Drouin, who was breaking in toward Montreal goalie Ken Dryden. Drouin was unable to put his stick on the puck, and it bounced off his skate and slid back to Hampson with one second left on the clock.

Hampson, swooping in from the left side, lifted the puck over a sprawling Dryden and into the net, but the red light signifying a goal never went on. It was a half second too late. The green light indicating that time had expired flashed first.

Mortified, the North Stars argued that the puck had gone in before the clock ran out. But referee Bill Friday held firm and did not allow the goal. "The green light was on so it had to be no goal," he later assured reporters. "If the green light is on, the red light that signals a goal *can't* come on."

"The last time I looked at the clock, there were five seconds to play," said Dryden. "Your internal clock starts counting a lot quicker in that situation, and it seemed like the game might be over, but I was playing the shot and got beat."

"I was on the ice at the time and I remember the goal," Tom Reid, the longtime North Stars defenseman, recalled years later. "In my mind I still say the puck was in the net [before time expired]. But I can't fault

Bill Friday because he had so much to look at. His vision was somewhat impeded by the amount of players on the ice because we had pulled our goaltender and were pressing pretty hard."

Clarence Campbell, described affectionately by friend Walter Bush as something of a "closet Canadiens fan," threw a fit when he saw Met Center's electric applause sign light up after the nongoal.

"You can't do that!" Campbell groused. "There's no cheerleading in hockey!"

Montreal won the game and the series, surviving a scare from the upstart North Stars before going on to beat the Blackhawks in the finals for their third Stanley Cup in four years.

A deflated Hampson said afterward, "It was the most important goal I ever scored that didn't count."

The conquered found solace in defeat. "Would we have won the series?" Reid wondered. "I don't know. But it was a great series for us. I remember walking off the ice, thinking how disappointed I was. And yet I was excited because we had done so well. We had so much confidence in ourselves after that series. We felt we could beat anybody. It helped that we had so much veteran leadership—a good mix of youth and experience. And our goaltending was terrific. You could call upon Gump and Cesare to win games for you, and they did that."

For a team battling to earn respect, the 1971 semifinals signified a major turning point for the North Stars and the rest of the class of 1967 because an expansion team had gone the distance with one of the Original Six. Many players from that Minnesota squad consider it one of their proudest achievements.

DID YOU KNOW?

Hall of Fame linesman Neil Armstrong worked Game Six of the 1971 semifinals between Minnesota and Montreal, the night of Ted Hampson's infamous "nongoal." His son, Doug Armstrong, joined the North Stars front office in 1991 and would eventually replace Bob Gainey as GM of the Dallas Stars.

NYET MEANS NYET!

Following the historic 1972 Summit Series between the Soviets and a team of Canadian NHLers, North Stars president Walter Bush let it be known that he was interested in signing Valeri Kharlamov, the great Soviet player who had become the talk of the eight-game tournament.

Bush was already familiar with Kharlamov from the Muscovite's previous visits to North America on exhibition tours with the Red Army Team. He saw a young man who could do virtually anything he wanted with the puck when it was in his possession.

4. Cartoonist Bill Johnson offers this commentary about Tom Reid's omission from the 1972 Western Division All-Star Team. Courtesy of the Dallas Stars

"Kharlamov," Larry Robinson observed, "wasn't subordinate to the usual manner of playing. In hockey, he was exclusively free and enterprising."

But in the eyes of the Politburo, Kharlamov was anything but free. Could an NHL team pry the gifted left wing from the clutches of the Soviet government, which viewed its players as property? When Bush put the feelers out to Red sports officials, he let green do the talking.

AROUND THE LEAGUE: 1972–1973

Two new teams join the NHL: the Atlanta Flames and the New York Islanders.

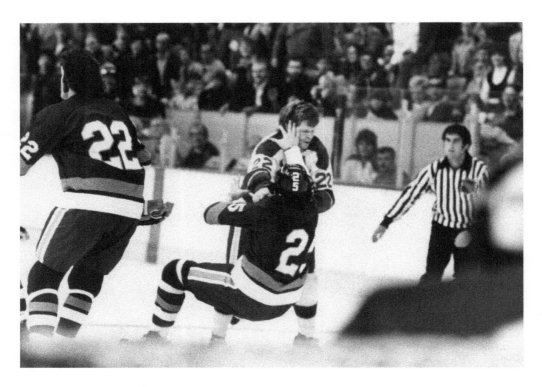

"We offered a big sum of money to the Russians, which I think got up to about $1 million," Bush recalled. "That was about half the franchise value. But we knew they wouldn't let him out because they hadn't let anyone else out. We took a chance. They were going to stick to their guns, even though that was a lot of money in those days."

In the end Kharlamov was forbidden to sign with the North Stars, but Bush's efforts underscored NHL teams' newfound willingness to scour the globe in search of talented players.

GROWING PAINS

Bill Goldsworthy had become a legitimate star, and his popularity in Minnesota was soaring. But there was always the sense that he could be better. By his own admission Goldy was the kind of player who needed a kick in the ass once in a while to stay motivated (Wren Blair was only too happy to oblige).

Left wing Dennis Hextall, picked up from the Seals in May 1971, brought a competitive spirit that impressed some teammates but chafed others. Not a big man, he played a big man's game and expected everyone to follow suit. When they didn't, he spoke up. It resulted in more than a few locker-room altercations.

"I think Dennis's heart was always in the right place," recalled Blake Dunlop, a center for the North Stars from 1973 to 1977, "but he was a very intense guy who wanted things to be a certain way. Sometimes, he bullied his way through things, and that did cause some friction and confrontations. But that was not totally uncommon in that era."

Minnesota opened its 1973–74 schedule with a 5–2 loss at home to Montreal, and that set the tone for the weeks to follow. By late October Jack Gordon's patience had dropped to dangerously low levels, and the coach openly began questioning his team's heart in the newspapers. Blair was ticked too and decided it was time for a wake-up call. On November 10 he traded team captain Ted Harris to the Red Wings for defenseman Gary Bergman.

The North Stars went on a minor roll, but just when it seemed like they might salvage the season, Gordon suddenly resigned, citing health reasons. His nerves were shot.

Blair immediately promoted Parker MacDonald, who had been coaching the North Stars' AHL affiliate in New Haven. MacDonald worked his tail off to get the North Stars within sniffing distance of a playoff berth, but the club remained wildly inconsistent.

Blair, architect of the club since its inception, was on the hot seat, and rumors were swirling that ownership would cause a shake-up of its own at the conclusion of the season. But it wasn't until April, when the team missed the playoffs for the first time since 1969, that Bird began to seriously worry about his job.

A few days after Minnesota's season ended, the ax finally dropped. Having invested so much of his time and energy into building the North Stars from nothing, Blair took the news of his termination especially hard. He went home that night, crawled into a bottle, and cried until the pain was washed out of his system. Within a year, however, he was back on his feet as an owner of the Penguins.

AROUND THE LEAGUE: 1974–1975

The NHL expands to eighteen teams with the addition of the Kansas City Scouts and the Washington Capitals. The league realigns into two nine-team conferences: the Prince of Wales Conference and the Clarence Campbell Conference. Clubs now play an eighty-game schedule.

When Jack Gordon came back to the North Stars that summer to assume the dual role of coach and GM, he began unloading many of the players whom Blair had worked so hard to acquire. A predominantly veteran team shifted gears to make way for youth, though some questioned the logic of trading away key contributors like Barry Gibbs, Fred Stanfield, Jude Drouin, and J. P. Parise, most of whom were still in their prime. Gordon's least popular (but in hindsight most sensible) move came in November 1976, when he dealt the

6. Before he struck oil in Edmonton, Glen (Slats) Sather was a journeyman left wing who spent his last NHL season (1975–76) with the North Stars before jumping to the WHA. Courtesy of the Dallas Stars

rapidly fading Bill Goldsworthy to the Rangers for Bill Fairbairn and Nick Beverly.

Gordon's rebuilding efforts threw team chemistry into a blender, and the resulting mix was never as good as it had been during the North Stars' formative years. Minnesota missed the playoffs from 1974 to 1976, while morale—and attendance—dipped to new lows.

"There were a couple of years where we'd have twenty games left in the season and no chance of making the playoffs," said Fred Barrett, one of the few veterans to survive Gordon's purge. "You have to become a survivor and basically work for your job for next year. It was a real learning experience."

Named for the International Hockey League's old St. Paul Saints, the Minnesota Fighting Saints of the World Hockey Association (WHA) fought, all right. But they were no saints, and a dangerous mystique, combined with cheap ticket prices, made them a popular alternative to the North Stars when Minnesota's NHL club hit the skids in the mid-1970s.

"WHA teams would have three, four, or five guys who did nothing but fight," ex-WHA player Cam Connor told the *Edmonton Sun*. "The Saints had these Carlson brothers who couldn't skate the length of the ice without falling down, although I think they got better later. Minnesota also had Curt Brackenbury, Gord Gallant, Paul Holmgren, and Johnny McKenzie. It was a tough lineup."

Whenever another team came into the Saints' rink, the St. Paul Civic Center, violence was the norm, and fans clamored to see the brawls. What they would never see, much to their disappointment, was an exhibition match between the two local pro teams. As far as North Stars personnel were concerned, the Fighting Saints did not exist.

They may not have been rivals on the ice, but the North Stars and the Fighting Saints were embroiled in a high-stakes, interleague battle for the loyalties of Minnesota's ticket-buying public . . . a battle with no winners. If the teams had home games scheduled on the same night, which was not uncommon, there might be twelve thousand fans at Met Center and eight thousand at the Civic Center. Neither team could draw enough to reach its break-even point, so both lost money.

"[The Saints] took the St. Paul crowd away from us," admitted Walter Bush. "That definitely had an impact. It's a shame too, because we were going along really well up to that point."

In the fight for survival, the North Stars came off as the establishment team—ironic, given the club's Expansion Six lineage—whereas the Fighting Saints were the rogue league bad boys willing to put up billboards just up the road from Met Center proclaiming: "WE'RE NOT THE OTHER TEAM ANYMORE." The North Stars tried not to acknowledge the taunt, but the temptation to respond became irresistible. Eventually they put up a billboard of their own that read: "IT'S NOT THE ONLY GAME IN TOWN . . . JUST THE BEST."

Like all NHL teams the North Stars were gravely concerned about player salaries, which had nearly doubled to keep pace with what WHA teams were paying. With that came the fear that players signed to long-term deals, in part to fend off marauding WHA teams, would never work as hard after receiving that kind of job security. (In 1972 the Saints tried to sign Bill Goldsworthy away from the North Stars, prompting Bush to lock Goldy up with a new three-year contract.)

Although the NHL had no love (and only begrudging respect) for the WHA, exhibition games be-tween the two leagues were common. The North Stars never played their neighbors from St. Paul, the Fighting Saints, but they did participate in eight preseason matches against other WHA teams, going 3-4-1:

October 6, 1974: Toronto Toros 3, North Stars 5
September 8, 1977: Winnipeg Jets 1, North Stars 2
October 1, 1977: Winnipeg Jets 4, North Stars 3
October 1, 1978: Quebec Nordiques 5, North Stars 2
October 3, 1978: Edmonton Oilers 4, North Stars 2
October 5, 1978: Winnipeg Jets 5, North Stars 5
October 7, 1978: Edmonton Oilers 3, North Stars 9
October 8, 1978: Winnipeg Jets 6, North Stars 5

Ultimately the WHA spent itself out of existence, but not before mak-ing life difficult for clubs like the North Stars.

The Saints folded midway through the 1975–76 season, returned the following year as the relocated Cleveland Crusaders, and then folded again in January 1977. Two years later the WHA was history.

Among the many players to skate for both the North Stars and Saints during their careers were Mike Antonovich, Henry Boucha, Wayne Con-nelly, Gary Gambucci, Ted Hampson, and Danny O'Shea.

THE ELECTRIC INDIAN

Henry Boucha (pronounced "BOO-shay") was a celebrated high school star from Warroad, Minnesota, who literally brought the Met Center crowd to its feet during the 1969 state high school championships. He was a tall and graceful skater whose dominating skills and Native Ameri-can heritage made him a media sensation.

A full-blooded Ojibwa, Boucha spent three years with the U.S. National Team and won a silver medal at the 1972 Olympics in Sapporo, Japan, before turning pro with the Red Wings. But after two seasons in the Motor City, one of Minnesota's most beloved sons came home to play for the North Stars in a trade for Danny Grant.

Hockey fans who had marveled at Boucha's exploits as a teen were ecstatic. It was also exciting for other North Stars players and front-office personnel, who welcomed "The Electric Indian" back to Bloomington with open arms. He soon developed a strong friendship with veteran center Murray (Muzz) Oliver and met his future spouse through Den-nis Hextall's wife, Becky.

Boucha intimidated through size and strength but was by no means a goon. He was a finesse player who fought on rare occasion. He is also

7. Jack Carlson.
Courtesy of the
Dallas Stars

Minnesota native Jack (The Big Bopper) Carlson, a rugged winger who spent two tours (1978–82, 1986) with the North Stars, almost achieved cinematic immortality. During the 1974–75 season, while Jack was playing for the minor league Johnstown Jets, the hockey classic *Slap Shot* was being filmed in town. Jack and his two brothers, Jeff and Steve, had been cast in the movie as a trio of siblings who were terrorizing the league with their hitting and fighting. But when Jack was recalled by the WHA's Minnesota Fighting Saints just prior to filming, his part had to be given to Johnstown teammate (and future North Star) Dave Hanson.

remembered for being the victim of one of the most vicious attacks in the history of sports.

When the North Stars hosted the Bruins on January 4, 1975, local media were concerned about whether the home team was tough enough to handle the visitors. Coached by the bombastic Don Cherry, the Bruins were notorious for bullying their opponents. And during a particularly chippy match between the two teams a few months earlier, the North Stars discovered that standing up to a bully sometimes has its consequences.

"That's how it started," Tom Reid recalled. "We were in Boston, and I remember Wayne Cashman slashing Dennis Hextall across the ankle as he was chasing up ice. Hextall turned around and pitchforked him with his stick."

The Bruins never forgot.

Back in Bloomington, Boucha was skating on the top line with Hextall and Muzz Oliver. Cherry countered with Boston's checking unit. The left wing on that line was Dave Forbes.

A five-feet-nine, 180-pound defensive forward, Forbes spent most of the first period trying to agitate Boucha, and when the two ended up together in the corner in Minnesota's end, Forbes took a run at the North Star with elbows high.

Boucha, who had just retrieved the puck, evaded Forbes as the Bruins winger sailed into the glass. A fight ensued. When the combatants went down in a pile, Forbes's linemate, Terry O'Reilly, jumped on Boucha's back. Officials broke up the scuffle, with Boucha and Forbes each sent off with two minutes for roughing and a five-minute major for fighting. O'Reilly, the third man in, was ejected.

The *Minneapolis Star* reported that, once in their respective penalty boxes, Forbes held up a clenched fist and shouted across to Boucha, "I'll get you and I won't use this, I'll shove my stick down your throat."

Meanwhile, Minnesota's equipment manager was upstairs tending to Reid's broken skate blade, while the trainer, Dick (Doc) Rose, was also off ice tending to Hextall, who had just been slashed in the face.

"In those days," said Reid, "the home bench was on the left side, and Boston's bench was on the right. But our penalty boxes were on opposite sides so we had to cross over each other's path to get to and from the penalty box area.

"I could see that Dave and Henry were yapping at each other in the penalty box. And when they stepped out of the box, their paths started to cross, and they came very close together. They were still yapping at each other when Forbsie came up with his stick—it was like that painting of the farmer with the pitchfork [Grant Wood's *American Gothic*]. He had the stick in that position, with his right hand wrapped around the top of the stick. As he came up with his fist, the blunt end of the stick came up and caught Henry above the eye. Dave didn't realize what he had done at that point, but Henry went down."

Maniago skated out of the net as both benches cleared. Though he was wearing only one skate, Reid jumped over the boards and raced over to the scrum, where an enraged Forbes was ramming Boucha's head repeatedly into the ice. Muzz Oliver, who saw the attack out of the corner of his eye, raced over to drag Forbes off his fallen linemate.

"Henry was rolling around on the ice in a pool of blood," said Reid. "Because it was around the eye, the wound bled quite a bit more than other areas. It was just pumping out. I pushed myself over and got Henry's legs around my head, trying to get him to hold still because I didn't know how much more damage could be done. Then some doctor jumped over the glass and onto the ice. He said, 'Hold him still; don't let him move!' So we got a towel and compressed it."

A stunned silence fell over the crowd as Boucha was gently hoisted onto a white stretcher and carried off the ice. Dazed and only semiconscious, he was flanked by shaken teammates.

Referee Ron Wicks slapped Forbes with a match penalty for deliberately causing injury, an infraction that carried an automatic fine of two hundred dollars. Maniago was penalized for leaving the crease, and Oliver, who may have saved Boucha's life, was ejected.

Final score: Boston 8, Minnesota 0.

Over at Minneapolis Methodist Hospital, an ophthalmologist was summoned to examine Boucha. Two sets of X-rays revealed no fractures to the bony structure surrounding the eye, and an early prognosis by team physician Frank Sidell suggested that once considerable swelling subsided, Boucha could soon be back in uniform.

The next morning the question on everyone's mind was how the league would react to this sickening orgy of violence. But before making a decision about supplementary discipline for Forbes, Clarence Campbell came to town and spoke with fans, players, and others who had witnessed the incident. He had to rely on interviews because the attack was not captured on videotape. Forbes and Boucha were still back near center ice while the Bruins were clearing the puck into Minnesota's end, and by the time cameras swung back toward them, Boucha was already face down on the ice.

Surely testimony collected during his investigation would compel Campbell to hand down a harsh, precedent-setting verdict. But in hindsight his ruling against Forbes seems appallingly lenient: a ten-game suspension without pay, which translated to about three weeks. These were different times, to be sure, but Forbes's attack would have drawn a yearlong ban or worse had it occurred under Gary Bettman's watch.

Perhaps Campbell showed mercy because Forbes, who said he had "no animosity at all towards Henry," appeared mildly remorseful.

Exasperated county officials weren't satisfied and filed criminal charges against the Boston winger. It was the first instance in the history of U.S. professional sports that an in-game incident resulted in court action, and Boucha, who suspected prosecutors were more interested in publicity than justice, was among the witnesses to offer testimony. But when the nine-day trial that summer resulted in a hung jury, the district attorney's office declined to pursue the matter further. Campbell was relieved. A conviction would have set a precedent affecting the NHL and potentially every other professional sports league by taking punishment for sport violence out of the arena and into the courts.

The North Stars later learned that Boucha's injury was more severe than doctors had originally thought. Further X-rays revealed a fracture at the base of his right eye socket, and he was plagued by double vision. Several operations were performed to correct the problem, but his eyesight remained impaired.

MILESTONE: FEBRUARY 8, 1975

North Stars rookie and Eveleth native Pete LoPresti records his first career shutout in a 5–0 win over the Flyers. LoPresti becomes part of the first father-son combo to record a shutout in the NHL. His father, Sam, had four shutouts in the 1940s as a member of the Chicago Black Hawks.

AROUND THE LEAGUE: 1976–1977

The California franchise relocates to Ohio to become the Cleveland Barons. The Kansas City franchise is transferred to Denver and becomes the Colorado Rockies. The Montreal Canadiens become the first team to win sixty games in a season.

Boucha filed a civil suit against the Bruins, Forbes, and the NHL in January 1976. The case, which involved extensive depositions of all parties involved, dragged on for five years. But just before the case was scheduled to go to court, all sides convened to discuss a settlement. The case never went to trial, and Boucha received an undisclosed amount of money from each entity named in the suit.

It was a small victory, as Forbes's assault had effectively ended Boucha's career. The towering Ojibwa attempted a comeback with the Fighting Saints before signing with the NHL's Kansas City Scouts. Moving with the franchise when it relocated to Colorado in 1976–77, he played just nine games into that season before retiring at the age of twenty-four.

Forbes played three more seasons in the NHL before finishing his career with Cincinnati of the WHA.

Clarence Campbell retires as NHL president and is succeeded by John Ziegler, a former member of the Detroit Red Wings ownership group. Six teams in the rival WHA apply for entry into the NHL but are rejected.

SWEET LOU TO THE RESCUE

Like Wren Blair before him, Jack Gordon discovered that being coach and general manager was the most stressful gig in hockey. As Bird once said, "The two jobs are too much for one man." So before he let the job consume him, Gordon hired a replacement to tackle the coaching chores. Then another. And another.

Charlie Burns, Ted Harris, and even former high school/junior coach Andre Beaulieu were among the sacrificial lambs thrown behind the North Stars bench. All met a similar fate.

The 1977–78 North Stars, which collected a mere four wins over the final two months of the season, probably had the most dreadful lineup that the organization had ever put on ice. A popgun offense was led by Roland Eriksson, Tim Young, Per-Olov Brasar, and Glen Sharpley, none of whom had more than twenty-three goals. In net Pete LoPresti and Paul Harrison routinely spotted the other team four goals a night.

A 3–0 loss to the Rangers on February 8, 1978, was the club's fourth in a row and fourteenth in seventeen games. Desperate, newly appointed team president Gordon Ritz and his colleagues began eyeing defenseman Lou Nanne as a possible coach and/or general manager. Nanne had been with the North Stars almost from the beginning, was a respected figure in Minnesota hockey, and was getting ready to retire anyway. Where was the risk in letting him run the show? The North Stars were already the worst team in the league.

The practice of using a player-coach had long been abandoned, so if Nanne wanted to swap his polyester jersey for a wool suit, he'd have to give up playing immediately.

"That Wednesday night I was a player," said Nanne. "We flew home on Thursday, and the ownership group asked me to come down and meet with them. We met on Friday morning, and that afternoon they offered me the job of manager-coach."

The sweat in Nanne's skates was barely dry when he accepted the offer, replacing Jack Gordon as the team's third GM at the ripe old age of thirty-six. He was behind the bench for Minnesota's final twenty-nine games, during which the North Stars went 7-18-4.

"The team was at an all-time low with players coming in and out," said Fred Barrett, a North Star blueliner for twelve seasons. "We weren't getting anywhere, and our draft picks weren't working out. Louie was

8. Fred Barrett.
Courtesy of the
Dallas Stars

well known in the area, having played college hockey in Minnesota. He'd
lived and worked there for years, so he was probably the most logical
choice. It's kind of tough to go from playing with a teammate, and then,
all of a sudden, he's your boss. You hope he appreciates what you bring
to the game every night and treats you accordingly. It was certainly very
challenging for Louie to deal with that whole situation."

That offseason Nanne faced the Herculean task of rebuilding a club
that had finished dead last in the league.

3

FLIRTING WITH GREATNESS (1978–1991)

If a depressing mood hovered over the dressing room and along the concourses of Met Center, matters were just as bleak over in the executive offices, where Walter Bush, Gordon Ritz, and their fellow investors were facing economic ruin and looking for a means to cut their losses.

"I spent a year working undercover, so to speak, to get the team sold because I could see what was happening," Bush said. "The other owners had family money and loved hockey, but it just became too difficult. I remember when Smokey Ordway said, 'Why don't we just charter a jet and buy season tickets for the team? Whoever wants to go see a game can just hop on the jet, because that would be cheaper than what we're doing now.'"

The solution would be found with the owners of another club with money problems, the Cleveland Barons. The perpetual losers formerly known as the Oakland (later California) Seals played to sparse crowds at the Coliseum in rural Richfield, Ohio, never finishing higher than last place in the Adams Division, and were leaking red ink. Brothers George and Gordon Gund had continued to lose money with the franchise since it was moved from California to the Buckeye State during the 1976–77 season.

Ritz hatched a revolutionary idea to amalgamate the two struggling clubs. The Gunds were amenable to the plan, and it was approved by the league in the summer of 1978.

"The deal went through just fine," said Bush, "but it was kind of strange because when we made our presentation to the Board of Governors, George Gund was in a wheelchair from a bad back, and Gordon, who is blind, was pushing him into the room. The board members must've wondered, 'What kind of guys are you bringing in?'"

The Barons and the North Stars were merged, and the Gunds assumed ownership of the Minnesota team while the Cleveland club folded. As a result all the players under contract with the Barons saw their rights transferred to the North Stars. In essence Lou Nanne had to identify the best of two of the league's worst franchises and then mesh them into one team.

The North Stars also had the top pick in the draft that year, which Nanne used to select a talented young center named Bobby Smith, a scorer of almost Gretzkyesque proportions in juniors.

So that he could focus his full attention on managerial duties, Nanne asked the former Barons GM, Harry Howell, to coach the North Stars. As classy an individual as you could find in all of hockey, Howell was a great defenseman in his day and would eventually become one of the game's most respected scouts . . . but he was no coach. Nanne had to find someone with aspirations to hold the post long term.

Less than two months into the 1978–79 season, Howell was replaced by former Gophers and Fighting Saints coach Glen Sonmor, who brought a level of experience and enthusiasm that had been lacking behind the North Stars bench.

Sonmor inherited a mess. The North Stars had missed the playoffs four times in the previous five seasons. Their lone postseason appearance, a two-game preliminary-round loss to Buffalo in 1977, hardly constituted an appearance at all.

Taking Cleveland's old spot in the Adams Division, the North Stars took the ice with eight former Barons, including left wing Mike Fidler, right wing Al MacAdam, and goalie Gilles Meloche. The sudden influx of talent didn't lead to an immediate change of fortunes for the team, which finished twelve games under .500 and missed the playoffs again. But in this period of transition there were hints of better days ahead. Bobby Smith went on to lead the club with thirty goals and seventy-four points, earning him the 1979 Calder Trophy as rookie of the year. Another new recruit, left wing Steve Payne, chipped in twenty-three goals. And at the draft that offseason, Nanne used his first three picks on Craig Hartsburg (sixth overall), Tom McCarthy (tenth overall), and Neal Broten (forty-second overall).

NORTH STARS IN THE SUPER SERIES

The Super Series were exhibition games between Soviet teams and NHL teams that took place in NHL arenas throughout North America from 1976 to 1991. The Soviet teams were usually club teams from the Soviet hockey league, although once, in 1983, the Soviet National Team represented the Soviet Union. The North Stars participated in six Super Series, going 1-5:

Super Series 1979: Soviet Wings 8, North Stars 5
Super Series 1983: USSR 6, North Stars 3
Super Series 1986: Red Army 4, North Stars 3
Super Series 1989: Dynamo Riga 2, North Stars 1
Super Series 1990: Red Army 4, North Stars 2
Super Series 1991: North Stars 6, Khimik Voskresensk 4

On January 7, 1980, Minnesota was scheduled to play the Flyers, who came to Bloomington riding the longest undefeated streak in the history of the NHL and major league sports, a thirty-five-game run that included twenty-five wins and ten ties. An all-time record Met Center crowd of 15,962 squeezed into the arena, which was the largest crowd to ever witness a hockey game in Minnesota up to that point and would remain the highest total in all twenty-six seasons of the North Stars franchise.

The Flyers jumped out to an early lead on a goal by Bill Barber at 3:49 of the first period, but it was all North Stars the rest of the way. Mike Eaves, Greg Smith, and Steve Payne scored, and Minnesota took a two-goal lead into the locker room.

The North Stars got a boost from killing off a five-on-three power play early in the second period, then lucked out when an apparent Paul Holmgren goal was disallowed after the referee had observed an extra skater on the ice. Rookie Craig Hartsburg scored a power play goal at 15:33, and Mike Polich scored twenty-two seconds later to put the North Stars ahead 5–1.

AROUND THE LEAGUE: 1979–1980

As a result of the NHL-WHA merger, the Edmonton Oilers, the Hartford Whalers, the Quebec Nordiques, and the Winnipeg Jets join the NHL. Protective helmets become mandatory equipment for all new players, but a grandfather clause gives veterans the right to choose not to wear them. Hartford's Gordie Howe becomes the first player to appear in an NHL game in five different decades.

DID YOU KNOW?

According to the *Toronto Star*, the North Stars were the first franchise to debut rink board advertising. The team sold eight pairs of rink boards at three thousand dollars per pair. Throughout the 1980s more ads began to appear on rink boards throughout the NHL, and today they are a fixture in arenas everywhere.

By the third period it was evident to everyone in attendance that the Flyers' impressive streak was about to end. The chant, "We're number one, we're number one," became louder as the period opened. Ron Zanussi and Bobby Smith capped the scoring for Minnesota to make it 7–1. Gilles Meloche made thirty-nine saves to earn his league-leading seventeenth win.

"Glen [Sonmor] had us real pumped up going into that game," Brad Maxwell recalled. "Here was this team coming in with a thirty-five-game undefeated streak up against a bunch of kids, and we just played a great game. We just dominated them from start to finish. I think the

Flyers were more upset that they lost such a one-sided game than they were about the streak ending. And I don't think they were tired. Maybe they thought we weren't really that good and they were going to breeze through the game and get the win. It didn't work out that way."

A fact that many people still forget about that night was that the North Stars were on a streak of their own. They managed to go eleven games without a loss at home and were one game away from tying a club record.

The North Stars finished with a 36-26-16 record and returned to the playoffs after a two-year absence. After sweeping Darryl Sittler's Maple Leafs in a best-of-five preliminary round, Minnesota advanced to the 1980 quarterfinals, where a most ominous opponent sat in wait: the four-time defending champion Canadiens.

The series opened on April 16 at the Forum. Meloche, who had supplanted Gary (Suitcase) Edwards as Minnesota's No. 1 goalie, turned away every shot he faced in a 3–0 shutout. The following night the North Stars took a 2–0 series lead when they beat the Canadiens 4–1.

But the Habs had too much pride to retire so meekly. Led by gritty winger Steve Shutt and one of the game's best defensive forwards, Bob Gainey, they reeled off three consecutive and decisive victories, reclaiming control of the series with scores of 5–0, 5–1, and 6–2.

The North Stars went home, studied some game tape, and thought about how they could get back into the series. Fred Barrett, Minnesota's steady defenseman, marveled at the Canadiens' incredible work ethic.

"It was pretty obvious that their guys, like Mario Tremblay and Yvon Lambert, were just getting to the puck and beating us in every battle," he said. "If you let the other team outwork you, you stand very little chance of winning. So we dug our heels in and got everybody to contribute. And we needed to hit. When you finish your checks, you send a message to the other guy that says, 'Hey, I'm here to play tonight.'"

Standing on the brink of elimination, Minnesota battled back to win Game Six, 5–2. "Our confidence started to come back," said Barrett, "and it was almost a toss of the coin as to who was going to work harder."

The series moved back to Montreal, where the North Stars hoped to steal Game Seven in hostile territory. The Canadiens had a 1–0 lead in the first period when Minnesota was assessed a penalty.

During Montreal's power play North Stars defenseman Brad Maxwell cleared the puck from his own end. It bounced off the boards and coasted into Montreal's zone as Guy Lapointe gave chase. Goalie Denis Herron came out nearly fifteen feet to his right to handle the puck, but when Herron passed it back, the disk banked off his own goal post. Before the goalie could retrieve it, North Stars right wing Tom Younghans swooped in and backhanded it into the net.

Minnesota took a 2–1 lead in the second period when Al MacAdam dug the puck off the right boards and passed it out front to rookie blue-liner Craig Hartsburg, who skated in from the right point and ripped a shot past Herron.

That's when desperation set in for the Habs, who moved Larry Robinson up from defense to right wing and forced a hobbled Serge Savard back onto the ice. They managed to get the tying goal at 5:23 of the third period, when Rod Langway went to the front of Minnesota's net and knocked in a pass from Tremblay.

The teams were deadlocked with 1:26 left to play when MacAdam scored the biggest goal of his life. The play began with Barrett passing the puck to Steve Payne, who flipped a backhanded pass to Bobby Smith along the left boards. Then Smith laid a soft pass in front, where Payne deflected it on goal. MacAdam got his stick on the rebound and chopped it back underneath Herron. It turned out to be the game and series-winning goal, effectively ending Montreal's last dynasty. The Canadiens were stunned. Fans sobbed.

But the North Stars were euphoric.

Ever the optimist, Glen Sonmor said it wasn't as big an upset as some believed: "We didn't think we couldn't win it. We didn't come here to wind up a respectable season. We came here to win."

It didn't hurt the North Stars' cause that Guy Lafleur and Pierre Larouche, a pair of fifty-goal scorers, were sidelined with injuries. But most Montreal players were classy enough not to use that as an excuse. They credited Minnesota's goaltender for playing one hell of a series. "This is the thrill of my life," said a beaming Meloche. "What more can I ask than to come into my hometown and win at the Forum?"

Bob Kurtz, who today is the radio play-by-play announcer for the Minnesota Wild, was in his first season doing play-by-play for the North Stars on KMSP-TV (Channel 9). "As a kid," Kurtz recalled, "growing up when the NHL was a six-team league, the Canadiens were THE CANADIENS. They're not what they are now. They were the New York Yankees of their time, maybe even more so. They won Stanley Cup after Stanley Cup, and they had that aura. When teams played in the Forum, especially in the seventh game, you knew you were going to lose. It was just a matter of some ghost coming out of someplace and causing something to work in the Canadiens' favor. Stunningly, on this occasion, it didn't."

It had taken every ounce of physical and emotional strength to beat an aging, banged-up Montreal team, and Sonmor's crew was worn out. Philadelphia took advantage of the North Stars' exhausted state in the semifinals, bouncing the Minnesotans in just five games.

An exciting season ended abruptly, but there was no denying that progress had been made. The merger with Cleveland, combined with

9. Before joining the North Stars, Gilles Meloche earned the nickname "The Robber Baron" because he robbed opponents of glorious scoring chances . . . and because he played for the Cleveland Barons. Courtesy of the Dallas Stars

the emergence of some homegrown talent, was beginning to pay dividends for the Boys from Bloomington.

THE BEANTOWN BRAWL

Perhaps because they had displayed some moxie by knocking off the mighty Canadiens the previous spring, there were hopes that the North Stars were finally ready to assert themselves as Stanley Cup contenders. They opened the 1980–81 campaign in fine fashion, posting a 25-12-11 record through late January.

But the team cooled in the second half, winning only ten games the rest of the way. And a particularly ugly incident that occurred during a five-game losing streak guaranteed the franchise its share of a dubious mark in the NHL record book.

On February 26, 1981, the North Stars took the ice at Boston Garden for what should have been just another midseason meeting between division rivals. But this game would be different. There would be no repeat of the "John Wensink incident" from a few years earlier, in which the Bruins ruffian—who bore a slight resemblance to *Slap Shot* goon Ogie Ogilthorpe—pummeled Alex Pirus, then challenged the entire North Stars bench. There were no takers.

"Management was trying to get the team on a roll," MacAdam recalled. "We were going into Boston, and I don't think Minnesota had won there for over ten years. So there was an edge to it. At our pregame meal, the talk was about how the Bruins weren't that intimidating anymore and that our team was just as physical."

"It was important for us, as a young team, to get some respect," Craig Hartsburg said, "and finally step up and stand up for ourselves."

Also a quick glance at the standings hinted at a likely Minnesota-Boston first round matchup. "There were pretty good odds that we were going to play those guys and that they'd have home-ice advantage," said Steve Payne. "The strategy was that we had to set some kind of tone. So it was decided we were going to go out and not worry too much about the score and show the Bruins that if they want to play rough, we'll kick the s—— out of them. And that's how it went down."

"Lou Nanne set up a big white dry-erase board in the meeting room of the hotel where we were staying," Maxwell remembered, "and all the Boston Bruins players were listed on one side and all the North Stars players were listed on the other side. And he starts drawing arrows back and forth to show which guys were going to take on which guys. He went down the list of every player."

Seven seconds into the game, Bobby Smith dropped his gloves against Boston's Steve Kasper, and within moments the ice was littered with discarded equipment as each North Star squared off against his Bruin counterpart. It really was like a scene out of *Slap Shot*.

Payne was wrapped up with Keith Crowder along the boards when a linesman stepped between the two to break up the skirmish. Crowder got loose and threw a punch at Payne's head.

"I got big-time pissed off that the linesman was holding me," Payne recalled, "so I punched him in the chest. That was not a good move. So I got twenty-nine minutes in penalties from that first altercation."

10. Would this young rough-neck look more familiar if he were wearing black-rimmed glasses and a Charlestown Chiefs jersey? Dave Hanson played twenty-two games for the North Stars in 1979–80 but is best known for portraying one of the Hanson Brothers (along with Steve and Jeff Carlson) in the 1977 film *Slap Shot*. Courtesy of the Dallas Stars

Slapped with two ten-minute misconducts, Payne was sent off to the visitors' dressing room since he wouldn't be playing again that period. He was soon joined by Hartsburg, and the two listened to the rest of the game on a portable radio. In their absence the first of several bench-clearing brawls broke out.

"So Hartsy and I charged back out, and I got into another fight just coming out of the dressing room," said Payne. "I got into it with Crowder again right down on the concourse. We were sliding around on the tile. Boston uniformed cops broke us up. They threw us back in our dressing rooms and locked us in. Then they threw the bolt down so I couldn't get back out. I was kicking the door, acting like an idiot."

A MacAdam–Ray Bourque scrap ignited the biggest fire of the period. Then Brad McCrimmon fought first Greg Smith and then Gordie Roberts. Later, as they exited the ice near the Boston bench, Crowder climbed out of the penalty box and into the exit aisle to get a second crack at either of them.

Referee Dave Newell called 341 minutes in penalties in the first session alone, but it took so long to sort them out that the period lasted over 90 minutes. Overall, twelve players were ejected: Payne, MacAdam, Hartsburg, Carlson, Roberts, Greg Smith, and Tom Younghans from Minnesota and Crowder, McCrimmon, O'Reilly, Milbury, and Peter McNab from Boston.

Hostilities didn't subside when the game ended.

The layout of Boston Garden was such that visiting teams got to their dressing room by leaving the ice via a runway alongside the Bruins bench. And the Bruins coach had to go through the same corridor to reach his office. It was there that Boston coach Gerry Cheevers went after Roberts, who had been tossed in the first period.

Then Cheevers exchanged words with Sonmor, who tripped over a spectator caught in the crush of bodies. Cheevers was eventually led off to the Bruins dressing room by security officers, but not before Sonmor fired off a parting shot. "If Cheevers wants to meet me in the runway in Minnesota," he bellowed, "he'd better bring along a basket for his head!"

The final score, a 5–1 Bruins victory, seemed almost inconsequential because the teams had combined for a then-record 406 penalty minutes including thirty-eight minors, twenty-six majors, seven 10-minute misconducts, and thirteen game misconducts.

"The whole night seemed to be geared toward that kind of behavior," said Hartsburg. "It got to be almost comical."

CINDERELLA STARS

The North Stars won four of their final seven regular season games to finish with a 35-28-17 record. The strong finish was due in part to a mid-season roster shake-up that introduced two former college players (Neal Broten and Kevin Maxwell), two from juniors (Brad Palmer and Ken Solheim), and one from the minor leagues (Dino Ciccarelli).

As expected Minnesota met Boston in the preliminary round because the Bruins placed second in the Adams Division, just ahead of the North Stars. Neither club went in with a decided advantage, but there were fears (or perhaps hopes?) that bad blood harbored from the record-setting melee back in February would resurface. For the most part, though, the teams concentrated on hockey.

Steve Payne's overtime goal in Game One gave Minnesota a 5–4 victory. Both teams abandoned the fundamentals of sound defense in Game Two, a rollicking 9–6 North Stars win. With Minnesota holding a two-games-to-none advantage, Boston set a playoff record in Game Three with three shorthanded goals. But the North Stars survived that scare, winning 6–3 and sweeping the best-of-five series.

Minnesota took a 3-0 series lead against Buffalo in the quarterfinals, but an overtime goal by Sabres defenseman Mike Ramsay in Game Four prevented a sweep. Rookie Don Beaupre, earning only his second start of the postseason, backstopped the North Stars to a 4–3 win in Game Five.

Up next were the Calgary Flames, making their first playoff appearance since relocating from Atlanta the previous summer. The club featured ornery rookie Jim Peplinksi, Swedish scoring sensation Kent Nilsson, and rugged winger Willi Plett.

The Flames hosted the first two games of the semifinal series at Calgary's Stampede Corral, a seven-thousand-seat facility used until the Saddledome opened across the street two years later. The teams split Games One and Two before heading back to Met Center, where the North Stars reeled off two more wins. Calgary responded with a 3–1 win in Game Five, cutting Minnesota's series lead to 3-2.

Two days later, the North Stars closed out Game Six and the series with a 5–3 win. For the first time in franchise history, Met Center would host the Stanley Cup Finals.

"It was a wild spring," said Payne. "Back then the fans could still tailgate at Met Center, and the entire parking lot looked like an old Indian reservation with all the smoke everywhere. People just sat there, taking it all in. It was their first chance to see the team in the Stanley Cup Finals, so it was euphoric. And it was like that for us too. We had a pretty young team. The average age was only about twenty-four. MacAdam was one of the veterans, and he was only twenty-eight. There wasn't a lot of finals experience there either, so we all just kind of went into it blindly together. There were jitters, but the good kind of jitters—the kind we'd figured out how to harness."

"We had good balance on our team," said MacAdam. "We had youth and a core of older, character players that fit right in nicely. We were a good skating team, and we battled for pucks. Anybody who had any doubts about our team or how we could play saw those doubts put to rest."

Standing between the North Stars and a Stanley Cup were the New York Islanders, who had reached the finals for the second time in two years. Like the North Stars the defending champs had encountered little in terms of serious opposition along the way. The only real threat the Isles faced came from a young Edmonton Oilers team that stretched them to six games in the quarterfinals.

The Islanders had already swept their hated archrivals from Manhattan in the semifinals, so for them the final series seemed a bit anticlimactic. They knew the North Stars had surprised some folks by making it this far but figured their luck was bound to run out eventually. Efficient and methodical, the Islanders held themselves to the highest standards. A second title was all but preordained. All they had to do was shake off the rust from a weeklong layoff.

The series opened on May 12, 1981, at Nassau Coliseum in Uniondale. Minnesota's objective would be to contain the top line centered by Bryan Trottier, the best playmaker in the league *not* named Wayne Gretzky, and create as much traffic as possible in front of their ankle-chopping goalie, Billy Smith. "And we had to get some breaks," said Payne. "We weren't so dumb as to think we were a better team."

The Isles jumped out to a 1–0 lead on Anders Kallur's first goal of the game, a tip-in of a point shot by Dave Langevin. A short time later the North Stars were licking their chops when New York's Bob Bourne was sent off with a five-minute major penalty for spearing. But three minutes into Minnesota's power play, the North Stars had managed only one shot.

Later in the period Kallur and Trottier scored a pair of shorthanded goals forty-seven seconds apart. With nine shorthanded goals in the playoffs, the Islanders had established a new NHL record.

Payne, hobbled by a spider bite from the night before that caused his thigh to swell, scored in the third period, but by then the game was well out of reach. New York rolled to a 6–3 win.

"You know what happened?" Islanders center Butch Goring boasted after the game. "We have the best power play in the league, and teams are a little leery of taking penalties against us. Now they have to be leery of going on the power play against us."

The contest was so lopsided that reporters assigned to cover the series were already talking about which Islanders player deserved the Conn Smythe Trophy as playoff MVP.

New York's specialty teams were put to the test early and often in Game Two. Ref Bryan Lewis whistled the Isles for two consecutive penalties in the opening frame, giving the North Stars a two-man advantage. Dino Ciccarelli scored on the power play, but Mike Bossy answered with a power-play goal of his own one minute later.

Bobby Nystrom's shot from the left circle and a Denis Potvin slap shot from the left point beat Don Beaupre, giving the Isles a 3–1 lead before the first intermission.

Brad Palmer's second period goal and Payne's conversion of a Gordie Roberts rebound early in the third knotted the game at 3–3. Billy Smith injured his arm on the play, jamming it against the goalpost. The sight of their goalie writhing on the ice in pain woke the Islanders from a brief slumber.

"Maybe my guys felt sorry for me to see me lying there," Smith said. "I don't think they let [Minnesota] get another shot at me until the end of the period. They came to my rescue like knights in shining armor."

With Fred Barrett off for high-sticking, Potvin took a pass from Goring and fired a shot over Beaupre's left leg. That power-play goal kicked off a three-goal third for the Isles, who skated to another 6–3 win.

The North Stars were visibly rattled. Respect for an opponent is healthy, but fear would result in a quick series.

"Maybe I was still basking in the glow of being in the Finals," lamented Glen Sonmor. "Maybe some of my players felt the same way. They didn't look very poised. They seemed hesitant and jittery. But the Islanders can do that to you. They give *me* the jitters."

One Minnesota player not easily intimidated was Ciccarelli. Signed as an undrafted free agent in 1979, the spunky kid from Sarnia, Ontario, appeared in only thirty-two regular season games but scored eighteen times over that span.

11. Dino Ciccarelli. Courtesy of the Dallas Stars

A Ciccarelli goal in Game Three gave him twenty-one points in the postseason, breaking Don Maloney's single-season rookie playoff scoring record. And it was an important goal because it capped off a late-game rally that cut New York's lead to one.

This was a wild affair that actually began with the Islanders back on their heels. The North Stars came out skating, hitting, and scoring. They struck twice on the power play, courtesy of Steve Christoff and Bobby Smith, and carried a 3–1 lead into the second stanza.

"We were losing the boards, losing the neutral zone, and even losing our own blue line," said Potvin. "In the second period we just took the game away from them."

That's when Nystrom scored once and Goring twice to give New York the 4–3 lead. Goring, who batted his second goal in out of the air off a Clark Gillies rebound, was emerging as the series' most exciting player.

Payne's backhander sailed past Billy Smith early in the third, tying the game. But as they had so often in the series, the Islanders let the North Stars play bigger than their britches before smacking them back down to size. Less than a minute later, Trottier capitalized on a gaff by Craig Hartsburg behind his own goal, swiping the puck and passing it out to Bossy at the top of the right circle. Bossy ripped a shot past Meloche and reclaimed the lead for New York. Goring tapped a Potvin rebound into the net to bag the hat trick about four minutes later.

Ciccarelli's goal at 13:35 of the third put his club one step closer to a tied game. So with fifty-nine seconds left to play, Sonmor pulled Meloche for the extra attacker. Minnesota turned up the pressure in hopes of scoring the equalizer, but Bossy managed to get his stick on the puck. He shuffled it to Trottier, who carefully flipped a thirty-footer into the empty net. The Islanders held on for a 7–5 victory before a sold-out Met Center crowd.

Sonmor called it his club's best effort of the playoffs. "And it *still* wasn't good enough," he said. "That tells you something. Every time you get careless, they score."

"We got beat, but we really outplayed them," Payne recalled. "A couple of hops went their way, and it cost us. If you ask anybody who was there, they'd say we should've won it. If we'd won that game, we would've gone back to Long Island tied up two apiece, and the whole complexion of the series would've changed."

Two nights later the North Stars faced elimination but were determined to avoid a sweep. Their mantra for Game Four was "not tonight." Those were the words scribbled on the blackboard in their dressing room. But since actions speak louder than words, the North Stars backed up that theme with their greatest performance yet against the Islanders.

Nineteen men took the ice that night for Minnesota, and it would take the very best from each to extend the series. But there would never have been a Game Five were it not for the individual efforts of two players: Steve Payne and Don Beaupre.

Payne was everywhere and doing everything, muscling his 202-pound frame into scoring position at will. Beaupre, the rookie who'd been alternating starts with Meloche, did what a future franchise goalie should do: stop all the routine shots and most of the tough ones too.

Isles defenseman Gord Lane opened the scoring, rifling home a slap shot from the left point. Hartsburg tied it halfway through the first period with a power-play goal preceded by two of the most intense minutes of the series. During the barrage Brad Maxwell launched a blistering shot from the point that beat Billy Smith. Or so it seemed. Neither referee Andy Van Hellemond nor the goal judge saw it, and play continued.

The North Stars took the lead five minutes into the second period when Al MacAdam scored from the top of the crease. Mike McEwen answered for New York, knotting the match two minutes later with a power-play slap shot that caromed in off the body of Gordie Roberts.

In the third Payne parked himself in front of the Islanders net, while players scrambled for the puck in the right corner. He knew linemate MacAdam would find a way to get possession of the puck and pass it back to Brad Maxwell at the point.

Payne managed to get away from Isles defenseman Bob Lorimer just as Maxwell took his shot then deflected the puck, backhanded, into the net. It was his seventeenth goal in seventeen playoff games and turned out to be the game winner.

Bobby Smith, whose goal at the end of the second period was waived off by Van Hellemond because it went into the net just after time had expired, added a power-play goal with 1:48 left to play, and the North Stars treated the home crowd to its first-ever win in the Stanley Cup Finals.

For perhaps the first time in the series, the North Stars played with intensity for a full sixty minutes and, unlike in the first three games, avoided any letdowns.

Over in the visitors' locker room, Billy Smith offered credit where it was due. "It wasn't meant for us to win tonight," he said. "Every time

I looked up, they were on the power play. They're a good hockey team, and you don't figure to beat them four straight."

Beaupre's goaltending was critical. "There wasn't any pressure on me," he said after the game. "We had lost three straight. We couldn't do any worse. The guys did a great job of clearing the puck in front of the net. Every time there was a shot, our guys either knocked them down or got the puck out of there. The Islanders don't waste many shots, so I did have some tough ones to stop."

"The team showed what real character they have tonight," Sonmor gushed. "They could have folded and the series would have been over, but instead they played their best game of the season."

Payne and Beaupre weren't the only heroes of the night. Minnesota received great performances from other cast members too. The line of Steve Christoff and rookies Neal Broten and Brad Palmer was sharp, outshooting the Islanders 6–0 over one two-minute span. MacAdam finished with a goal and two assists. Brad Maxwell, playing with a bruised right shoulder, collected four helpers.

And Paul Shmyr, Minnesota's captain, was back in the lineup and making Sonmor look rather foolish for not utilizing him sooner. One of the team's oldest players at thirty-five, Shmyr had yet to play a postseason game since the quarterfinals against Buffalo but helped stabilize the North Stars defense. He set the tone early with a big hit on Potvin. "Whoever doesn't think I can play anymore," a defiant Shmyr said in a veiled dig at Sonmor, "well, this is my way of showing them."

The Islanders' nonchalance cost them a chance to wrap up the series right away.

"We knew they'd throw everything at us," said Islanders coach Al Arbour. "We knew they wouldn't fold. We made way too many mistakes, and our intensity was spotty. We have to regain that, shift after shift after shift."

The Stanley Cup, on hand in Bloomington and ready to be awarded in case of an Islanders sweep, was packed up for the return trip to Long Island.

Back in Uniondale, Arbour reminded his squad that the series was still New York's to win or lose. They didn't want the North Stars to believe for a millisecond that a comeback was possible.

Just over five minutes had elapsed in Game Four when Goring put New York ahead 1–0 with a power-play goal. It was 2–0 just twenty-five seconds later, when Wayne Merrick converted on a John Tonelli pass from behind the net. Later in the period Clark Gillies was knocked into the boards by North Stars defenseman Curt Giles, but the puck was near his skates as he tumbled forward. Gillies managed to get off a pass to Goring, who promptly scored his second goal of the game.

12. The (almost)
last line of defense:
Curt Giles. Courtesy
of the Dallas Stars

Regarded by some as the heart and soul of that Islanders dynasty, Goring had established himself as a big-game player. He lacked the pure talent of a Trottier, a Bossy, or a Potvin but had become just as indispensable. "We knew what to expect from their dominant guys," said Sonmor, "but I don't think we were prepared for so much offense out of Goring."

Minnesota received an unassisted goal from Christoff late in the first, but by then the game had already been decided. New York was so determined to close out the series that night, Gillies said, "We could have been down eight guys and won."

Still Arbour was worried because even though his team thoroughly dominated the second period, they had yet to score. Those concerns were put to rest when Bob Bourne beat Beaupre with thirty-nine seconds left in the period. McEwen scored New York's fifth goal late in the third.

When the final buzzer sounded, the Isles had a 5–1 win and their second Stanley Cup. Goring deservedly received the Conn Smythe, while the pumped up Coliseum crowd sang along to Queen's "We Are the Champions."

And the humbled North Stars, who delivered moments of excellence but few they could sustain, prepared for a long flight back to Bloomington.

"I really feel we played better than the four-games-to-one final would indicate," Payne said years later. "I felt we deserved at least one other win. I can't speak for the rest of the guys, but after Game Four we felt like we probably made our mark as best we could. We went out and tried hard in the last game, but they had a team that was better than us, could finish us off, and was at home. You couldn't get the odds any greater against us."

"You don't want to just be happy that you're in the finals," said Mac-Adam, "because you don't know if you're going to get back there next year. That's the kind of push that a team has to have. And I'm not sure that everybody had that. I can say that we were beaten by a really good team, but I prefer to say that if we had played at the top of our game, it might've been closer."

BIG MEN ON CAMPUS

Credit the Minnesota North Stars for being the first NHL team to make extensive use of college-trained athletes. This was due in large part to the presence of John Mariucci, the team's longtime assistant GM and Lou Nanne's former coach at the University of Minnesota.

Mariucci was the godfather of Minnesota hockey. As a young man "Maroosh" went from his native Eveleth to the U of M, where he starred on defense and helped transform the Gophers into a national power. After graduation he earned a spot on the Chicago Blackhawks blue line. At that time the NHL employed only a handful of Americans and even fewer ex-collegians. All the while, he endured the taunts of Canadian players, though a well-timed bodycheck was usually sufficient to silence most hecklers.

When Mariucci returned to the U of M to coach in 1952, he broke with tradition by recruiting kids from in state and throughout the western United States instead of the top Canadian players. He believed it would advance the cause of American hockey. And he was right.

Nanne, a Mariucci disciple, knew how much untapped talent there was on America's college campuses, and when he became GM of the North Stars in 1978, he decided to break with tradition too.

There had long been a stigma against hockey's scholar-athletes. Since junior circuits like the Ontario Hockey League (OHL) and the Quebec Major Junior Hockey League (QMJHL) were the traditional paths to NHL stardom, many general managers assumed that kids who opted for college over juniors lacked the desire to pursue a pro career. Better than any of his colleagues, Nanne understood the benefits of college hockey and recognized the intensity and enthusiasm those players brought to their game every night. Most college-trained players also had the benefit of instruction in the fundamentals of hockey—the kind of training they might not get in juniors.

Of the fourteen players selected by the North Stars at the 1981 draft, eight were current or incoming collegians.

It's fair to say that Nanne's conviction, combined with the success of North Stars like Neal Broten (U of M), Curt Giles (Minnesota–Duluth) and Mike Eaves (University of Wisconsin) had a major impact on the advancement of college players to the pro ranks, a process that has gained momentum in subsequent decades.

ONE STEP FORWARD, TWO STEPS BACK

A team that exceeded all expectations by reaching the Stanley Cup Finals in May 1981 still had a strong, youthful nucleus that autumn, and Dino Ciccarelli, Don Beaupre, Craig Hartsburg, Bobby Smith, and Neal Broten would be asked to build on the previous season's success.

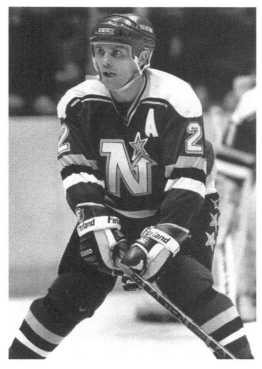

13. Curt Giles. Courtesy of the Dallas Stars

The North Stars' attack was devastating. Up front Smith and Ciccarelli became the first Minnesota players to score over one hundred points in a season. Hartsburg was coming into his own too, establishing personal and club highs in goals (seventeen), assists (sixty), and points (seventy-seven) for a defenseman.

The team went 37-23-20 and captured its first Norris Division title. Expectations of another deep postseason run were ruined, however, when Minnesota met Chicago in the division semis. Game One ended at 3:34 of overtime, when Blackhawks defenseman Greg Fox scored the first and *only* playoff goal of his NHL career. It gave Chicago momentum and damaged the North Stars' tender collective psyche. The Hawks went on to win the best-of-five series, three games to one.

That summer the club acquired Willi Plett from Calgary in exchange for Steve Christoff, Bill Nyrop, and a draft pick. Plett was a prototypical power forward who had topped the twenty-goal mark five times while reg-

NOVEMBER 11, 1981: JETS CRASH IN BLOOMINGTON

The North Stars pound the visiting Winnipeg Jets, 15–2, setting club records for most goals in one game, most goals in one period (eight), most power-play goals (five), biggest margin of victory (thirteen goals), and most players scoring at least a point in one game (seventeen). Bobby Smith's seven points (four goals, three assists) also sets a single-game franchise record.

14. Bobby Smith (left) and Neal Broten celebrate a North Stars goal. Courtesy of the Dallas Stars

ularly recording over two hundred penalty minutes. He and rookie sniper Brian Bellows added to Minnesota's extensive arsenal. And while the 1982–83 North Stars finished with a franchise-best 40-24-16 record, they fell in the second round of the playoffs to familiar foe Chicago.

The 1983–84 season began on a sour note with Bobby Smith requesting a trade. The North Stars complied, dealing their unhappy playmaker to Montreal for Keith Acton. The club didn't miss a beat, however, winning thirty-nine games and reclaiming the Norris Division crown. They made it as far as the Conference Finals, where they ran into Wayne Gretzky, his dynasty-bound Edmonton Oilers . . . and referee Bruce Hood. In Game Two of the series, Hood allowed a goal by Edmonton's Jari Kurri that proved to be the difference in a 4-3 Oiler victory, even though it appeared that the puck did not cross the goal line. Hood ruled that the puck had crossed the line while it was being cradled in Beaupre's catching glove.

Gretzky dominated the series, which the Oilers would win in four straight, accentuating a virtuoso performance with a penalty-shot goal against Beaupre in Game Three. It didn't help that Gordie Roberts, an integral piece of Minnesota's defense corps, missed most of the series with a bruised back.

The next season brought more disappointment as key players like Ciccarelli, McCarthy, and Hartsburg missed major stretches because of injury. That contributed to an off year from Broten, who never found a rhythm playing with different linemates. The goal-addicted North Stars tied for the fourth-lowest output (268) in the league, finishing eighteen

---

AROUND THE LEAGUE: 1981–1982

Teams realign within existing divisions, with new groupings based on geographical areas. Edmonton's Wayne Gretzky sets an NHL record for most goals in a season (92) and becomes the first player in history to score 200 points in a season (he'd finish with 203).

AROUND THE LEAGUE: 1983–1984

To decide regular season games that are tied at the end of regulation time, teams play five-minute sudden-death overtime. An eighteen-year-old goalie, Buffalo's Tom Barrasso, wins the Calder and Vezina trophies.

15. Brian Bellows.
Courtesy of the
Dallas Stars

games under .500. They qualified for the playoffs and even swept the Blues in the division semis, but their run was cut short by—who else?— the Chicago Blackhawks, whose Darryl Sutter scored two overtime winners in the division finals.

In 1985–86 Minnesota added a just-past-his-prime Kent Nilsson to boost its sagging goal output. Broten became the first American-born player to break the one-hundred-point mark, while his linemate, St. Paul's Scott Bjugstad, shocked everyone with a forty-three-goal effort that seemed to come out of nowhere. Ciccarelli and Bellows also had strong seasons, and Beaupre assembled a club-record fourteen-

February 14, 1985: It is Valentine's Day at Detroit's Joe Louis Arena, but Cupid is clearly out of arrows. Referee Ron Wicks has already called six fighting penalties in the first period when Willi Plett and ex–North Star Greg Smith drop their gloves at center ice. Their bout spills into the Detroit bench, where Dino Ciccarelli and Danny Gare exchange blows. In the chaos an irate Glen Sonmor jumps into the melee to get at injured Red Wings goalie Greg Stefan. Detroit coach Nick Polano tries to restrain Sonmor, and the two wrestle for nearly five minutes. The game ends in a 5–5 tie, and the North Stars are later fined $2,500 by the NHL.

MILESTONE: NOVEMBER 11, 1986

Dino Ciccarelli scores twice in his fifteenth game of the season, setting a modern NHL record for the fastest twenty goals from season's start, in a 2–2 tie against the visiting Capitals. Montreal's Joe Malone holds the all-time record with twenty goals in eight games in 1917–18.

game win streak. From February to April the North Stars were virtually unbeatable.

But it seemed that no matter what gains they made during the regular season, the North Stars could never win when the games mattered most. A first-round playoff meeting with St. Louis ended the way so many had before: with the Minnesotans cleaning out their lockers before the first of May.

The knock on those North Stars teams of the 1980s was that they were tall on talent but short on character—the kind that excelled in getting coaches fired. But for a club that relied on the professionalism and leadership of players like Broten, Keith Acton, Curt Giles, Dirk Graham, Al MacAdam, and others, that criticism hardly seems fair.

"The North Stars' problem was always that they would have a good year," Al Shaver opined, "and instead of taking it another step toward winning a Stanley Cup, they'd slide backwards. They were an inconsistent team over the years. John Mariucci used to have a saying that a hockey team is like a chain—it's only as strong as its weakest link. The North Stars never did replace those weak links adequately. They didn't make the deals that would've gotten them someone a little bit better."

IN NEED OF A MIRACLE

Glen Sonmor's battle with the bottle had been a disruption throughout the decade, and on a number of occasions the much-beloved coach was forced to leave the team to seek treatment for his alcoholism. He eventually got himself sober and took a job as the club's director of player personnel, but he stepped behind the bench one last time in February

1987, after the North Stars fired Lorne Henning with just two games left in the season. The team missed the playoffs that spring for the first time since 1979.

Lou Nanne had been trying for years to get his good friend Herb Brooks, the local legend who'd engineered the "Miracle on Ice," to coach the North Stars. He'd come close in 1978, but negotiations broke off because Brooks demanded more job security than the Gunds were willing to offer. Nanne almost got his man after the 1984–85 season, but Brooks was just coming off his firing by the Rangers and didn't feel prepared to coach again so soon.

In April 1987 the courtship culminated with Nanne finally getting Brooks' signature on a two-year contract. "It's been a long time coming," Nanne said at the time. "Herbie and I have been romancing one another for nine years. Sometimes it takes a long time to get a girl to the altar."

More than two hundred people packed the media room at Met Center for the press conference introducing Brooks as the fourteenth coach in the history of the North Stars (and seventh of the Nanne regime).

"A joke made the rounds at the club's offices that the press conference should be held on the shores of some nearby lake," Austin Murphy wrote in *Sports Illustrated*. "That way, the wiseacres said, after the announcement was made Herb could walk on the water."

That was an indication of how deeply revered Brooks was (and still is) in Minnesota, a state as hockey-mad as any of the Canadian Provinces. As coach at the University of Minnesota, he led the Gophers to three national championships. Any anonymity he enjoyed up to that point evaporated in 1980 when he coached the U.S. team to a gold medal at the Winter Olympics in Lake Placid.

Brooks had sternly and cleverly molded that unlikely collection of college kids and former college players into the best-prepared team at the tournament. Turning the North Stars into a Stanley Cup contender represented a very different challenge for the St. Paul native, who, by his own admission, had mellowed with age. He didn't feel it was neces-

GOOD-BYE, MAROOSH

A beloved member of the North Stars family since its inception, John Mariucci (1916–87) left an indelible mark on the sport in Minnesota and America. Lou Nanne, Glen Sonmor, and Herb Brooks were all disciples of the tough but fair-minded former Gophers coach. Mariucci held a number of positions with the North Stars, mostly in the field of collegiate scouting. But there was more to "Maroosh" than hockey. Described as "a man for all seasons . . . not only for hockey season," Mariucci loved opera, could converse on a wide range of topics, and had a great sense of humor. To honor this influential figure, the North Stars wore a "JM" patch on their jerseys for the 1987–88 season.

sary to act like a "wacko" (his word) to get the most out of professional athletes and actually cut out many of the rules and fines that were on the books before he was hired. He did, however, ban chewing tobacco in the dressing room and insist that players wear a suit and tie to all games, home and away . . . standard procedure nowadays.

Herbie still had plenty of fight left in him though. During a November game against the visiting Bruins, Boston scored three times in a nine-minute span in the second period. Between periods Brooks hurled a chair and broke a big-screen TV in the team meeting room. A month later, with his North Stars about to lose 8–3 to the Red Wings, a frustrated Brooks called Detroit coach Jacques Demers a "milk truck driver" (Demers had actually driven a Coca-Cola truck). Demers went ballistic and challenged Brooks to a fight on the ice. Both coaches had to be restrained by their players.

If he didn't know it from the start, Brooks came to realize that the North Stars—woefully thin behind Neal Broten, Dino Ciccarelli, and Brian Bellows and showing age at other key positions—didn't yet have the talent to be contenders. "You don't just get well overnight in the NHL," he said, doing his best to temper expectations. "All the clichés—'We're so close we can taste it' and 'We're building a dynasty'—are marketed, sold, ingrained without any basis in reality. Then, when you don't win the Stanley Cup, people ask, 'What the hell's wrong?'"

MR. VERSATILITY

A reliable penalty killer, Bob Brooke broke into the league as a center but was capable of playing every forward position. Out of necessity the Yale grad was also used as a defenseman for much of the 1987–88 season.

With a new coach and a new system, it wasn't much of a shock when the team started out slowly under Brooks. Then came a wave of injuries. Broten, the player Herb expected to spearhead Minnesota's offense, missed part of the season with a separated shoulder. Scott Bjugstad, two years removed from his breakout forty-three-goal effort, missed most of the season with a torn ligament in his right knee. A separated shoulder and a hernia limited Craig Hartsburg to just twenty-seven games. A shattered kneecap wiped out most of Dennis Maruk's season. And Steve Payne played only nine games before retiring due to a neck injury.

In the face of this adversity, Brooks knew he had to adjust his tactics. On offense he'd always preached creativity and flow, but with many of the North Stars' top scorers hobbled, he instituted a more conservative style. Yet the team continued to struggle. Back-to-back victories over the

Red Wings and the Blackhawks right before New Year's interrupted a pair of eight-game winless streaks.

The stress of losing was taking its toll on Herbie's boss. The previous spring Nanne had undergone a battery of tests at the Mayo Clinic to figure out why he'd lost twelve pounds in ten days when the North Stars missed the playoffs for the first time in eight years. A year later he was still losing sleep over the team's struggles . . . literally. Once Nanne admitted that he'd woken up in the middle of the night hyperventilating after having a dream that he'd traded Brian Bellows to Hartford for an imaginary player named Cliff Norris. It was a sign that something needed to change. In January 1988 Louie stunned the organization and hockey fans throughout the state by announcing that after the season, he would step down as GM.

As bad as the North Stars were, the Norris Division was so weak that year—only the Red Wings finished with a winning record—that Minnesota was actually in contention for a playoff spot going into the last day of the season. A loss to the Maple Leafs not only kept the North Stars out of the playoffs but assured them of the worst record in the league.

At the conclusion of what had been a brutal season, Brooks looked forward to turning things around the following year. Much would depend on who the Gunds chose as Nanne's successor. Herbie already knew he wouldn't get to be coach *and* GM since the Gunds had made it clear they weren't keen on one man trying to juggle both jobs (and, truth be told, even if they did think one man could do it all, they weren't enamored of Brooks).

AROUND THE LEAGUE: 1987–1988

In a December 8, 1987, game against the Bruins, Philadelphia's Ron Hextall becomes the first goalie in NHL history to score a goal by shooting the puck into the opponent's empty net.

BOB WOYTOWICH, 1941–1988

An original North Star and the team's first captain, Bob (Augie) Woytowich died on July 30, 1988, in a motor vehicle accident in his native Winnipeg. It was believed that Woytowich, forty-seven at the time of his death, suffered a heart attack while driving his pickup truck. The vehicle veered off the road and struck a utility pole.

Ironically, one of the people interviewed for the GM job was Craig Patrick, Brooks's assistant coach at Lake Placid and his former boss in New York. Ultimately, the Gunds went with Jack Ferreira, a former teammate of Brooks and Nanne on the 1967 U.S. national team who had been working as director of player development for the Rangers.

Nanne, the person who had acted as a buffer between Herb and the Gunds, had accepted a promotion to become team president, casting doubt on Brooks's future with the club. Initially, Ferreira seemed inclined to keep Brooks around. But when the job eventually went to former Flames assistant Pierre Page, Brooks felt blindsided. The *Minneapolis Tribune*'s John Gilbert recalled the episode in his extraordinary book *Herb Brooks: The Inside Story of a Hockey Mastermind*. In it Brooks reveals that Ferreira telephoned him and asked him to stay on as coach, then had to renege on the offer because the Gunds wanted someone else.

"To be frank," an angry Brooks told Gilbert, "I have no desire to work for the Minnesota North Stars. That is in no way a reflection on the players, who were a great group to be associated with. All season, we were decimated by injuries and had little to show for our effort other than a good attitude. The players didn't quit or blame others. They stepped on the scale of adversity and measured up very well."

DID YOU KNOW?

Lou Nanne and Walter Bush were behind efforts to get Herb Brooks named head coach of the U.S. Olympic Hockey Team leading up to the 1980 Winter Games. Nanne, who had just been named the GM of the North Stars, offered Brooks the team's head coaching job, but Brooks declined, saying that it was instead his goal to coach the Olympic team.

In addition to Brooks, six players from the "Miracle on Ice" squad also spent portions of their NHL careers with the North Stars: Neal Broten (1980–93), Jim Craig (1983–84), Steve Christoff (1980–82), Steve Janaszak (one game in 1979), Mark Johnson (1981–82), and Mark Pavelich (1986–87). Another Olympian, Phil Verchota, was drafted seventy-fifth overall by Minnesota in 1976, but he opted to play overseas rather than sign a contract with the North Stars.

HARD LESSONS

If the ice at Met Center had become a stage for scenes of heartbreak and folly, so too had the draft table.

In 1983 the North Stars reserved their top pick for left wing Brian Lawton, a New Jersey native and the first U.S.-born player to be selected first overall. He had enjoyed two impressive seasons at the revered Mount St. Charles Academy in Rhode Island, scoring eighty-five goals in only forty-nine games. Only three months removed from his eighteenth birthday, Lawton joined the North Stars and appeared in fifty-eight games during the 1983–84 season. Though he managed just ten goals, the club was convinced that the dynamic offensive talents Lawton displayed on the high school level would eventually resurface in the NHL.

But Lawton, pressed into service before he was ready, never lived up to the hype that accompanied his status as a No. 1 pick. His twenty-one goals and forty-four points in 1986–87 both marked career highs. By 1988 he was property of the Rangers and within five years, out of hockey.

Imagine how different the North Stars' fortunes might have been had they passed on Lawton in favor of future Hall of Famers Pat LaFontaine or Steve Yzerman, who were drafted third (by the Islanders) and fourth (by Detroit) respectively. Other top-ten selections that year included Tom Barrasso, Cam Neely, Russ Courtnall, and John MacLean.

Minnesota didn't fare too well in subsequent years either, drafting Dave Quinn, Stéphane Roy, Warren Babe, and Dave Archibald with its first selection in consecutive drafts. Quinn, whose career was derailed due to a rare blood disorder, would never play a game in the NHL. Roy, the kid brother of Patrick Roy, was a fixture on the Canadian National Team but appeared in only a dozen NHL games, all with Minnesota. Babe was a highly regarded prospect with size, strength, offensive skills, and, sadly, a habit of getting concussed. He retired at twenty-two. And Archibald, chosen sixth overall in 1987 after scoring fifty goals in his last season of juniors, was dropped into the league as an eighteen-year-old and expected to be the North Stars' savior. He wasn't.

16. Herb Brooks. Courtesy of *USA* Hockey

NORTH STARS ADD SOME IRON

The NHL's reigning Iron Man, Doug Jarvis, played 964 consecutive games with Montreal, Washington, and Hartford. Shortly after retiring in 1988, the four-time Stanley Cup winner joined the North Stars coaching staff as an assistant under Pierre Page. Jarvis would stay with the Minnesota/Dallas franchise for fourteen years, becoming the longest-tenured assistant coach in the NHL.

Proving the old adage that even a blind squirrel finds an acorn every now and then, the North Stars did manage not to bungle the second overall pick in 1982 when they chose goal-scoring machine Brian Bellows. And in 1988 the team used the top pick on a chipmunk-cheeked speedster from Livonia, Michigan, named Mike Modano.

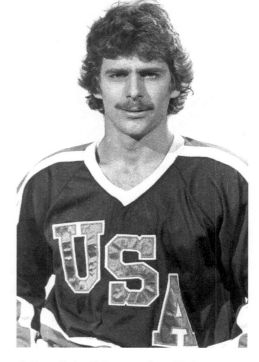

17. Neal Broten. Courtesy of *USA* Hockey

18. Steve Christoff. Courtesy of *USA* Hockey

CLOAK AND DAGGER

Drafted thirty-eighth overall by the North Stars in 1983, Frantisek (Frank) Musil was blocked from coming to North America by the Communist regime in his native Czechoslovakia. The story of how he achieved his dream of playing in the NHL would make a great movie.

In the summer of 1986, after three years of careful planning and covert messages exchanged in brief encounters between Musil and Lou Nanne, a scheme to get the big defenseman out of Czechoslovakia was put in motion. With the aid of Nanne and agent Ritch Winter, Musil staged an elaborate defection while on vacation in the former Yugoslavia. Nanne and Winter obtained an American work visa for Musil and used it to trick the border guards, who had no idea that Musil was a defecting hockey player. No one in Musil's inner circle—not his parents, not his brother, not even his girlfriend—knew of his plans to defect until after it was all over. Absolute secrecy was a necessity. There was a lot more than a hockey career at stake if the plan backfired.

Nanne waited until Musil completed his Czech military obligation before helping him leave his homeland. Had he been caught defecting while serving in the army, he could have faced execution.

"I told Louie if one of us has to go over there and get shot," Glen Sonmor joked, "it wouldn't be me because I don't make enough money. But if I was going to get shot over a player, this would be the guy."

Musil joined the North Stars that fall, providing the club with a steady blue-line presence for just over four seasons.

19. Frantisek Musil. Courtesy of the Dallas Stars

Some new faces helped put Minnesota back in the 1989 playoff hunt.

After several years of backup and minor league duty, hot goalie prospect Jon Casey was ready to wrestle the No. 1 job from Don Beaupre.

Dino Ciccarelli was still a marquee talent and probably the best goal scorer the North Stars ever had, but he enhanced his bad-boy image with a 1987 arrest for indecent exposure. A changing of the front-office guard pointed to the end of his days in Minnesota, and in March 1989 Jack Ferreira dealt Ciccarelli and defenseman Bob Rouse to the Washington Capitals for a pair of future Hall of Famers: puck-moving defenseman Larry Murphy and right wing Mike Gartner, whose consistency (nine consecutive seasons with thirty-five or more goals!) and professionalism were beyond reproach. And compared to Dino, Gartner—a born-again Christian—was a choirboy on skates. Dave Gagner, a former first-round pick of the Rangers, broke out with thirty-five goals after being called up from IHL (International Hockey League) Kalamazoo.

REMEMBERING DOC ROSE

Richard (Doc) Rose, the team's longtime trainer, was the ultimate North Stars fan, and he had a front-row seat for all the action from 1970 until a bad back forced him into retirement after the 1989–90 season.

Rose, who passed away in September 2012 at age seventy-four, worked tirelessly in an age when NHL trainers doubled as equipment managers. Needed a skate sharpened? A glove restitched? A bruise iced? Doc was your man.

"He would stay at the rink all day long," Lou Nanne recalled in an interview with the *Star Tribune*. "He'd make the players come in for their treatments. He'd stay all night. The locker room was his home, and the players were his family."

Loving the game as he did, and being so emotionally invested in his care of the players, Rose sometimes found it difficult to temper his excitement.

One night, during a February 1982 game between the North Stars and the Hartford Whalers, Bobby Smith and Hartford's Russ Anderson were whistled for matching roughing penalties. Rose expressed his disapproval by gesturing with his hand to his throat, implying that referee Denis Morel choked and blew the call. Morel gave Rose a bench penalty, and the Whalers scored on the power play in a game the North Stars won 8–7.

Strengthened by these new additions, the North Stars placed third in the Norris Division but were easy prey for St. Louis in the semifinals, which won that series four games to one.

In addition to strong efforts from Casey (a league-high thirty-one wins), Brian Bellows (fifty-five goals), and Neal Broten (sixty-two assists), the 1989–90 campaign was significant because it offered everyone in the

North Stars' universe an exciting, extended look at the young man who would one day rewrite the team record books. Rookie Mike Modano, who had made his pro debut during the 1989 playoffs, scored twenty-nine goals and seventy-five points. The kid looked like a shoe-in for the Calder Trophy, but that award was eventually given to Calgary's Sergei Makarov. "Mo" had to settle for Rookie of the Year honors as voted by scribes at the *Hockey News*.

In a cruel twist of fate that surely felt to the hockey fans of Minnesota like someone's idea of a sick joke, the North Stars drew the Blackhawks in the semifinals by virtue of Chicago winning the division. The series went the distance, but with the benefit of home-ice advantage, the Hawks won Game Seven and snuffed out Minnesota's Stanley Cup hopes. Again.

HEARTBREAK ON LAKE NOKOMIS

"I got hit with a puck at a North Stars game when I was a kid. My dad was with me, and I couldn't have been more than eight years old. The ushers came down to check on us, which I remember very clearly because they wore these bright red blazers. I didn't take a direct hit—the puck ricocheted off a few other people before grazing my left cheek. A guy sitting a few seats to our left ended up catching it. I was crying like a baby, so he handed it to me. I thought that puck was the coolest thing ever. It was a really cherished item of mine, and I'd show it off to the neighborhood kids. Then I made the mistake of using it to play pond hockey on Lake Nokomis in Minneapolis . . . which is how I lost it. Why my dad actually let me use that puck to play hockey is beyond me. He probably told me not to, and I did it anyway."—Bud Kleppe, St. Paul

---

HOCKEY BUSINESS 101

In the late 1980s revenue-generating amenities like luxury suites were becoming more and more important to arena managers. When Met Center added twenty suites in 1988, they sold right away. But the Gunds wanted about forty-five more at a price tag of $15 million—an expense they asked their landlord, the Metropolitan Sports Facilities Commission, to shoulder. The brothers' reasoning was that additional improvements to Met Center were essential to keeping the North Stars in Minnesota. The commission considered the Gunds' request, then voted unanimously to reject it.

Season ticket sales were down, thanks to a string of public relations disasters, most notably the Bobby Smith trade and the firing of Herb Brooks. Corporate support for the North Stars was dwindling too. Met Center had been built in Bloomington, right next to Metropolitan Stadium, in part so that the North Stars would be identified with the Twins and the Vikings. Walter Bush and the original owners envisioned the hockey team as one of the "big three," but then the Twins and the Vikings moved to downtown Minneapolis, and much of the corporate support went with them.

By 1990 the economic strain on the club had become unbearable. Citing losses in the neighborhood of $16 million, the Gunds filed a formal application with the league to move the club to California unless a suitable local buyer stepped forward.

"Minnesota does not want [the North Stars]," Gordon Gund prophetically told his colleagues on the Board of Governors. "The only way you'll get Minnesota to want it is to let us leave; then maybe two years later, they'll want an expansion franchise."

As it happened, expansion was again on the NHL's agenda, and the league set $50 million as an acceptable buy-in fee.

Gordon was a respected member of the board who had chaired a number of important subcommittees, but he raised the ire of some peers by insisting that the North Stars would not be sold for anything less than the expansion fee, arguing that doing so would actually devalue existing franchises.

There was the belief among many governors that by demanding at least $50 million for the North Stars, the Gunds were actually attempting to dissuade any local investors, including Minneapolis envelope mogul Harvey Mackay, from buying the team, thus clearing the way for a West Coast move.

Mackay wasn't the only potential buyer. Peter Karmanos, the Compuware CEO who would later purchase the Hartford Whalers and move that team to the hockey hotbed of North Carolina, put in a bid for the North Stars well below the Gunds' asking price. Karmanos was so confident that a deal would get done that he announced, rather tactlessly, that former NHL goalie Jim Rutherford would eventually replace Jack Ferreira as GM.

Meanwhile, Hollywood movie producer Howard Baldwin (*Mystery, Alaska*) was interested in applying for an expansion team in San Jose. No stranger to the pro hockey business, Baldwin was the founder and former owner of the Whalers who'd helped broker the NHL-WHA merger.

However, San Jose was about thirty miles from the San Francisco Bay, where the Gunds were hoping to move the North Stars. Under league rules an NHL franchise had the exclusive right to operate within a fifty-mile radius of its home city. Thus, a team located in Oakland, San Francisco, or San Jose would have the exclusive territorial rights to all three cities.

The league's chief counsel and eventual president, Gil Stein, chronicled the tense negotiations that ensued in *Power Plays: An Inside Look at the Big Business of the National Hockey League.* According to Stein, the Board of Governors feared that if the Gunds succeeded in relocating the North Stars, it might undermine the league's expansion plans. But if they weren't, then the NHL could be drawn into lengthy and ugly litigation.

Norman Green, a part owner of the Calgary Flames and boyhood friend of Baldwin's partner, former Budget Rent-A-Car CEO Morris Belzberg, believed he had a solution. Green suggested that the Gunds sell the North Stars to the Baldwin-Belzberg group at a more affordable price, and then, as part of the same transaction, the league would award the Gunds an expansion team in the Bay Area for the full $50 million entry fee. The proposal would give everyone what they wanted and allow all parties to save face, and it was generally met with much enthusiasm.

The Gunds, however, were not keen on the idea of having to start from scratch with an expansion team. They had stocked the North Stars with some good young players and wanted to be competitive the moment they touched down in California.

NHL president John Ziegler encouraged the Gunds to work something out with Baldwin. When the two parties emerged from negotiations, they presented a complex and laughably unfair deal that would see Baldwin and Belzberg purchase the North Stars for $31 million but have its players for only one year. Then the Gunds' new Bay Area franchise would acquire *all* of Minnesota's NHL and minor league players as well as its entry draft picks in 1990 and 1991.

"The obvious one-sidedness of the deal," Stein recalled, "was a testament to either the genius of Gordon Gund as a negotiator, the weakness of the Baldwin-Belzberg financial position, or, more likely, a little of each."

Board members were appalled. But at the same time, they were afraid that if the Gunds did not get their way, they would drag the NHL into court. Several governors urged Ziegler to let the deal go through to avoid a certain lawsuit, but the league president was resolute in believing that the player portion of the transaction was unacceptable and succeeded in leading the majority of governors to oppose it.

Faced with the prospect of filing an antitrust action against the NHL or tinkering with the original plan, the Gunds opted for the latter. The revised plan—and one ultimately approved by the Board of Governors— was just as complicated as the first but more equitable in terms of player distribution: Minnesota and the Bay Area franchise, which later became the San Jose Sharks, would hold an intraclub draft and player exchange in June 1991 in which the Sharks would get to claim players from Minnesota's reserve list.

Baldwin and Belzberg purchased the North Stars but soon ran into trouble raising enough money to complete the transaction. Calgary's

20. A short-lived partnership: Howard Baldwin (left), Norm Green, and Morris Belzberg pose with a replica Stanley Cup. Courtesy of the Dallas Stars

Green, itching to become the controlling owner of an NHL club, sold his interest in the Flames so that he could buy a 51 percent stake in the North Stars. Not long after assuming the team presidency, Green bought out his partners.

THE SAVIOR

A tall and charismatic character with slicked-back silver hair, Norm Green made his millions building shopping malls in Canada. He burst onto the Twin Cities scene with his Rolls Royce, a pair of English spaniels, and a determined belief that he could transform the North Stars into Stanley Cup champions. His enthusiasm seemed boundless.

Calling his acquisition of the North Stars "a hockey entrepreneur's dream," Green sounded and acted like a man who would be committed to his investment over the long haul. The real estate mogul sought to distinguish himself from the Gunds by offering assurances that a team run as a business under *his* stewardship would not lose money: "I have a chance to take a poorly managed team, one that lost $16 million over four years, in a good hockey market, and make it profitable in its first season. It's as if I were in heaven."

But to Green, there was nothing heavenly about the terms of the franchise agreement that Howard Baldwin had helped negotiate with the Gunds. He felt it was far too generous to San Jose and potentially damaging to the North Stars. Green, who bought into the team after the deal was made, talked about wanting to renegotiate, but the Sharks saw little benefit in doing that. They were soon informed that their scouts would no longer receive free passes for games at Met Center.

Before selling off his share of the North Stars, Baldwin had hired Bob Clarke to be the new GM (Jack Ferreira and his assistant, Dean Lombardi, followed the Gunds to San Jose). Clarke had been running the Flyers for the previous six seasons and helped guide Philadelphia to the Stanley Cup Finals in 1985 and 1987. One of his first priorities would be to fill the coaching vacancy created when Pierre Page resigned to become the new general manager of the Nordiques. John Paddock, Paul Holmgren, and Terry Crisp were all linked to the job, which wasn't surprising, since all three had played with Clarke.

Instead Clarke chose Bob Gainey, a five-time Stanley Cup winner with the Canadiens who, at just thirty-six, was already a rising star in the coaching ranks. The two men knew each other well: Gainey had served as vice president of the Players' Association when Clarke was president; and they were teammates in Canada Cup tournaments and competed against each other throughout the seventies and eighties. Together they were about to play a role in one of the most exciting postseason runs in the history of the NHL.

A BRUSH WITH MAGNIFICENCE

Clarke busied himself revamping the North Stars' defense corps. In the expansion draft he added character and leadership in veteran Rob Ramage and size in Allen Pederson. He also claimed Dave Babych, then traded him to Vancouver for Tom Kurvers, who in turn was moved to the Islanders for shot-blocker extraordinaire Craig Ludwig. Clarke then traded Larry Murphy to Pittsburgh with Peter Taglianetti for two local boys: Jim Johnson and Chris Dahlquist.

DID YOU KNOW?

In September 1990 the North Stars joined the Montreal Canadiens on a preseason barnstorming tour through the Soviet Union called "Friendship Tour '90." Games were played in Moscow, Leningrad, Kiev, and Riga. Soviet hockey fans greeted the visitors enthusiastically, but they were also eager to see how their national teams matched up against the visitors from North America. The Soviets proved to be stronger, finishing with a 5-3 record against their NHL counterparts.

The North Stars got off to a slow start in the 1990–91 season. It took longer than expected for a few of Clarke's offseason acquisitions to gel, but the team also missed Basil McRae, the enforcer and de facto captain who sat out half the season recuperating from an injury suffered during the preseason. His dressing-room presence was not easily replaced.

21. Minnesota's emerging star Mike Modano jockeys for position with some pesky Devils. Courtesy of the Dallas Stars

It also took time for Bob Gainey, the rookie coach, to fully comprehend the strengths and weaknesses of his squad and use players in situations where they stood the best chance of being successful.

After the All-Star break, a phenomenal metamorphosis occurred. The North Stars became more proficient in their own end and played with a sound, disciplined style. Dave Gagner, Brian Bellows, Ulf Dahlen, and Mike Modano returned to form after sluggish starts. At age thirty-two Brian Propp dipped into the fountain of youth to deliver a twenty-six-goal, seventy-three-point effort. Though Stew Gavin missed half the season due to injury, a strong defense corps got stronger with the continued maturation of Mark Tinordi, the hulking twenty-four-year-old who contributed at both ends of the rink and established himself as Minnesota's MVP.

"At home we were extremely confident," said Gagner. "We didn't care who we played. We had all the pieces: youth, experience, and good team speed. Guys like Neal Broten were in the prime of their careers. Bobby Smith came back after having a lot of success in Montreal. We had young guys on defense like Shawn Chambers and Neil Wilkinson who were playing really well. Johnson and Dahlquist gave us a lot of consistency and grit. And Brian Propp was a centerman's dream because he did all the little things well. He was the best left winger I ever had . . . but don't tell Basil McRae I said that."

What looked at first glance like a fairly average hockey club was getting above-average results. The North Stars went 15-11-6 over their final thirty-two games, including 12-1-2 at Met Center, finished as the eighth seed in the West, and drew first-place Chicago in the first round of the playoffs.

Mike Keenan's Blackhawks had won the President's Trophy for finishing with the league's best record (49-23-8), and their formidable arsenal included Jeremy Roenick, Steve Larmer, and Michel Goulet. Chris Chelios anchored the defense. And any chinks in the club's collective armor would be plugged by Ed Belfour, one of the best young netminders in the game. To beat a club that good and that deep, the North Stars would have to play with extraordinary discipline.

Gainey's troops did just that, winning Game One in overtime on a goal from Propp. Games Two and Three went to the Blackhawks, but Minnesota evened the series in Game Four with a 3–1 victory.

In Game Five the Blackhawks lost their composure and took a series of stupid penalties. Growing increasingly confident on the power play, the North Stars capitalized on their chances and humiliated the Hawks, 6-0, at Chicago Stadium.

Two nights later Minnesota closed out the series with another 3–1 win, becoming the first team in twenty years to upset a top-ranked club in the first round. Revenge was sweet, although no one could have predicted at the time that the sixth postseason meeting between these fierce rivals would be the last.

Next up was St. Louis, which had the second-best record in the league and a lethal one-two punch in sharpshooter Brett Hull and his setup man, Adam Oates. The pair had combined for over 240 points during the regular season, and Minnesota's chances hinged on its ability to contain this dynamic duo.

The North Stars employed the same tactics against St. Louis that had worked so well against Chicago. Stew Gavin and Gaetan Duchesne shadowed Oates and Hull throughout the series, while Tinordi's defensive play seemed to get better with each passing game. Once again Minnesota closed out a series on a heavily favored opponent in six games.

The Blues and the Blackhawks were tough, but Edmonton, reigning Stanley Cup champ and the last team standing five times in the last seven years, posed a unique threat in the Conference Finals. A superpower in decline, the Oilers had begun to unload some of the heroes from their glory years, but the ones they had left—Mark Messier, Glenn Anderson, and Grant Fuhr, to name a few—were full of pride and would not go quietly into that good night.

Minnesota's strategy was pretty simple: continue converting on power plays and protect leads when they had them.

After a 3–1 win in Edmonton, the North Stars found themselves on the wrong end of a 7–2 rout in Game Two. The turning point of the series came in Game Three when Modano and Bellows sparked Minnesota's attack with a pair of momentum-shifting breakaway goals. The North Stars struck five more times that night and rolled to an easy 7–3 win. Minnesota's victory was so decisive that it prompted Oilers owner Peter Pocklington to remark, "They play like we used to play."

Game Four saw Minnesota win another lopsided match, but the fifth game in Edmonton was a much closer contest. With the game tied at 2–2 early in the final frame, Stew Gavin carried the puck into the Oilers' zone and fed a breaking Bobby Smith, whose long reach stretched around a frozen Grant Fuhr for what would become the game- and series-winning goal.

The North Stars, a team that finished the regular season with just sixty-eight points (sixteenth overall), had stunned the hockey world by advancing to the championship round for the second time in franchise history. There they would face the Pittsburgh Penguins. For the first time in almost sixty years, the Stanley Cup would be contested by two teams that had never won it.

In the first three rounds, Minnesota upended three supposedly superior foes by assessing and then exploiting each team's weaknesses. If Pittsburgh had a vulnerability, it wasn't readily apparent. Making their first appearance in the finals, the Penguins finished first in the Patrick Division despite toiling for most of the season without their best player and captain, Mario Lemieux. His lieutenants, including Mark Recchi, Paul Coffey, and Kevin Stevens, played well in his absence, and the team was strengthened by the late-season acquisitions of center Ron Francis and defenseman Ulf Samuelsson.

Unfortunately for the North Stars, No. 66 was ready to play when the series opened on May 15, 1991, at Pittsburgh's Civic Arena, a dome-shaped, concrete colossus nicknamed "The Igloo."

The Pens outshot Minnesota 17–9 in the first period, but the North Stars, who gave Pittsburgh a series of early power plays, received goals from Neal Broten and Ulf Dahlen and carried a 2–1 lead into the first intermission.

Lemieux tied the game with a shorthanded breakaway goal early in the second. North Stars winger Marc Bureau answered with a shorthander of his own three minutes later. Less than a minute had elapsed when Pittsburgh's Scott Young tied the game on the power play with a shot from the left point. With about three minutes to go in the period, Broten scored his second goal of the game.

22. Mark Tinordi stickhandles through a flock of Penguins. Courtesy of the Dallas Stars

Bobby Smith's conversion of a Dahlen feed 1:39 into the third period gave the North Stars their second two-goal lead of the night. Joe Mullen cut that lead back to one halfway through the third, when he was hit by Jaromir Jagr's wraparound attempt at the left post.

Shifting gears Minnesota clogged up the neutral zone with all five skaters, employing its team defense concept almost perfectly over the game's final six to eight minutes. The Pens pulled Tom Barrasso for the extra attacker and generated some good scoring chances in the closing minute, including one glorious, last-second attempt by Lemieux that missed by inches, but the North Stars held on for a 5–4 win.

Without great goaltending and penalty killing, the North Stars would have been toast. Shorthanded *eight times*, Minnesota's skaters limited the Penguins to only one power-play goal.

It was the fourth consecutive series that the North Stars kicked off with a victory and the fourth the Penguins opened with a loss—a neat little factoid at the time but completely useless in trying to predict who'd win the cup.

There was cause for concern, however, about the condition of Brian Bellows. During Game One, Ulf Samuelsson nailed Minnesota's leading playoff scorer with a low hit that left the winger with a severe charley horse. Bellows played through pain the rest of the series and was far less effective.

More bad news: Paul Coffey, who was expected to miss at least the first four games of the finals with a broken jaw, was coming back early.

Coach Bob Johnson announced he would use the speedy defenseman as a power-play specialist.

The Penguins were nursing a 2–1 lead late in the second period of Game Two when Lemieux scored one of the most breathtaking goals of his career. The play began with Lemieux taking the puck from teammate Phil Bourque at the top of the circle in Pittsburgh's zone. He carried it up the middle of the ice, slipped between defensemen Neil Wilkinson *and* Shawn Chambers, and while sliding to his knees, flipped a backhander past Jon Casey.

"The sleight-of-hand required to complete the play at the speed Lemieux was traveling was astounding," Jay Greenberg recorded in *Sports Illustrated*. "The spectacle was also deflating for the North Stars, who had all but shut down [Brett] Hull and other potent scorers in the first three rounds."

Pittsburgh Press writer Dave Molinari called it "the kind of play on which a series can turn." At the very least Mario's goal helped the Penguins knot the series at 1–1 before heading back to Minnesota.

The North Stars were welcomed home by a frenzied Met Center crowd of 15,378 for Game Three. What fans did not know at the time was that Lemieux had pulled a muscle in his back while taking off his skates after warm-ups. Fifteen minutes before the opening face-off, the Pens learned they would be taking the ice without their superstar captain.

This was nothing new for Lemieux's teammates. The North Stars expected them to play hard, and they did not disappoint.

Casey and Barrasso matched each other save for glorious save through the first period and up to the seven-minute mark of the second. Then Minnesota broke through.

Modano, crossing the blue line at center ice, spotted a streaking Dave Gagner coming down the left side and dished the puck to him with a perfect tape-to-tape pass. Gagner zipped around defenseman Peter Taglianetti, cut to the front of the goal, and stuffed the puck between Barrasso's legs.

Just thirty-three seconds later, Bobby Smith capitalized on a Pittsburgh turnover, retrieving a pass from Bellows and firing a shot that sailed over Barrasso's shoulder. It would turn out to be his fifth game-winning goal of the playoffs, tying an NHL record.

Phil Bourque spoiled Casey's shutout bid early in the third, but Gaetan Duchesne added an insurance goal for Minnesota forty-six seconds later. The North Stars won 3–1, giving them a 2–1 series lead.

Could this really be happening? Were the North Stars really two wins away from a Stanley Cup? Destiny seemed to be guiding Minnesota's Little Team That Could, and nobody wanted to jinx it.

"We said all the right things to the media after games," Gagner recalled. "Bob Gainey would tell us what to say. He'd say, 'Be humble, always be respectful of the other team, and don't give them a reason to hate you. If you do that, they'll want to beat you that much more.' We did what he said, but after Game Three the media in Minnesota started talking about where they were going to hold the parade. That just wakes up the other team. It pissed them off a little and made us ripe for the picking, I guess. Five minutes into Game Four, the bubble burst."

Sure enough the Penguins torched Casey with three goals in the first *three* minutes. Stevens, Francis, and Lemieux were on the board before the North Stars knew what hit them, though Gagner scored with 1:38 left in the period.

Bryan Trottier, the ex-Islander great who had victimized the North Stars in their previous Stanley Cup Finals appearance a decade earlier, scored halfway through the second period to put the Penguins up, 4–1.

A pair of power-play goals from Propp and Modano cut Pittsburgh's lead to one. In the third period, when Troy Loney was whistled for high-sticking Mark Tinordi in the face, the North Stars were given a five-minute power play and a golden opportunity to get the tying marker. Instead they were held without a shot for almost four minutes. Phil Bourque added an empty-netter with fifteen seconds remaining, and Pittsburgh held on for a 5–3 victory.

The discipline Minnesota employed with so much success against Chicago, St. Louis, and Edmonton had eroded, and its record-setting, deadly efficient power play was beginning to sputter.

It was also becoming increasingly difficult to contain Mario Lemieux. Whispers that he received preferential treatment from officials were growing in volume, but that could not mask the undeniable truth that he was talented enough to win games all by himself and deeply driven to be considered a star on par with Wayne Gretzky. Only a Stanley Cup would accomplish this.

The North Stars were in trouble, spotting Pittsburgh a four-goal lead in the first period of Game Five. The onslaught began when Minnesota defenseman Brian Glynn was sent off for cross-checking Lemieux behind the net (Gainey thought it was "just a push"). Lemieux scored on the ensuing power play, then assisted on two goals from Mark Recchi at even strength, driving a rattled Casey from the net. Backup Brian Hayward stepped in and tried to stop the bleeding.

The North Stars cut Pittsburgh's lead to two with shorthanded goals from Broten and Gagner. Barrasso, who suffered a first-period groin injury, was replaced by Frank Pietrangelo to start the second. He also turned in a solid effort in relief.

Francis put the Pens up 5–2 late in the second, but as they had so many times in the series, the Penguins allowed the North Stars to claw and scrape their way back into the game.

Dahlen and Gagner scored third-period goals, cutting Minnesota's deficit to one. But with less than two minutes to go in the game, ex–North Star Larry Murphy rifled a shot at Hayward, while Loney, a tall left wing, crashed the net. The puck ended up behind Hayward, and Loney, who had muscled his way past Broten, was credited with the goal. Murphy collected his fourth assist against his former club, and the Penguins skated to a 6–4 victory.

The North Stars trailed in the series for the first time. Worst of all they now faced elimination on home ice. All anyone could expect or demand of the club when it returned to Bloomington two nights later was its best effort yet. Having lost only two of their previous twenty-four home games, the North Stars had recent history on their side.

But the sixth game began as most in the series had: with Minnesota having to play catch-up.

Barrasso was back between the pipes, his achy groin tightly wrapped. The North Stars knew he was hurting, so they went at him early and often. He was bumped twice before Broten was finally whistled for interference nine seconds into the game.

With thirteen seconds left on the man advantage, Trottier won a face-off deep in Minnesota's zone and got the puck back to Taglianetti at the right point. Taglianetti slid it across to Ulf Samuelsson, who fired a shot that sailed between the legs of a screened Casey.

A string of penalties to both teams prevented the game from taking on any kind of offensive flow, but when it did, it flowed in Pittsburgh's favor. With the Penguins playing three-on-four, Larry Murphy banked the puck off the boards to his left. Lemieux picked it up, broke in alone on Casey, and slid a backhander into the net. A Joe Mullen power-play goal followed fifty-five seconds later.

That was it for Casey, who was clearly not on his game. Brian Hayward took over in the second period, but he didn't fare much better.

Where the Penguins had too often become complacent after jumping out to early leads, they now understood that a sustained attack might be enough to bury the North Stars for good. And bury them they did, striking again at 13:53 of the period, when Bob Errey poked in a curl-in attempt by Jaromir Jagr. Goals from Francis and Mullen followed. By the second intermission the Pens led 6–0, and Bob Gainey's crew was out of gas and out of answers.

There were no late-game comebacks this time—no more magic tricks up Gainey's sleeve. Murphy and rookie Jim Paek tallied in the third, and the Penguins, outshot 39–28, cruised to an 8–0 win and their first championship.

All the Met Center crowd could do was offer polite applause as NHL president John Ziegler handed the Stanley Cup to Lemieux, who also skated away with the Conn Smythe Trophy. One man can't win it all by himself, but "Le Magnifique" certainly gave the Pens a lift when they needed it most.

For the North Stars, it was a fun ride while it lasted. "It's an unbelievable feeling when you go to the rink and just know you're going to win," said Gagner. "Nobody expected us to do well in the playoffs, but we got to within two games of winning the Stanley Cup. It was definitely the most fun I've ever had."

"Reaching the finals in 1991," Dahlen said, "was the best hockey memory of my career. The whole city was going crazy. I wish it had been like that the whole time, because I really enjoyed playing in Minnesota. We beat Chicago and really felt like we had a realistic chance. We just kept the momentum going against St. Louis and were really riding high against Edmonton, and everything started to go really fast, including the first few games of the final. We felt that we had a chance to win no matter who we played. We kept getting stronger and stronger with every win, but then Mario really turned it up a notch."

4

GREENER PASTURES (1991–1993)

The dispersal and expansion drafts to stock the incoming San Jose Sharks were held via conference call on May 30, 1991, less than a week after the Stanley Cup Finals.

In the dispersal draft the Sharks claimed four active players from Minnesota's roster—goalie Brian Hayward, brawler Shane Churla (who was reacquired days later in a swap for center Kelly Kisio), and defensemen Neil Wilkinson and Rob Zettler—as well as ten from their system, including goalie Arturs Irbe and defenseman Link Gaetz, a six-feet-three, 240-pound bruiser who showed up at the '88 draft with two black eyes suffered in a bar fight the night before. Of Gaetz (aka "The Missing Link"), Lou Nanne famously said, "In the first round we drafted Mike Modano to protect the franchise, in the second round we drafted Link to protect Mike, and in the third round we should've drafted a lawyer to protect Link."

Though they improved in terms of points, up by two to seventy, the North Stars (32-42-6) dropped from sixteenth to eighteenth overall in 1991-92. Progress made the previous season didn't carry over for players like Jon Casey, who took until the end of the year to recapture the form that had made him a playoff hero in the spring of '91. Up front the team didn't get the same kind of offensive production from guys like Neal Broten and Brian Propp, who combined for only twenty goals.

And the team suffered through a variety of injuries to its defense corps: Mark Tinordi missed seventeen games after suffering nerve damage in his leg, while Rob Ramage and Allen Pedersen were also lost for extended periods. That put extra pressure on rookie defenseman Kevin

23. To celebrate the team's twenty-fifth anniversary, the North Stars wore on their uniforms a commemorative patch of this design. It depicts Bill Goldsworthy, wearing a green uniform, facing off against Mike Modano, wearing the club's new black uniform. Author's collection

MILESTONE: NOVEMBER 30, 1991
Bobby Smith scores his one thousandth career NHL point with an assist (and later adds a goal) in Minnesota's 4–3 win over the Toronto Maple Leafs.

Hatcher, but even he was out of action for thirty-plus games because of an ankle injury and a league-imposed suspension.

The North Stars squeaked into the 1992 playoffs and actually grabbed a surprising 3-1 series lead on Detroit in the division semis. Then the Red Wings rallied to win three straight, and with a wave of Steve Yzerman's wand, hockey season in Minnesota disappeared.

That June Bob Clarke went back to Philadelphia to become senior vice president of the Flyers, leaving Bob Gainey to take on the dual role of coach and GM of the North Stars. Preferring to focus on his coaching duties, and not wanting to end up a burned-out mess like Wren Blair, Gainey left much of the off-ice minutiae to assistants Doug Armstrong and Les Jackson.

AROUND THE LEAGUE: 1991–1992

As the NHL celebrates its seventy-fifth anniversary season, it also becomes a twenty-two-team league with the addition of the San Jose Sharks. The 1991–92 regular season is suspended due to a players' strike on April 1, 1992. Play resumes eleven days later.

STORM CLOUDS

Norm Green's relationship with Minnesota was beginning to sour. There are plenty of theories about when and why the honeymoon ended, but it's likely the seeds of disdain were planted years earlier when the Metropolitan Sports Facilities Commission (MSFC) nixed his grandiose plan to develop the land around Met Center.

"Like the Gund brothers, Norm had some very good plans to not only remodel Met Center and add more luxury suites but also have a skyway connecting the arena with Mall of America," said Wally [son of Al] Shaver, the team's former advertising sales director and color commentator for KITN-TV in Minneapolis. "He also wanted to add some retail. That was his background: shopping centers. That's where he made all of his dough. He knew how one could support the other."

Green called his proposed $30 million development Arena of the Stars. He believed that revenue from the retail outlets would help offset the rising cost of player salaries, but he wasn't going to foot the entire bill for a project of that magnitude out of his own pocket. So he took his case to the MSFC, owners of Met Center and the surrounding land.

Essentially, Green wanted the MSFC to hand over the land for free—with no property taxes—and in exchange he offered to sign a long-term lease to keep the North Stars in Bloomington for up to twenty-five years. The commission wanted no part of it.

"He didn't want to pay for it," the MSFC's executive vice president, Bill Lester, told the *Star Tribune*, "and that was not acceptable to us."

The commission was willing to sell the land . . . for $28 million. It was too big a price tag for Green, who felt he'd be doing Bloomington a favor by developing potentially lucrative property that was sitting unused.

There may have been other, less obvious forces working against Green, like the festering rivalry between suburban Bloomington and cosmopolitan Minneapolis. It's been suggested that, with six of seven MSFC members from Minneapolis, the commission was really just looking to stymie further competition from Bloomington. Would Green's development siphon business away from the new downtown Minneapolis Convention Center and other commercial interests in the city?

"The Metropolitan Sports Facilities Commission put the death nail into the North Stars' coffin," Shaver opined. "The MSFC, which was largely comprised of Minneapolis business people, had a mission statement to support professional sports, but they rarely lifted a finger to help the North Stars. They were more involved with trying to get a dome built for the Vikings and Twins downtown. That took both those teams out of Bloomington. Well, Bloomington had an opportunity to build the Mall of America when Minneapolis said they didn't have room for it. That really pissed off a lot of the politicians and big business people in downtown Minneapolis. They didn't think there was a hope in hell the mall would move out to Bloomington. There was a vendetta there. They won't admit it, but there was. It all goes back to the ties people on that commission had with the political and business community in Minneapolis. Up to that point, the Gunds paid for any remodeling that was done. The commission didn't do a thing. It was an easy excuse that there was no money left for Green, but it was really because they didn't want to help him. They wouldn't approve of any project even if Green wanted to spend his own money."

Green's pleas for municipal aid might have been more favorably received had he forged stronger ties with the captains of local industry. While he could be charming and initially took great pains to befriend local media, it was said that he didn't have many allies in Minnesota's business community. Conspiracy theorists suspect that might have been by design.

During his very brief tenure as owner, Howard Baldwin had spent a lot of time and energy shaking hands and kissing babies. He engaged himself with the Twin Cities' inner circle of movers and shakers, trying to align himself with the Fortune 500 companies in town because he recognized that he was going to need their help in order to be successful.

"Green, on the other hand, was going to do it all by himself, sink or swim," said Robb Leer, a former reporter at KSTP-TV in Minneapolis. "And the suspicion was that he would much prefer to sink because he had a lifeboat waiting that nobody really knew about."

Relocation.

The owner's idiosyncratic behavior belied a real shrewdness. He had been savvy enough to maneuver himself into a position to buy out Baldwin and Belzberg and knew that if the North Stars continued to lose money, he could muster support at the league level to take the team elsewhere. He also knew that the NHL was thinking seriously about expanding into warm-weather markets like Florida and Texas in order to become more attractive to advertisers and broadcast partners.

NO QUARTER FOR QUINN

Seeking to add depth at center ice, the North Stars signed the offensively talented (and well-traveled) Dan Quinn as a free agent in October 1992. But eleven games into the 1992–93 season, Quinn was suspended indefinitely by the North Stars after a local woman accused him of rape. The woman reported the alleged sexual assault to police, and Quinn was arrested. He spent a short time in jail before being released on a $30,000 bond. Quinn, who was never formally charged, insisted that the sex had been consensual. He was vindicated when the Hennepin County attorney's office announced it would not file charges against him. Although Quinn had been cleared of any wrongdoing, his reputation was shot. Rather than stick by their player, the North Stars released Quinn on November 24, 1992, claiming he'd violated team curfew rules on the night of the alleged assault.

Attendance at Met Center, where single-game tickets averaged about twenty-one dollars (lowest in the league at the time), was good but not great. The arena could accommodate a little over fifteen thousand for hockey, but the North Stars routinely drew several thousand less.

"We were probably two or three thousand shy of capacity most of the time," Dave Gagner remembered, "and it wasn't a huge rink. One thing that really bothered us as players was that the year after we went to the finals, we only had about eight or nine thousand for opening night the next season. Opening night is usually a big kickoff when tickets sell out pretty fast. After the playoff run we had the year before, we were all really shocked at that. That was probably the day Norm Green said, 'I'm taking this team out of here.'"

Complicating matters for Green were allegations of sexual harassment. Early in the 1992–93 season, Green's former executive assistant, Karen (Kari) Dziedzic, was one of three women quoted in a *Pioneer Press* story as saying the North Stars owner had acted inappropriately around the office (ogling, groping, overtly sexist comments, and the like). Kari was the daughter of a well-known and well-liked city council member, Walt Dziedzic, and sister of former NHL player Joe Dziedzic. Fairly or otherwise, the accuser had instant credibility because she came from a prominent local family, whereas the accused had been living off his own press clippings.

Green, who claimed his behavior had simply been misconstrued, desperately needed someone to lean on or a discernible voice of support to shout his virtues. If that voice was out there, it never rose above a whisper. Absent allies, Green began to feel persecuted. He tried to make some in the media feel that it was their responsibility to promote the North Stars, to encourage people to buy tickets, and to paint the team and its owner in a favorable light. So he bristled at criticism from the press and was said to have been hurt less by the sexual harassment charges than by the local media's exhaustive coverage of them and subsequent jokes made at his expense.

"He loved the media because he loved the attention," said Leer. "He was chartering planes for the media on Stanley Cup trips. He'd walk up and down the aisle asking reporters, 'OK, guys, where do you want to go for dinner tonight?' And he'd take sixteen people out to dinner. He was very philanthropic because he thought he could control his own public relations. That all changed when the media had the audacity to report something as personal as his inappropriate behavior. Then he wanted to distance himself and became very guarded. He clearly, from that day on, couldn't trust the press."

AROUND THE LEAGUE: 1992–1993

Gil Stein, former vice president and general counsel of the NHL, becomes league president. Only four months later, in February 1993, former NBA executive Gary Bettman is named the first NHL commissioner. The league expands to twenty-four teams with the addition of the Ottawa Senators and the Tampa Bay Lightning. Clubs play an eighty-four-game schedule. Winnipeg's Teemu Selanne sets NHL rookie scoring records with seventy-six goals and 132 points.

MILESTONE: NOVEMBER 27, 1992

Mike Modano scores his one hundredth career NHL goal as the North Stars tie the visiting Rangers, 4–4.

That December the NHL Board of Governors granted Green the right to relocate the team within one year. He hadn't yet ruled out the possibility of staying at Met Center, provided he could get a commitment from the community for 10,000 season tickets. Trouble was that the club's season-ticket base—fewer than 6,500 were sold for the 1992–93 season—had never been very strong.

When Green entertained offers to relocate to Target Center in downtown Minneapolis or to the St. Paul Civic Center, it gave Minnesotans hope that they could still keep their North Stars, upon whose uniforms the team's traditional logo had been replaced with a crest reading "Stars." The word "North" was suspiciously and conspicuously absent.

Under the Target Center plan, it was reported that Green would have received all the revenue for sixty-four of the building's sixty-eight luxury suites, valued at about $80,000 each. He also would have gotten $2.5 million from his 45 percent take on hockey and basketball advertising. The catch with the Target Center option, however, was that it hinged on either the city or the MSFC purchasing the property from Harvey Ratner and Marv Wolfenson (aka "Harv and Marv"), co-owners of Target Center and the Timberwolves who were having financial problems of their own. There wasn't a lot of enthusiasm for investing taxpayer dollars in what would have amounted to a bailout for the North Stars *and* the arena.

And St. Paul? The city tried stroking Green's sizable ego by temporarily renaming Kellogg Boulevard "North Stars Boulevard" and staging a rally at the Civic Center, but its offer—a package including revenues from season tickets, concessions, parking, corporate sales, and team merchandise—just wasn't tempting enough to hook the North Stars owner.

Green also toyed with the idea of moving the club to Anaheim, about ninety minutes from his home in Palm Springs. But it was an expansion year, and the Walt Disney Company had its sights set on Anaheim too. The league approved Disney's bid, so Green's search continued.

While speculation about a possible move hovered over the North Stars into January, Gainey had players focused enough to tune out most of the off-ice chatter. Under the circumstances it's remarkable that the team played as well as it did over the first fifty-four games of the 1992–93 season, compiling a 28-18-8 mark. It was the sixth-best record in the NHL at the time, and Minnesota was on a 7-1-2 run going into the All-Star break.

Mike Modano and Jon Casey were chosen to play in the All-Star Game in Montreal, with Casey winning the goaltenders' competition. Averaging better than a point per game before the break, Modano certainly didn't look out of place among the NHL's biggest stars. Statistically at least, he was well on his way to having the best season of his career. But stats never tell the whole story.

There were lingering doubts about whether Modano, recently made the highest-paid player in team history, was ready to take himself and the North Stars to the next level. Gainey, looking ahead to a stretch of games within the Norris Division when the Stars would jockey for playoff position, suggested that Modano would have an opportunity to prove his mettle when the stakes were higher. Mo responded to that challenge by scoring just four goals and nine points over the last sixteen games against Minnesota's divisional rivals and went scoreless over the last nine games of the season, when the team was battling just to make the playoffs.

Green, meanwhile, had tired of negotiating with officials from Target Center, since it was looking less and less likely that a public takeover of the privately owned arena was going to happen (in fact, it did happen, in 1995). He also shot down a possible offer from a local investor to buy the team for $55 million, stating that the club wasn't for sale, and even it were, he wouldn't take less than $60 million—almost double what he paid in 1990.

He chose All-Star Sunday to announce that the bids he'd received from the Target Center and the Civic Center weren't good enough and that he would begin to negotiate seriously with Dallas.

With its beloved Cowboys fresh off a 52–17 trouncing of Buffalo in Super Bowl XXVII, Dallas had long held a certain allure for Green. He had been making secret trips to Big D (among other places) ever since the Board of Governors gave him permission to move. City officials like Mayor Steve Bartlett, corporate leaders, and owners of other sports teams took turns romancing the North Stars owner, and together they helped convince Green that Dallas had the makings of a great NHL town.

"All of the surveys I have done," Green told the *Star Tribune* shortly after touring the city with former Cowboys quarterback Roger Staubach, "point to the North Stars being very successful in Dallas."

Minnesota governor Arne Carlson and others delivered last-minute pleas for Green to stay put, but Carlson conceded there was only so much they could (or would) do to keep the team: "In 1991, we came into office with a huge, multibillion-dollar deficit. We were still digging ourselves out of a financial hole through 2001. There was no way the government had the capacity to solve [Met Center's] problems, and Norm really wanted a better facility. I think something could've been worked out, but my recollection is that Green was pretty determined to go."

On March 10, 1993, with his wife, Kelly, at his side and sporting a tie adorned with stars, Green stood in the Dallas City Council chambers and announced before a media scrum that the team would move to Texas for the 1993–94 season.

On the surface there was nothing spectacular about the deal Green was getting from Dallas city officials. It included a ten-year lease with three five-year options to play at 16,800-seat Reunion Arena. Green would pay ten thousand dollars a game in rent but would receive a percentage of concession revenues, parking, and corporate advertising sales. He had no guarantee of season ticket sales and knew going in that revenue from luxury suites would be zilch because, unlike Target Center, Reunion had no suites. He also had to spend four million dollars of his own money to renovate the building for hockey.

Stars fans barely had time to digest the crushing news when they learned that Kari Dziedzic was suing Green for sexual harassment. Green countersued, claiming defamation.

He put forth a valiant effort, but Bob Gainey couldn't completely insulate his players from the endless conjecture that preceded Green's bombshell announcement or the anger and confusion that followed. The specter of moving became something that the coach could no longer manage, something that grabbed players' attention from hockey and never let go. After March 10 the Stars went into a tailspin, going 4-11-1.

"You say that none of the outside stuff should distract you," Bobby Smith told *Sports Illustrated*, "and it shouldn't. But it had to have some effect. Everyone was talking about it, and if you weren't talking about it, someone was asking you about it. It was the only subject of conversation."

"The last two months in Minnesota were a disaster," said Gagner. "We were well within a playoff spot, but after the announcement was made, we just threw in the towel. I guess guys were a little too distracted. Players worry about being traded, getting sent down, and what's happening at home—all the things that distract you from being a successful athlete. With a whole team, you can multiply that by twenty. You worry about schools for your kids and whether your wife is going to enjoy the new city. Back then players weren't used to that type of distraction. Nowadays, there's so much talk about ownership changes and collective bargaining and such, guys are just immune to it."

Green hoped that a little spousal support might alleviate some of the pressure players were feeling. "Norm Green did a smart thing," said Al Shaver. "Before the move he took all the wives on a charter flight down to Dallas, so they could look the city over and check out some places where they might want to buy or rent a house. Some guy who sold cowboy boots took all the wives to his store and gave them all boots. They came home with glowing things to tell their husbands about what life was going to be like in Dallas. I think that eased the players' minds about what they were going to find down there."

FROM HERO TO ZERO

Fans who once lined up to shake his hand on the Met Center concourse and affectionately chanted, "Norm! Norm! Norm!" during the playoffs two years earlier now referred to the beleaguered owner as "Norm Greed," branded him a carpetbagger, and took every opportunity to convey their newfound loathing.

Later that March the University of Southern California men's basketball team journeyed to Minneapolis to play the Golden Gophers in the third round of the 1993 National Invitational Tournament. Because the University of Minnesota's Williams Arena was being renovated and the Timberwolves had a home date at Target Center, the game was played in Bloomington.

In his college hoops memoir *Life's A Joke*, former USC associate head coach Jack Fertig recalled that fans started taunting Green midway through the second half, shouting, "Norm Green sucks! Norm Green sucks!"

The cheer perplexed USC's head coach, George Raveling.

"[George] was as good at playing to visiting crowds as anyone," Fertig recalled. "He had no idea what the commotion was about. He walked to the end of the bench and asked some of the jeering fans, 'Who's Norm Green?'"

"He's the SOB who moved the North Stars to Dallas," a fan responded.

"Oh, yeah," Raveling concurred, "he *does* suck."

"We got beat," Fertig said later, "but that line did make the night memorable."

So vilified was Green that "Norm Sucks" merchandise became something of a cottage industry. There were T-shirts, hats, buttons, and bumper stickers—mostly sold by hawkers outside Met Center before games, with little or no interference from Met Center security personnel—to complement the hundreds of homemade posters, banners, and placards that dotted the crowd.

But Green was rarely on hand to experience the full potency of fans' venom. He had been absent from the Twin Cities area since announcing the move, well insulated at his mansion in Palm Springs. The only time he dared attend a North Stars game in their closing weeks was on the road one night at the Forum in Los Angeles. As the story goes, a Minnesota fan found him in the press box and dumped a full cup of beer on his head.

In light of such incidents, Green and his wife wisely scrapped plans to spend their summers at a house they had recently purchased on a lake in Minnesota. The daily newspaper sitting on their doorstep would have been unreadable because, like the prize buck lined up in the scope of a hunter's rifle, Green had become the easiest of targets for local scribes who unsheathed their poison pens and wielded them with ruthless efficiency. Some showed mercy, but most were downright mean.

Tom Powers, longtime columnist with the *Pioneer Press*, issued this ominous warning to the expectant hockey fans of Dallas: "Norman is an operator. He could sell sand to the Saudis or ice hockey to Texans. His ability to do the impossible and the ridiculous appears limitless." Powers added, "[Green's] commitment is to his cash register. And like the biblical mustard seed sown onto rock, he will blow away during the first ill wind."

The press also had its hands full gathering material from current and former employees who were eager to share horror stories about Green. They helped tear down the public image Green had carefully crafted of himself as a savior of hockey in Minnesota, revealing him to be an

24. "Norm was the savior of the franchise once," Mike Modano said. "Then, a couple of years later, they all wanted to hunt him down." Courtesy of the Dallas Stars

impulsive and paranoid egomaniac. Patty Reid, the team's longtime director of public relations, recalled for the *Star Tribune* how she'd been fired four days after Green took over the team because he didn't sense any "chemistry" between them. When Reid asked Green what he meant by chemistry, he told her she wasn't someone he'd want to date. Eric Kruse, the former director of operations at Met Center, remembered how Green had once ordered him to knock down a firewall at the arena only hours before the North Stars were to play a playoff game. Green either didn't know or care that by law the City of Bloomington had to approve any major structural changes to the building. City officials found out about the work from a newspaper article the next day and called to complain. Green was livid and had Kruse fired.

Clearly there was a lot not to like about Green. But those who have suggested that he intended to move the North Stars from day one either overlook or choose to forget his efforts to make the team successful. Only someone who truly cared would pop open a bottle of champagne to celebrate a relatively paltry one thousand new season tickets, as he did on the eve of the 1991 playoffs, or bother to put ice cubes in Met Center urinals. ("It helps the appearance," he explained, "and it also takes care of the smell.")

"He would come into our building once a month, pick our brains, and try to get marketing ideas to apply in Minnesota," said Jim Lites, the former Red Wings executive who eventually became president of the Dallas Stars. "I'm not a Norm apologist, because he did a lot of things wrong, but he got a really bad rap in Minnesota. He tried. He *really* tried. When the

NAME THAT TUNE

Paul Metsa, a singer-songwriter from Eveleth, found a great outlet for his anger toward Norm Green: he wrote a song about it. Sung to the tune of "Come On Ilene," Metsa's "Goodnight, Norm Green" went in part, "He came from the desert with a suntan and a dream. / He sat with his dogs in a private box and stole our hockey team." The song, performed by Twin Cities country singer Billy Acorn, actually got some airplay at Met Center . . . sort of. Some mischievous Met Center staffer found a way to pipe the song into the arena's voicemail system, so every time employees phoned in to check for messages, they would hear Acorn singing, "Someday on a rink up in Eveleth, frontier justice, it will be done. / The ghost of Mariucci will take old slick Norman on one on one."

Red Wings met the North Stars in the '92 playoffs, I went to Met Center for those games and couldn't get over how much Norm had put into the building. He painted every wall, created new club seats, and dressed up the main concourse. He even had cheerleaders, but it was done with a real wholesome approach. He tried his darndest to lift the franchise up."

"GOOD NIGHT AND GOOD-BYE"

The North Stars took Met Center ice for the last time on April 13, 1993, against the Blackhawks. Perhaps it was fitting that this old and familiar enemy would close out the home schedule.

"The crowd was loud and very supportive," Bobby Smith recalled. "Everybody felt it was the end of an era—a game that people didn't want to miss. It was a special night for all of us."

A scoreless first period saw Enrico Ciccone drop the gloves with Chicago's Stu (The Grim Reaper) Grimson in the last of countless bouts between the two rival squads.

Stephane Matteau and Greg Gilbert scored second-period goals for the Blackhawks, and Brent Sutter gave the visitors a 3–0 lead early in the third. Jon Casey was strong in net for the North Stars, who staged a late rally on goals from Russ Courtnall and Mike McPhee. But the 3–2 score held up until the final clock ticks as the capacity Met Center crowd bid farewell to the NHL in Minnesota.

"It was a very good game," said Smith. "A lot of the players who had been around for a long time played particularly well that night. Neal Broten had a strong game and although my last season wasn't a stellar one for me personally, I also played well. It was one of those special moments you get to experience as professional athletes, and one you never forget."

But the sense of betrayal felt by fans only contributed to their anger and disappointment, and predictably a boorish minority used the episode as an excuse to behave like animals. Ezra Marcus, a former news reporter at KSTP-TV, saw their hostility manifest itself in some ugly ways. "That's what we saw in Bloomington that final home game," he said. "Anger, frustration, disappointment, and betrayal. The fans felt cheated. And they took it out on one another, the team, the news media, even the arena itself—ripping out seats from Met Center before hightailing it out to the parking lot."

Once outside, small but rowdy crowds began to form around the local TV stations' satellite trucks. Fans, some more inebriated than others, taunted camera crews and pounded on the sides of news vehicles. "I remember having to climb onto the roof of KSTP's van to do my live report that night for the ten o'clock news," Marcus said. "Bloomington police quickly sent the would-be mob packing before things turned truly ugly."

Here is one anonymous fan's vivid recollection of how the night unfolded:

Me and a buddy decided to head out to the Met really early in the morning the day the tickets for the last game went on sale. There was quite a crowd waiting in line at the arena from sunrise until they opened the doors at 10:00 a.m. When they finally opened, about a half-dozen people walked in and got their tickets. Then a manager or Stars rep came out to inform the crowd that the game was sold out in ten minutes because Ticketmaster sold tickets over the phone as well. Everyone was pretty upset about that, but what could you do? So it was on to the scalpers. We went out to the parking lot a few hours before game time and landed standing-room seats for sixty dollars each. I think the face value was ten dollars—not too bad.

In the parking lot we saw a Met Center employee who was waving traffic along and he had a beer in his hand. One of us yelled something at him, jokingly asking about the beer. He said something like, "What, am I going to get fired on my last day?" then had a chuckle with his coworker as they gave each other a "cheers" and took a swig of brew.

Inside the Met there was kind of a strange but lively atmosphere, like it was Game Seven of a playoff series or something, except that if the Stars were to lose this game, it was the end of the franchise. I remember Enrico Ciccone getting into a fight with Stu Grimson early in the first period, and the place went nuts. The game was back and forth, very exciting.

After the game I recall some players coming back out or waving to fans for a few minutes while a thundering standing ovation was taking place for at least ten minutes. But the place got quiet real quick when a tribute to the team was played on the scoreboard. Once that finished, people tried to tear the Met apart: seats, signs, whatever was available. Hundreds of people littered the ice with the long black plastic arm pieces from the seats. I tried like hell with my friends to loosen and take a seat home, to no avail.

Some people just sat there for minutes after the game, watching the scoreboard or just looking around, soaking it in for one last time. We decided to get out of there and head over to the mall for a few more beers, where we ran into a number of Blackhawks players and chatted with some of them.

I'm glad I was able to be a part of the last NHL game ever at the Met. I wish it was still standing or they could have done something with it rather than tear it down for Mall of America parking. It would be cool to walk around in there one last time.

Two days later the North Stars limped into Detroit for their last game of the season and, trailing by only one point in the standings behind eighth-place St. Louis, needing a victory to have any chance of making the playoffs.

But Paul Coffey's power-play goal early in the third period sparked a three-goal explosion for the Red Wings, who skated to a 5–3 victory. It erased the dimmest hopes that a happy ending could still be written for this long, eventful chapter in the history of Minnesota hockey.

Here's how an emotional Al Shaver signed off that night's broadcast:

To all the North Stars over the past twenty-six years, we say thank you, all of you, for so much fine entertainment. It's been a pleasure knowing you. Minnesota's loss is definitely a gain for Dallas—and a big one. We thank you, though, from the bottoms of our hearts, for all the wonderful nights at Met Center, when you've given us so much entertainment, and you've been such a credit to the community in which you played. We will still remember you as the Minnesota North Stars. Good night, everybody. And good-bye.

SCORCHED EARTH

At one time the Twin Cities region was the smallest market in the country by population to be represented by each of the four major North American team sports. This was a tremendous source of pride for many of the 2.5 million people who lived and worked in the metropolitan area. No midwestern podunk, it was vibrant enough commercially to attract Fortune 500 conglomerates like General Mills, Andersen Windows, Radisson Hotels, 3M, and Honeywell.

And while the years immediately following the North Stars' Stanley Cup run were filled with disappointment and frustration, it was still a pretty good time to be a sports fan in Minnesota. The Twin Cities had recently played host to college basketball's Final Four, Super Bowl XXVI, and the U.S. Open golf tournament. The Twins won the World Series in 1987 and 1991. And in 1989 St. Paul and the NBA welcomed the expansion Timberwolves.

So why, in a hockey-mad place like Minnesota, weren't the North Stars selling out every home game and making it impossible for Norm Green to move the team? One theory is that the money people had to spend on nonessentials like sporting events had been flat for years and with the allure of new casinos and the Mall of America, there was simply less discretionary income to go around. But Green's critics, of which there was no shortage, didn't want to hear about "entertainment saturation" and scoffed at his claims of losses approaching $24 million.

"I think many North Star fans feel, despite low turnout at games, Green should have respected their emotional connection to the team," said KARE-TV's Scott Goldberg, the reporter who scored a rare, exclusive interview with Green in 2008. "'You can't take hockey out of the State of Hockey' is what I hear over and over—that having professional hockey here is somehow a birthright, regardless of the financial reality. That said, I certainly don't think fans are the only people to blame. The Metropolitan Sports Facilities Commission and the legislature could have stepped in with money for stadium improvements or a new stadium. But fans played a role. It's a chicken-and-egg thing; either fans weren't going because the team stopped winning and the venue was bad, or the team stopped winning and the venue was bad because fans weren't going. Either way the North Stars were losing money, and that's not a sustainable business model."

Green has repeatedly insisted that his actions were necessitated by financial concerns and nothing more. To this day, however, there are still many who steadfastly believe that embarrassment over that sexual harassment episode—along with some wheedling by Green's wife—was at the root of his decision to leave Minnesota. It's a theory that gained some traction when Pat Forciea, the team's former vice president of communications, testified during depositions for Kari Dziedzic's sexual harassment suit that Green admitted in private that he'd decided to move the team because of the pending legal actions against him. The credibility of this witness is suspect, though, since Forciea would later plead guilty to federal fraud and embezzlement charges.

Whatever the causes, Green's flight delivered a direct body blow to the region's collective self-esteem. "There was an overwhelming sense in the days and weeks that followed that something in the community was broken—something big and irreplaceable," Ezra Marcus said. "It would have been one thing if the North Stars had picked up and moved to Milwaukee or Indianapolis. That might have been a little easier to swallow. But the fact that the franchise was headed south underscored a subtle but very deep-seated insecurity felt by many who lived and worked in the Twin Cities. How was Minneapolis-St. Paul supposed to compete with similarly sized metros like Dallas, Houston, Phoenix, and Miami if they couldn't even hold on to their beloved North Stars? In becoming a three-sport market, the Twin Cities lost its stature among other major pro sports markets like Chicago, Detroit, Philadelphia, and New York."

Once it was certain that Green and the North Stars were leaving, the MSFC began looking for a new hockey team to play at Met Center. A rumor that Hartford Whalers owner Richard Gordon might move his club to Minnesota turned out to be just wishful thinking, while Target Center's courtship of Edmonton Oilers owner Peter Pocklington went nowhere. Major League Hockey, a pro circuit that never took off, also expressed some interest in the Twin Cities.

The IHL eventually placed a team in St. Paul—the Minnesota Moose—but it relocated to Winnipeg after only two years due to lack of support.

The MSFC came to realize that the real estate upon which Met Center sat was far more valuable than the arena itself. Unable to attract new tenants and obsolete by modern standards, the old barn was eventually (but not easily) torn down.

The Kari Dziedzic soap opera wrapped up too. In February 1994 Green and his accuser agreed to accept a mediator's recommendation and drop their respective lawsuits. An undisclosed settlement gave Dziedzic some financial security, but she still found it tough to put the episode behind her, thanks to harassing phone calls and verbal attacks from cretins who made her the scapegoat for the team leaving town.

KARI ON

After the Norm Green scandal, no one would have faulted Kari Dziedzic for wanting to retreat from public view to live and work in quiet anonymity. But being a Dziedzic, Kari was inevitably drawn to politics, and in 2012 she won a seat in the Minnesota Senate.

The passage of time and the return of the NHL to Minnesota in the form of the Wild have dulled Minnesotans' pain, but the old wound has never fully healed. Mike Modano knows that better than anyone. He was still answering questions about Green, a personal friend, when he hung up his skates in 2011.

Maybe one day the hockey fans of Minnesota will get to experience the same unbridled joy that Dallas Stars fans felt in 1999. And as the Stanley Cup rides in a motorcade down Kellogg Boulevard in St. Paul or Nicollet Mall in Minneapolis, and the entire State of Hockey lets out one, colossal collective sigh of relief, the locals will find it in their hearts to forgive Norm Green.

Maybe.

5

FAN FAVORITES

KEITH ACTON (1983–1988)

To compensate for a lack of size—he was listed at an elfish five feet eight, 170 pounds—Keith Acton made a name for himself in the NHL by battling for every possible competitive advantage. This was especially true of his work in the face-off circle, where he would use his entire body on draws to gain the leverage necessary to win control of the puck. Or he might do something to distract the official and snap the concentration of his opponent.

A strong forechecker with good speed and an underrated scoring touch, Acton was also an expert agitator, flapping his gums all night long to knock opposing players off their game. He was probably punched in the kisser more times than Roberto Duran, but his willingness to scrap helped get his team more involved physically and emotionally.

But Acton knew that a smart pest also knows when to keep his mouth shut. "Those types of players have a lot of experience at going about the business of bothering people," he said. "They probably always have been that way, even before getting to the NHL. They know what they're doing. I think you have to trust them to know what's the right time to agitate, when does the team need a lift, and, just as important, when the game is nice and quiet and you want to keep it that way."

Off the ice Acton was a locker-room jester who did anything and everything to keep teammates upbeat. That's the mark of a true professional because those close to Acton knew he never wanted to be a North Star.

After a productive junior career with the OHA's Peterborough Petes, Acton was drafted 103rd overall in 1978 by the Montreal Canadiens. Two seasons later he was playing between Steve Shutt and Guy Lafleur, having rapidly secured top-line duty because of his feistiness and proficiency on face-offs. He may have hated the Canadiens as a child growing up in Stouffville, Ontario—Maple Leaf country—but Acton now bled *bleu, blanc, et rouge* and figured to play a major role in the Habs' resurgence in the mid-1980s.

25. Keith Acton in
action. Courtesy
of the Dallas Stars

Instead, he was dealt to Minnesota along with Mark Napier and a draft
pick for Bobby Smith in October 1983. Initially, the trade was as warmly
received in the Acton household as an IRS audit.

But he adapted to his new surroundings quickly and emerged as a
leader for the North Stars. He was a natural choice to serve as interim
captain when Craig Hartsburg was sidelined with injuries during the
1986–87 season.

Rather than try to replace Smith, the offensive dynamo for whom he
was traded, "Woody" just focused on being himself: a good two-way
player who never backed down from anyone or anything.

Upon reflection it's a shame that the North Stars did not realize their
fullest potential during Acton's five-year tour of duty with the club. Every
year Minnesota's season ended earlier, while Acton's chances of winning
his first Stanley Cup grew dimmer.

DID YOU KNOW?

In 2012 Keith Acton and former North Stars teammate Craig Hartsburg were reunited on the coaching staff of the Columbus Blue Jackets.

In January 1988 the North Stars mercifully traded the wily pivot to Edmonton for journeyman defenseman Moe Mantha. Acton won a Stanley Cup with the Oilers that spring, but in his absence the North Stars won only five of their last thirty games.

In fifteen NHL seasons, he also played for the Philadelphia Flyers, the Washington Capitals, and the New York Islanders.

Acton's hockey smarts and leadership skills made him a natural at coaching, and he worked as an assistant for several teams after his retirement as a player in 1994.

DON BEAUPRE (1980–1989)

Don Beaupre defended his crease like a mother bear protecting its cubs. Just ask Ric Seiling, the ex–Buffalo Sabre whose foray into Beaupre's turf one night in 1984 resulted in Seiling getting clubbed over the head.

That momentary lapse of reason earned Beaupre a six-game suspension but was somewhat out of character for a highly competitive goaltender who always wanted to improve. Beaupre was respected for his desire to rebound strongly after playing a weak game or surrendering a soft goal.

With a great glove hand, quick feet, and a knack for cutting down the angles, "Bobo" first caught the gaze of NHL scouts while playing for the OHA's Sudbury Wolves.

As one of the top-rated goalies in the 1980 Entry Draft, Beaupre didn't last very long and was claimed thirty-seventh overall by the North Stars.

Since he never expected to make the team out of his first training camp, low expectations helped keep Beaupre on an even keel. But the rookie beat out Gilles Meloche and Gary (Suitcase) Edwards for the starting job on opening night on October 11, 1980, a 9–3 win over the Hartford Whalers.

"If I was thinking, 'Boy, I really have to go and make it,' I probably wouldn't have," Beaupre said. "The pressure would have probably got to me. Being naive probably helped my chances then."

Veterans recalled being impressed by the young goalie's composure. "He was only nineteen or so when he came to Minnesota," said Al MacAdam, "and I found him to be quite mature. He looked after himself and wasn't running around. I met his parents, and if you met them, you wouldn't be surprised by it. He came from a very stable family."

26. Don Beaupre.
Courtesy of the
Dallas Stars

It was a whirlwind year for the nineteen-year-old netminder, who won eighteen games, started in goal for the Wales Conference in the 1981 All-Star Game (becoming the youngest starting goaltender in NHL history), and played six postseason matches as the North Stars advanced to the Stanley Cup Finals. He was in net when Minnesota posted its lone victory of the series.

Beaupre served the club well in eight years of service but never improved on the success of his rookie season. However, he did backstop Minnesota to the 1984 Campbell Conference Finals, recording a then-impressive 3.07 goals against average in thirteen postseason games. And in 1985–86 he set an NHL record for most consecutive victories by a goaltender (fourteen, from February 6 to March 19, 1986) and tied the record for most penalty minutes in one season by a goalie (thirty-four).

The emergence of AHLer Jon Casey began to eat away at Beaupre's playing time, and after first being placed on waivers and then sent to the minors, he requested and was granted a trade to Washington in November 1988. In return the North Stars received Claudio Scremin, a blue-line prospect from the University of Maine.

Scremin's NHL career spanned all of seventeen games (with San Jose), while Beaupre, still in his prime, played another eight seasons with the Capitals, the Ottawa Senators, and the Maple Leafs.

Beaupre returned to Minneapolis after his retirement in 1997 and worked as co-owner of Power Lift, a company that rents and leases heavy construction equipment.

BRIAN BELLOWS (1982–1992)

Had the chips fallen as most experts predicted, Brian Bellows would have broken into the NHL as a Boston Bruin. But some crafty draft-day maneuvering by GM Lou Nanne allowed the North Stars to win "The Bellows Sweepstakes."

In major junior hockey Bellows played on perhaps one of the most talented teams of all time in Kitchener, where he was a teammate of future NHLers Mike Eagles, Al MacInnis, and Scott Stevens. His last season in the OHL culminated with a Memorial Cup title, and he played under the blinding glare of media attention. Blessed with leadership skills rarely seen in an eighteen-year-old and a goal scorer's instincts, the talented youngster was expected to be the first overall selection in the 1982 NHL draft.

Bellows was a sure thing if ever there was one, and teams scrambled for a chance to obtain a higher drafting position to get a crack at him. That included the Bruins, who had previously acquired the top pick from the Colorado Rockies. But if Boston GM Harry Sinden had his heart set on Bellows, he wasn't saying.

"I'll be very surprised if the Bruins don't take him," commented one NHL scout. Indeed, Bellows hoped and fully expected to end up in Boston.

The night before the draft, Bellows, his father, and his agent were out at a bar and saw some Bruins executives. They saw him too but didn't come over to say hello or shake his hand.

"That's when we figured out something was up," Bellows later revealed.

Something *was* up. An offseason deal with Detroit in August 1981 gave the North Stars the option of swapping first-round picks with the Red

27. "Because he was young," Lou Nanne said of Brian Bellows, "he was a little abrasive." Courtesy of the Dallas Stars

Wings in the following season's draft. They exercised the option, moving up from the No. 17 spot to second overall, but had one more deal to make.

In exchange for Brad Palmer and prospect Dave Donnelly, the Bruins agreed to pass on Bellows, instead selecting Gord Kluzak, a highly skilled but injury-prone defenseman. Bellows went next to Minnesota.

Bellows had a stressful rookie campaign. Fans unfairly expected another Wayne Gretzky because both players had been prolific point producers in juniors. But halfway through the 1982–83 season, Bellows found his rhythm and finished with an impressive thirty-five goals.

"There was a lot on his shoulders when he was younger because a lot was expected of him," said Nanne. "And because he was young, he was a little abrasive. It was tough on him. But he became a terrific player for the North Stars and was another guy who never shortchanged you in a game. He always worked hard. He worked every night."

In his second year Bellows was asked to stand in for Craig Hartsburg as captain of the North Stars when Hartsburg underwent knee surgery. At nineteen Bellows became one of the youngest players in league history to assume leadership duties—a role in which he excelled. However, the pressure of wearing the captain's "C" was not so daunting as to distract the wily winger from what he did best: score. Bellows improved on his rookie year totals with forty-one goals and eighty-three points.

He went on to become one of the game's most consistent snipers, scoring 342 goals in 753 games as a North Star while representing Minnesota at two All-Star Games (1984 and 1988).

But there were hints of discontent along the way. When he complained about the quality of his linemates during the 1989–90 season, coach Pierre Page partnered Bellows with playmaker Neal Broten and sniper Mike Gartner. He responded by scoring fifty-five goals and ninety-nine points, both career highs.

"I enjoyed when Brian and I played on the same line together in 1991," said Bobby Smith. "You knew when you went to the rink that Brian was going to give you his best. That's not to say we didn't butt heads once in a while, but in a good way."

"Brian was a terrific, tenacious competitor," said Nanne. "He had a great career here. In the 1991 playoffs, Mike Modano, Jon Casey, and Bellows were our three best players."

But when Bellows suffered a leg injury in Game One of the Stanley Cup Finals—courtesy of an Ulf Samuelsson hip check—it dealt a serious blow to the club's championship aspirations.

"That really hurt us," said Dave Gagner. "He was really a catalyst for us offensively—so strong on the puck. He was a bear in the corner. He'd have three guys on him, throw them all off, and come out with the puck. When he was determined to do something, he could do it. He wasn't really able to compete at his level in the finals because of the injury."

Unfortunately for Bellows, the North Stars finished below .500 in seven of the ten seasons he wore the green and gold. Perhaps because he was a former No. 1 draft pick and considered by some to be Minnesota's best player, he shouldered a disproportionate share of the blame for the team's poor record. When Bob Gainey took on the dual role of coach and general manager in 1992, he decided to shake things up by trading Bellows to Montreal for Russ Courtnall.

"It's not without risk or fear that we've taken [Bellows] out of our lineup," Gainey said in defense of the deal. "But the bottom line is that seventy points [in the final team standings] is not enough in the Norris Division anymore, and Brian has been in the lineup. It's time to take the risk and find another player who can help us improve our position."

The trade ended months of speculation about Bellows's status with the club. Given a fresh start with the Canadiens, Bellows won a Stanley Cup in Montreal the following spring. He played another six seasons in the NHL, including stints with Tampa Bay, Anaheim, and Washington.

After Bellows retired in 1999, he moved back to Minnesota, where he became a financial trader.

NEAL BROTEN (1980–1993)

His ascension from high school and college star in his native Minnesota to NHL icon took a short but memorable detour through Lake Placid, New York. But of all the postpubescent heroes to emerge from the euphoria of America's "Miracle on Ice," none forged so long or as successful a career in hockey as Neal Broten.

The North Stars' third choice (forty-second overall) in the 1979 draft, Broten was a five-feet-nine, 175-pound dynamo who led the University of Minnesota to an NCAA championship and two years later captured the first-ever Hobey Baker Award as the nation's best collegiate player.

Former teammate Gordie Roberts, a Detroit native who has spent nearly half his life living in Minnesota, admits to being a bit envious of

28. Neal Broten.
Courtesy of
USA Hockey

the "storybook" hockey life Broten has experienced. "It's the perfect story," Roberts said. "If you played high school hockey in Minnesota, then starred for the Gophers, then played in the NHL for the North Stars or the Wild, you're a rock star forever."

Neal was actually the first of three brothers (along with Aaron and Paul) to attend the University of Minnesota, jump to the NHL, and play for the Minnesota/Dallas franchise.

The eldest Broten was a wonderfully talented player with great agility, intelligence, and playmaking skills. Despite his small stature he could rarely be knocked down or intimidated (his five-second bout with Edmonton's Wayne Gretzky on December 22, 1982, was one of the few fights for either player, with Broten the clear victor).

During the early to mid-1980s, Broten did more than put the North Stars back on the hockey map; he proved that U.S.-born players could become superstars in the NHL. In his first full season, he finished runner-up to Winnipeg's Dale Hawerchuk as rookie of the year and fell just two points shy of becoming the first American to reach the 100-point plateau. He would accomplish the feat four years later with a 105-point effort that included a single-season team record of seventy-six assists.

Neal went on to represent the North Stars in two All-Star Games (1983 and 1986) while working his way up the club's all-time scoring list.

> Broten did more than put the North Stars back on the hockey map; he proved that U.S.-born players could become superstars in the NHL.

But numbers, titles, and awards tell only part of his story. Bobby Smith called Broten the most unselfish person with whom he had ever played. "He seemed to delight in the accomplishments of his teammates," said Smith, "more than his own accomplishments."

Dave Gagner was a young center trying to crack the Minnesota roster in 1987 when Broten, by then the team's first-line pivot and one of the game's most accomplished stars, made a gesture of sportsmanship that Gagner never forgot.

"I was struggling to make the team and had a two-goal game one night," recalled Gagner, Broten's roommate for over five seasons. "The other team had pulled their goalie. Neal was out there, but he came off the ice after only about ten seconds because I was up. At the time he was getting criticized very badly in the papers because he wasn't producing. But he was the kind of guy who wanted to help me. He was so unselfish. Even when people were picking on him for a lack of production, it was more important to Neal that he be regarded by his teammates as a good team guy."

"Neal was pretty quiet," added Mike Modano. "We were both quiet guys, but Neal had a real inviting kind of attitude and personality where you could come to him and talk about anything. He was very supportive of me. And he was a great guy to watch. Bob Gainey would tell me, 'Hey, just watch Neal and see how he plays.'"

But Broten's tenure with the North Stars wasn't all peaches and cream. Although he valued his time in Minnesota and had every intention of retiring as a North Star, he also wanted to be paid accordingly.

When he became a free agent in 1991, Broten sought a substantial pay increase, but contract negotiations with the team took an ugly turn when he rejected the North Stars' initial four-year, $2.6 million offer and, in protest, signed a one-year contract to play in Germany. (Actually, the deal paid Broten $50,000 for only seven weeks of hockey, after which he had the right to return to the North Stars or join the 1992 U.S. Olympic team.) That put GM Bob Clarke on the hot seat to get Broten back in a Minnesota uniform. And quick.

The two sides remained at an impasse through the summer, training camp, and the first weeks of the 1991–92 season until Broten finally accepted a revised $3.4 million deal. Clarke never budged on his refusal to include a no-trade clause but did give Broten his word that he would never be traded to a Canadian team.

When the Stars moved to Texas, Broten moved with them, and on October 5, 1993, he scored the first goal in the history of the Dallas Stars, against the Red Wings. But his scoring declined as the decade progressed, and in February 1995 he was dealt to New Jersey for Corey Millen.

Once revered for his offensive prowess, Broten was cast by the defensive-minded Devils in the role of checking forward and face-off specialist. He adapted well and won a Stanley Cup with the Devils that spring.

Broten retired in 1997 and moved to Wisconsin to manage the Sally Broten Horse Company with his wife, a former rodeo competitor. He also worked for the expansion Minnesota Wild, making public appearances on behalf of the team.

His number, 7, was retired by the Dallas Stars in 1998, and two years later he was inducted into the U.S. Hockey Hall of Fame.

JON CASEY (1983–1993)

For six magical weeks in the spring of 1991, Jon Casey took North Stars fans on a ride they will never forget—a ride that ended two victories shy of a Stanley Cup.

Quiet during games but a funny and likable guy off the ice, Casey was an intense competitor who won at every level in which he played. A native of blue-collar Coleraine, Minnesota, he moved to Grand Rapids as a junior in high school when his dad got a job at the Blandin Paper mill in town.

As a senior during the 1979–80 season, Casey led Grand Rapids High to a state title. That threw some gasoline on an already combustible rivalry between Grand Rapids and Coleraine's Greenway High since Casey had tended goal for Greenway as a sophomore. Greenway was upended in the section playoffs that year, and folks in Coleraine are convinced to this day that had Casey stayed with the Raiders, they would have won their third state title instead of Grand Rapids.

29. Jon Casey.
Courtesy of the
Dallas Stars

In 1980 Casey accepted a scholarship to the University of North
Dakota. While there he was a strong performer and was named to the
Western Collegiate Hockey Association First All-Star Team. In 1984 he
was selected to the NCAA West First All-American Team and was also
named a finalist for the Hobey Baker Award, eventually losing out to
Minnesota–Duluth's Tom Kurvers.

Casey skipped his senior year at North Dakota and signed as a free
agent with the North Stars. His early years with the organization were
anything but easy, and from 1984 to 1988, he saw only limited NHL action.
Instead, he honed his skills in minor league towns like Baltimore, Springfield (Mass.), Indianapolis, and Kalamazoo. With patience he slowly
worked his way up the North Stars' depth chart. He finally earned a
shot at the starting job in Minnesota when Don Beaupre was traded to
the Capitals in 1988.

But first-round playoff losses in 1989 and 1990 hadn't done much to
alter people's unenthusiastic perception of the club and did even less to
boost Casey's stock around the league. That all changed in 1991.

"Jon really played well down the stretch," recalled Brian Propp. "Our
team as a whole had taken all year to get to the point where we built up

confidence in each other. Jon caught on to this also. His attitude changed towards the end of the season when he realized that he was good enough to carry the North Stars in the playoffs. His mental attitude got better down the stretch, and he started believing in himself. Once he had that feeling, he was consistently better every game. Consistency was what really impressed me. He had been prone to off games early on, but he took himself to a new level towards the end of the season."

Indeed, there were moments when Casey looked downright unbeatable.

Since his slightly built frame didn't cover much of the net, Casey had to rely on fast reactions and a thorough understanding of the angles he would need to play to stop opposing shooters. A scrambling, reflexive goalie, he wasn't afraid to go roaming, often ranging far from the crease to cut the angle on an opponent's shot. Sometimes the tactic worked so well on breakaways and one-on-ones that Casey could startle a shooter into making a mistake before the puck ever left his stick.

"I could tell that he enjoyed coming to the rink for games and practices later in the 1990-91 season," said Propp. "I had seen many other goalies go through the same process, so I knew he was turning the corner. Jon accepted the challenge of the playoffs and was outstanding in beating Chicago, St. Louis, and Edmonton. Then we ran out of steam against the Penguins. It was a great year for North Stars hockey, and it created a number of lifetime friendships for the whole team."

> Casey could startle a shooter into making a mistake before the puck ever left his stick.

Unlike Pete Babando, Mel (Sudden Death) Hill, and Stephane Matteau, whose celebrity was predicated on ephemeral moments of postseason glory, Casey's career should not be defined solely by his heroics in the 1991 playoffs.

From 1988-89 to 1992-93, a five-year stretch during which he was the undisputed workhorse of the North Stars goalie corps, Casey appeared in 228 games, winning 105. He led the league with 31 wins in 1989-90 and represented the North Stars at the 1993 All-Star Game.

After the North Stars missed the playoffs in 1993, Casey was traded to the Bruins for Andy Moog to complete an earlier transaction that sent Gord Murphy to Dallas. At the time he ranked third on the team's all-time list in wins (128), third in games played (325), second in shutouts (12), and fifth in goals against average (3.28).

Casey spent one successful season with the Bruins before closing out his career with St. Louis. In 1997-98 he played his final season of pro hockey with the IHL's Kansas City Blades.

He settled in Missouri after his retirement.

DINO CICCARELLI (1980–1989)

What fans loved most about Dino Ciccarelli was the way he battled adversity in every shape or form. He took his lumps and never backed down when confronted by a bigger opponent.

The "experts" said the kid from Sarnia was too small and that he'd never skate like a pro. And when he broke his leg in his second season with the OHL's London Knights, well, that just about squashed any hopes he had of ever being drafted by an NHL team.

Nineteen years and 1,200 points later, Dino proved to the naysayers that he belonged in the NHL.

Every member of the twenty-one-team league passed on the high-scoring right wing from Sarnia, Ontario. They worried that Ciccarelli's leg, which had required the insertion of a metal rod, would not withstand the rigors of NHL play. GM Lou Nanne, however, was not convinced (Glen Sonmor figured it was because Lou liked little Italians with lots of determination, being one himself), and he invited Ciccarelli to North Stars training camp as a free agent in 1980.

Dino didn't make the squad initially but was recalled from Oklahoma City of the Central Hockey League (CHL) halfway through the 1980–81 season; he scored eighteen goals in thirty-two games as a rookie while helping the North Stars reach the Stanley Cup Finals. And that metal rod? He kept it as a souvenir.

"Dino had that simplicity about him that I liked," said Al MacAdam. "He was a simple guy who loved to score goals. He went into those rough areas, and it appeared to me that everybody on the other team just hated him. But he approached the game like a little kid would—with a lot of enthusiasm. It was important for guys who were a little older on the team to see. That's why you bring youth to your team—so the older guys will see that."

What the North Stars loved most about the five-feet-nine, 185-pounder was his tenacity. He was a bull in the corners and a pest in front of the net, especially on the power play. Ciccarelli was fond of parking himself in the slot where he could trawl for rebounds, redirect shots, or harass the goalie.

And while he was busy poking his stick at the goalie's pads or trying to pin the netminder's stick against the post, opposing defenders employed any and all means to knock him off-balance. "Nobody teaches you to take that abuse," said former Buffalo Sabres great Dave Andreychuk. "It comes down to being smart about your positioning and being mentally prepared to sacrifice your body."

Andreychuk emulated Ciccarelli's style well enough to become the game's all-time leader in power play goals. "I watched [Ciccarelli] before

I got to the NHL and kept on watching him his entire career," Andreychuk told the *Hockey News*. "Dino was all determination and heart. He got goals for one simple reason: because he was willing to absorb punishment that other players wouldn't. And you can bet the punishment comes—crosschecks in the back, slashes to the back of the legs, punches to the head."

Ciccarelli saw it all. A player of his temperament and obvious skill made for an easy target, especially in hostile environs like Chicago Stadium or St. Louis Arena. But opponents quickly learned that he could respond in kind when provoked. A rookie defenseman named Luke Richardson found that out one night in 1988 when the North Stars visited Maple Leaf Gardens.

Richardson was a big kid: six feet four, 210 pounds and eager to make an impression. When he nailed Ciccarelli with a bodycheck from behind, it sent the winger into a rage. The North Star, convinced the hit was illegal, turned and twice clubbed Richardson over the head with his stick.

Richardson wasn't seriously injured, but immediately after the game, Ciccarelli was arrested by some overzealous Toronto police officers and charged with assault. He was slapped with a $1,000 fine and forced to spend the night in jail, where he passed the time by signing autographs for his cellmates.

> "It appeared to me that everybody on the other team just hated him." • *Al MacAdam*

But that episode didn't attract nearly as much negative press as when Ciccarelli went out to his front step to retrieve the morning newspaper and forgot one very important detail: his pants. Unfortunately, a seven-year-old neighbor spotted Dino dressed in his birthday suit and alerted her mother, who in turn called the police. Ciccarelli was charged with indecent exposure. He pled guilty and served fifty hours of community service.

In hindsight one wonders if the deadline trade that sent Ciccarelli and Bob Rouse to Washington for Mike Gartner and Larry Murphy in March 1989 was purely a hockey decision or one prompted by Dino's run-ins with the law.

Whatever the reason, there can be no denying that while in his prime, the four-time All-Star was one of the best pure goal scorers the game has ever seen, and certainly one of the best to wear a North Stars uniform. He was the only player in club history to score fifty or more goals twice and held the team record for most hat tricks with fourteen.

In nineteen NHL seasons Ciccarelli also played for the Detroit Red Wings, the Tampa Bay Lightning, and the Florida Panthers, finishing with 608 career goals.

30. Dino Ciccarelli's dreams of stardom were almost snuffed out by a severe leg injury suffered in juniors. A few years later, he was a fifty-five-goal scorer in the NHL. Courtesy of the Dallas Stars

Once asked if he believed that a tarnished reputation had prevented his name from joining those of other six-hundred-goal scorers in the Hockey Hall of Fame, Ciccarelli replied, "That's not for me to say. I don't know. I got myself into pathetic situations in my career, so possibly."

"He should be in the Hall of Fame," said Nanne, one of Ciccarelli's biggest boosters, "because he not only scored goals, he scored big goals. He scored 'em in big games and in the playoffs. The guy really had a knack."

The Hall of Fame induction committee agreed, and in 2010 the call that Ciccarelli had waited nearly a decade to receive finally came. That Dino didn't get a chance to share the good news with his parents made the occasion bittersweet. His father, Benito (Vic) Ciccarelli, an Italian immigrant who came to Canada from Italy in the 1950s, had passed away four years earlier, while his mother, Celeste, died only months before the hall announced Dino as one of its newest inductees.

ULF DAHLEN (1989–1993)

When Swedish hockey legends like Anders Hedberg, Ulf Nilsson, and Börje Salming came to North America in the 1970s, they were maligned by old-guard NHL types as being "soft." Unlike those pioneers, who performed their artistry in open ice, Ulf Dahlen practiced his unsung art along the boards, where he became known as one of the best cornermen in the game.

"I'm not a great skater," Dahlen said, confirming a fact known to the hockey world for years, "so I always wanted to be good along the boards, even back home. The game is played there a lot, and that is where I know I can contribute."

31. Ulf Dahlen.
Courtesy of the
Dallas Stars

The New York Rangers had lofty plans for the six-feet-two, 195-pound right winger when they selected him seventh overall in the 1985 draft. A solid rookie campaign in Manhattan was followed by a somewhat disappointing 1988–89 season. So the Rangers, rarely a team to employ much patience with developing prospects, shipped Dahlen to Minnesota for Mike Gartner in March 1990.

Few North Stars fans knew anything about Dahlen, except that it had taken the kid three seasons in the league to score seventy-one goals—good but not *Mike Gartner* good. And where Gartner wowed fans with his superb skating and agility, they noticed that Dahlen chugged up the ice and dug the puck out of the corners. By the end of the season, fans were complaining that the North Stars had sacrificed too much skill and speed just to get a little younger and shave some salary off their payroll. To them it was looking like the team's worst trade in years.

The more savvy observer recognized that although flash and quickness didn't figure strongly into Dahlen's game, balance and the ability to absorb a hit certainly did. Dahlen virtually patented a move in which he carried the puck into the offensive zone while turning sideways. At that angle he could better protect the puck with his body from oncoming defenders. In his first full season as a North Star, he scored twenty-one goals and factored in the team's storybook 1991 playoff run with his sound, two-way play.

"There's a lot more to the game than flash, eh?" Bob Clarke said, more than a little satisfied that Dahlen was proving the naysayers wrong in his own understated way. "A lot of players skate like hell and nothing ever happens. Ulfie brings substance to the game. He plays well in traffic, and he comes up with the puck when two or three guys are around it. He's not a bad skater; he has kind of a different stride, but he's agile on his feet, and he gets there fast enough. And when he gets there, he does something. He makes something happen."

Interestingly, Dahlen and most North Star veterans had played the entire 1990–91 season knowing that they could be headed to the Bay Area as part of the complicated expansion draft arrangement between the North Stars and former owners George and Gordon Gund, who owned the incoming San Jose Sharks. But Clarke admired Dahlen's tenacity and found a way to keep him in Minnesota. Ulfie went on to have the best offensive seasons of his career, pacing the North Stars with thirty-six goals in 1991–92 and adding thirty-five more in 1992–93.

> "A lot of players skate like hell and nothing ever happens. Ulfie brings substance to the game." • Bob Clarke

Dahlen went on to play over nine hundred NHL games with the Rangers, the Stars, the Sharks, the Blackhawks, and the Capitals. He returned to Sweden in 2008 to coach in the Swedish Elite League.

JUDE DROUIN (1970–1975)

Even if some occasionally questioned his effort, ability was never an issue with Jude Drouin.

As a Canadiens prospect playing for the AHL's Montreal Voyageurs, the small but skilled playmaker won the league scoring title and captured Rookie of the Year honors in 1970 before he was traded to Minnesota for center Bill Collins.

Drouin went on to lead the North Stars in scoring the following season, and when his exceptional play carried over into the 1971 playoffs—he had twelve points in twelve games—the club thought it had a burgeoning superstar on its hands. He finished runner-up to Buffalo's Gilbert Perreault in Calder Trophy voting and set a rookie record (since broken) with fifty-two assists.

"Jude was a terrific talent," recalled Lou Nanne. "He was a wonderful playmaker with great hands, great acceleration, good speed, and for a small guy, he was tough. He'd play through traffic like he weighed 240 pounds."

As much as Drouin loved the game, he seemed to love the life of a hockey player almost as much. That landed him in hot water on a few occasions, like on October 18, 1972, when he and six teammates went out to an Atlanta bar to celebrate their 6–0 win over the Flames. When their late-night carousing got out of control, the cops showed up and hauled the players away on charges ranging from public drunkenness to "creating a turmoil."

"He loved the party life," said Tom Reid, "but he always came to play."

Cesare Maniago wasn't so sure. "Unfortunately," Maniago said, "maybe Jude's priorities were mixed up. I thought he was capable of playing a little better than he showed. But maybe because he didn't put more of his heart into it, that's why he didn't stay in the league that long."

In January 1975 the North Stars traded Drouin to the New York Islanders. J. P. Parise followed in a separate deal, so the two ex–North Stars were reunited and placed on the same line. In fact, it was Drouin who assisted on Parise's famous, series-winning, overtime goal in the 1975 playoffs against the Rangers.

Drouin, who later opened a chain of seafood restaurants on Long Island, sat out the entire 1978–79 season in order to achieve unrestricted free agency. He signed with the Winnipeg Jets the following year, narrowly missing out on the Islanders' Stanley Cup dynasty.

DAVE GAGNER (1987–1993)

It's hard to believe that a man who ranked fifth on the club's all-time scoring list was once so disenchanted with his hockey career that he almost quit to become a stockbroker. But the determination that became Dave Gagner's trademark held despair at bay just long enough for the offensive-minded centerman to achieve stardom in Minnesota.

In a bigger man Gagner's intensity would have been frightening. He routinely played to about twice his size and zipped around the rink like an angry hornet looking for someone to sting.

"It was never hard for me to get up for games," he said. "I was always able to get my emotions going, though coaches always said that my strengths could be my weaknesses if I let my emotions get the best of me. I used to try to manufacture some anger before a game—think about something to get me going. On the flipside of that, I wasn't always the easiest guy to play with."

Indeed, there was a Jekyll-and-Hyde dimension to Gagner's character. The same man who often appeared on the verge of homicide during games turned into Clark Kent when the skates came off.

"But it's a good transition," said Mike Kennedy, assigned to Gagner's line as a rookie in 1994-95. "It's an intensity you need to have out there. It's an intensity that works."

It also helped get Gagner noticed as a teen skating for Brantford of the OHL, where he teamed with future NHLers Bob Probert, Shane Corson,

32. Dave Gagner was always looking for a competitive advantage, as the Islanders' Mick Vukota discovers. Courtesy of the Dallas Stars

and Mike Lalor. In 1982–83 he paced the Alexanders with 121 points and shot up the Central Scouting Bureau's prospect rankings.

Impressed by his skill and spunk, the Rangers selected him twelfth overall in the 1983 NHL draft. It seemed like a perfect match: the Blueshirts of the early 1980s had a fondness for talented but undersized players, and Gagner certainly fit the bill. After representing Canada at the 1984 Olympics in Sarajevo, he was eager to begin his pro career in Manhattan.

But it never quite worked out with the Rangers. He couldn't crack a lineup featuring established centers like Pierre Larouche, Mark Pavelich, and Mike Rogers, and coach Herb Brooks, the person who seemed most interested in Gagner, was fired four months into the 1984–85 season. After three years of extended demotions to New York's AHL affiliate in New Haven, Gagner grew frustrated and resentful.

"If I wasn't a really motivated kid," he said, "I probably wouldn't have been playing after my third or fourth year. As a kid you don't realize that you have to earn your job every day. In the pros you have to succeed *before* you get the ice time. That means playing well with less minutes. It's not all about talent—it's about dealing with adversity. I didn't have the understanding of that when I was with the Rangers. I can cry about it and say they didn't give me a chance, but honestly, I probably didn't deserve the chance."

After clearing waivers in 1987, an experience Gagner called the biggest wake-up call of his career, he requested and was granted a trade by GM Phil Esposito, who shipped the pivot to Minnesota along with Jay Caufield for Jari Gronstrand and Paul Boutilier.

Believing he still had something to prove to his new employers, Gagner didn't mind splitting his first season in the North Stars system between Bloomington and Kalamazoo of the International Hockey League (IHL). But another demotion the following season—his eighth in five years—pushed Gagner to the brink of an early retirement.

"I had a really strong camp, but they sent me down again," he said. "I was labeled a minor league guy and an underachiever. That's when I thought about quitting. There are only so many rejections you can take. I was going to go back to school, maybe play in Europe the next year. But my wife was very influential in my decision to stay. She said, 'This has been your dream your whole life. You're hurt right now—don't let your feelings get the best of you.'"

"I wasn't always the easiest guy to play with." • *Dave Gagner*

Gagner reported to Kalamazoo as ordered but was recalled after only one game. It was his last stint in the minors, and over the next six seasons, he never scored fewer than thirty goals, topped the forty-goal mark twice, twice led the club in points, twice was named team MVP, and represented the North Stars at the 1991 All-Star Game. Only Brian Bellows scored more points for Minnesota during the 1991 playoffs than Gagner, who would've earned serious consideration for the Conn Smythe Trophy as playoff MVP had the North Stars defeated Pittsburgh in the finals.

Gagner stayed with the club after it moved to Dallas in 1993. His fifteen-year NHL career also included stints with the Maple Leafs, the Calgary Flames, the Florida Panthers, and the Vancouver Canucks.

After his retirement in 1999, Gagner founded Custom Ice Rinks, a company that builds ice rinks in people's backyards. In 2008 he was named director of player development for the Canucks.

CURT GILES (1979–1991)

At five feet eight, 175 pounds, he lacked the brawn traditionally favored in a defensive defenseman. But Curtis Jon Giles was a strong, agile skater

33. Curt Giles (left) tries to prevent ex–North Star (and current St. Louis Blue) Blake Dunlop from screening goalie Gilles Meloche. Courtesy of the Dallas Stars

adept at breaking up opposing rushes, and he knew how to throw a mean hip check. In fact, he once hit Philadelphia center Dave Poulin so hard that the Flyers captain swallowed his tongue.

"He always amazed me with his ability to throw those checks," said Al Shaver. "I always used to tell him, 'Hell, you make all these hits because they can't see you—you're so short!' I always wished Curt could've been about three feet taller than he was, but, God, he was a solid little player and very, very competitive."

"Solid as a rock," was the appraisal offered by former defense partner Craig Hartsburg. "And not just his play but also his personality and character. He was always there, whether things were going well or not."

Dyed-in-the-wool Minnesota hockey fans knew all about "Pengy" (that's short for Penguin) long before the North Stars tabbed him with the fifty-fourth pick of the 1978 draft. He had a superb collegiate career at the University of Minnesota–Duluth, where he was twice named to the NCAA West First All-American Team.

Giles opened the 1979–80 season with the CHL's Oklahoma City Stars but was put on the fast track to Bloomington when injuries decimated the North Stars' defense corps. He stepped in and showed surprising poise for a rookie while helping the team reach the semifinals.

The steady rearguard was a regular for almost seven years in Minnesota and helped the squad reach the Stanley Cup Finals for the first time in 1981. The next year, after Minnesota was upset in the first round of the playoffs, he hooked up with Team Canada and helped his countrymen win the bronze medal at the World Championships.

Giles missed the end of the 1985–86 regular season after doctors discovered a tumor in the bone of his left ring finger. A portion of the finger was amputated in March, and he returned later that spring to compete in the 1986 playoffs.

Traded to the Rangers early the following season, Giles was dealt back to Minnesota a year later. In 1990–91 his veteran savvy helped the North Stars reach the Stanley Cup Finals for the second time, though he missed the final series due to a knee injury.

The following season Giles left the North Stars as a free agent and spent most of the 1991–92 season with the Canadian National Team and was a member of the Canadian squad that won silver at the Albertville Olympics. After the Olympics he signed with the St. Louis Blues. He retired in 1993 and six years later was named coach of the Edina High School hockey team. In 2010 Edina won the state title.

Giles's 760 games as a North Star ranks second only to Neal Broten's 876.

BILL GOLDSWORTHY (1967–1977)

The term "original North Star" has a double connotation when applied to the late Bill Goldsworthy, a freewheeling winger whose on-ice exploits were overshadowed by a troubled personal life.

Older fans remember Goldsworthy for "The Goldy Shuffle," a comical, arm-pumping dance he performed every time he scored a goal. He was also the first major talent in the history of the North Stars: an animated, charismatic player who gave the expansion team an identity. Thus he was, in every way, an original.

"Goldy was electric," said longtime friend and teammate Lou Nanne. "He was the kind of guy the crowd could relate to. He was flamboyant, he was big, he was strong, he had blond hair, and he was unpredictable. And because of all those things, he was very attractive to the hockey public."

"Goldy was one of my favorite guys," said Jim Lorentz, a former Buffalo Sabre who played junior hockey with Goldsworthy on the OHA's Niagara Falls Flyers. "He was another tough guy to play against. He was more aggressive with his stick than, say, Lou Nanne. He was just a very good competitor, an excellent skater, and just a big, strong guy. We won a Memorial Cup together in Niagara Falls, so I was pleased to see him do well in the NHL."

William Alfred Goldsworthy was a natural athlete like his father, a hockey player who also pitched in semipro baseball. Young Bill was skating on outdoor rinks at five and playing in organized leagues by seven, wearing rolled up magazines under his stockings as shin guards.

He ran with a bad crowd as a teenager and, in between fistfights, was arrested for stealing some records from a music store. He got off with

34. Cesare Maniago (left) confers with Bill Goldsworthy. Courtesy of the Dallas Stars

a warning but was only half-joking when he later said that sports saved him from a life of crime.

Hockey was Goldsworthy's passion, but he also enjoyed football because it gave him a chance to do what he loved most: hit. "I just loved to come—bang—and just crucify guys," he said. "I liked contact. I was that way off the field. If I thought someone had taken my bike, I'd beat him up first, then ask for the bike. And on the ice I was a hitter before I could skate with any speed or shoot worth a darn."

Drafted by the Boston Bruins and later claimed by Minnesota in the 1967 expansion draft, Goldsworthy spent the next ten years rousing North Stars fans from their seats.

Never a skilled stickhandler or passer, he could be a lethal marksman when he had the puck in scoring position. In the 1967 playoffs he led all players in scoring with eight goals and fifteen points. But his listless play the following season resulted in a temporary demotion to the minors. His unpredictability drove coaches nuts.

"I remember telling Goldy I'd make a hockey player out of him if it killed both of us," Wren Blair said. "For a long time I wasn't sure I'd make it. I needled him so hard it sometimes came out the other side. He didn't like it. We literally bumped heads sometimes. But some guys you encourage with smiles, kind words, and pats on the back, and some guys you get going with frowns and taunts and kicks in the backside. Goldy was the second kind, and I grabbed him and dragged out of him what he had in him."

Said Cesare Maniago, "[Blair] would work on Goldy constantly. I can remember Goldy breaking lots of sticks in the dressing room. Blair would chastise him, and once he finished, Goldy would go somewhere and you'd hear SNAP, and a stick would be flying in all directions. But then he'd come back, calm down, and go on to play a hell of a game. He was volatile but had talent galore."

"Whether you were a teammate of his or not," said Tom Reid, "you never knew what to expect from Goldy in a game. You never knew how he was going to react in certain situations."

Goldsworthy was never short on motivation to fight, and the temper that got him into so much trouble as a kid landed him in the penalty box more often than management would have liked. He was prone to dropping his gloves with anyone who made him look bad, though it's likely that opponents knew Goldy could be easily provoked into taking dumb penalties. He learned to restrain his emotions somewhat in later years but could never fully suppress them.

He was also the type of player who didn't handle adversity well, and scoring droughts usually left him depressed and discouraged. Halfway through the 1969–70 season, he had only six goals and was down in the dumps again.

Just as he was ready to write off the whole campaign, inspiration hit him squarely in the head. In practice one day he collided with linemate J. P. Parise and suffered a severe concussion. It was the third major blow to the head he had taken, and doctors convinced him to wear a helmet to decrease the likelihood of further injury. When he returned, the new-look Goldsworthy went on a scoring tear seldom seen in that era. He scored in six consecutive games, missed one, then scored in seven straight. Then he scored ten times in eleven games, giving him twenty-three in twenty-six contests. Then in back-to-back games against Los Angeles and Vancouver, he lit the lamp seven times.

Goldsworthy went on to represent Canada at the 1972 Summit Series, played in four All-Star Games, and was the first player from an expansion team to score 250 goals (he finished with 283). He was the last remaining North Star from the team's inaugural season when GM Jack Gordon traded him to the Rangers for Bill Fairbairn and Nick Beverly on November 11, 1976, a deal necessitated as much by Gordon's desire to make the North Stars a little younger as by John Ferguson's goal of making the Rangers a little tougher.

But Goldsworthy's career took a nosedive after that, and he played out his days in Edmonton of the WHA before calling it quits in 1979.

His autobiography, *The Goldy Shuffle*, was a bestseller in the Twin Cities, and in 1992, the North Stars retired his number, 8, in a gala ceremony at Met Center.

Most fans who adored Goldsworthy for his achievements as a hockey player never knew that he led a troubled personal life. He drank heavily in the years after his retirement, leading to a bitter divorce.

After fourteen seasons in the NHL and two in the WHA, Goldsworthy struggled to find his place in the world. Hockey was all he had ever known, and though he tried his hand at scouting and briefly coached son Sean on the CHL's San Antonio Iguanas, nothing filled that gaping void in his life. Goldy was single and out of control.

In November 1994 he entered a Memphis hospital for treatment of blood clots in his legs and a bout with pneumonia. Tests revealed that he had contracted the AIDS virus—the result, he later admitted, of promiscuity.

At the age of fifty, he was given less than five years to live.

Goldsworthy returned to his home in Edina, where he struggled with the prospect of leaving behind a family he still loved and grappled with the decision to go public about his plight.

Unlike NBA star Magic Johnson, who spoke out almost immediately after learning he had the virus, Goldsworthy waited several months. "I talked to some of my former teammates, like Lou Nanne, Tom Reid, and J.P. [Parise]," Goldsworthy said in a CBC radio interview, "and they'd heard some rumors about this. I sat down and talked to them about it. I didn't want this to come out in an ugly manner. I was concerned about my family and friends."

Their reassurance, combined with Johnson's candor, helped Goldy find the confidence he needed to reveal the truth. But he also hoped that his story would serve as a warning to others—a warning that no one is invincible. Not even professional athletes.

"We think that it can never happen to us," he said. "We think we can fight anything off. And we do at times. I've had broken noses and operations and have always rebounded. But when you get diagnosed with something like this, you have to fight it in a different way."

The response was overwhelming. Former players, teammates, and even kids whom he had once coached in hockey schools called or wrote letters expressing love and support.

Goldsworthy pledged to fight the disease and become a more active voice in the cause of AIDS awareness. He worked for the Minnesota AIDS Project, attended a benefit in the Twin Cities with Magic Johnson, and continued to take his medication.

> "If I thought someone had taken my bike, I'd beat him up first, then ask for the bike."
>
> • Bill Goldsworthy

As a player it had been said of Goldy that he was at his best when the chips were down. He was facing the biggest challenge of his life now and for a time appeared to be making progress. More than a year after he was first diagnosed, doctors were encouraged that he made it through the previous winter without any infections or other setbacks.

But Goldsworthy could not keep the disease at bay forever, and his continued dependence on alcohol accelerated a decline in his health. Loved ones who hoped against hope that Bill would reach or exceed the life expectancy predicted by physicians could only watch helplessly as he drank away his last days on earth.

On March 29, 1996, Goldsworthy died at a Minneapolis hospital.

"If you knew Goldy, you knew he had a great big heart," said Nanne. "As unpredictable as he was, he was a loyal guy and a caring guy."

DANNY GRANT (1968–1974)

There was a time when the Montreal Canadiens had so many talented players on their roster and stashed away in other corners of the hockey world that it was impossible to keep them all. Luckily for the North Stars, Danny Grant was one of those players.

In 1967 Grant turned pro with the Habs following a stupendous junior career with the OHA's Peterborough Petes. But he was low on Montreal's depth chart—just another kid playing behind established veterans with proven track records like Yvan Cournoyer, Bobby Rousseau, and Claude Provost. The incumbents were there to win championships, not tutor promising rookies.

After appearing in just twenty-two games with the Canadiens, Grant was dealt to the North Stars in June 1968. The trade offered the Fredericton native less pressure and more opportunities to show off his pinpoint wrist shot. He adapted quickly to his new environment. Teammates called the New Brunswick native "Tuna," and he made friends quickly because he never took himself too seriously and he was a terrific storyteller.

"He had some great stories," Tom Reid agreed. "They weren't always true, but they were good."

35. They called
Danny Grant
"Tuna," but he had
sharklike instincts
around the net.
Graphic Artists/
Hockey Hall
of Fame

"He was a typical Maritimer," Cesare Maniago said. "He was so easy-going that you could tell him the world would cease tomorrow and he'd still have his rum and Coke and not worry about it. I've yet to see one Maritimer that I've played with or against who got uptight."

"Danny was a fun, fun guy," added Lou Nanne. "He had a personality that you loved because he was funny and he made fun of himself. But he was also a guy who had tremendous skill on the ice that just came naturally to him. He was maybe the best pure goal scorer I've ever seen."

DID YOU KNOW?

Danny Grant set the North Stars club record for most consecutive games played with 442.

By the end of his first full NHL season, Grant set rookie scoring records for the time, netting thirty-four goals and finishing the year with sixty-four points. He was rewarded with the 1969 Calder Trophy as the league's top rookie, though that came as little surprise to anyone familiar with his abilities.

"I played against Danny in juniors," said longtime Bruins winger Wayne Cashman. "He was a tremendous scorer. He was on a line with Andre Lacroix and Mickey Redmond in Peterborough. He was a good, solid goal scorer, but being in Minnesota, he didn't get the recognition around the NHL that he would have gotten if he'd played in another area. When he played with a centerman who knew how to get the puck to him, he could finish. He was a great finisher."

> "Being in Minnesota, he didn't get the recognition around the NHL that he would have gotten if he'd played in another area."
>
> • *Wayne Cashman*

The first setup man with whom Grant really clicked was Danny O'Shea, center on Minnesota's "GOL Line." Right wing Claude Larose rounded out the trio.

Despite the lack of fanfare surrounding much of his career, Grant won acclaim for his productivity and durability. He recorded six seasons of twenty-nine or more goals in his first seven full years (including six as a North Star) and while in his prime played in 566 consecutive games. He represented the North Stars at three consecutive All-Star Games from 1969 to 1971.

In 1973–74, the team finished seventh in the eight-team West Division. Sensing (correctly) that this might be the beginning of a prolonged funk, and not thrilled with some of the personnel moves the club was making, Grant reluctantly decided to approach management after the season to request a trade.

"I didn't want to do it," Grant recalled. "I had so many friends on the team and at one point even imagined myself retiring in Minnesota. But I went into Wren Blair's office and said, 'Wren, I think it's about time I moved on.' Well, he got very upset. He jumped up from his desk and said, 'You're not going anyplace as long as I'm here. You've been a part of this franchise for six years and you're going to be a part of it for six more. Now go home, have a good summer, and get back here ready to play in the fall.' A short time later I'm driving along in my car, and I hear on the radio that I've been traded to Detroit for Henry Boucha. When I got home, before I even had a chance to tell me wife, the phone rang. It was Wren. And Wren said, 'I'm just calling to tell you that you were with the North Stars for as long as me, because they fired me fifteen minutes before you were traded.'"

Grant retired in 1979 as a member of the Los Angeles Kings. In later years he worked for a natural gas company in New Brunswick and as an assistant coach with the men's hockey team at St. Thomas University.

CRAIG HARTSBURG (1979–1989)

When his body cooperated, Craig Hartsburg was one of the best offensive defensemen in hockey—the kind who could slow a game down and control it.

"I just tried to be the best two-way player I could be," he said. "You're not going to get me to say much more about myself than that."

If Hartsburg won't toot his own horn, we'll let Lou Nanne do it for him. "Craig was the best defenseman who ever played for the North Stars," Nanne said. "It's not even close. He dominated the game with his unbelievable ability to handle the puck in close quarters and come out with it to make plays."

Voted the OHL's most outstanding defenseman at the age of seventeen, Hartsburg left Sault Ste. Marie a year later to sign with the WHA's Birmingham Bulls. It turned out to be a great experience for young players like Hartsburg because it helped prepare them for the NHL.

"That last year in the WHA, it was a good league," he said. "There were only six teams left so there was a high level of play and great rivalries. For our first crack at pro hockey, it certainly was a great learning experience. Off the ice and on the ice, we saw a lot of different things. Most of us were living on our own for the first time."

36. Craig Hartsburg. Courtesy of the Dallas Stars

Once compared to Canadiens legend Serge Savard, Hartsburg became eligible for the NHL draft in 1979 when the Bulls folded and the WHA ceased operations. He was selected sixth overall that June by Minnesota.

"We were simply astounded—and overjoyed—when Craig Hartsburg was available on our first turn in the draft," said Nanne, who took the Stratford, Ontario, native two spots ahead of Hall of Famer Ray Bourque.

Poise. Grace. Intelligence. Those were the hallmarks of a ten-year NHL career spent entirely in Minnesota and included All-Star Game appearances in 1980, 1982, and 1983. Hartsburg also captained the North Stars from 1982 to 1988.

While he never won the Stanley Cup as a player, Hartsburg was a key member of Canada's 1987 Canada Cup–winning team. He also represented his country at three World Championships and was named that tournament's best defenseman in 1987.

His career suffered a number of setbacks due to injury. In 1983–84 it was torn knee ligaments. In 1984–85 a fractured hip. His production and professionalism were missed.

"Craig was the best defenseman who ever played for the North Stars. It's not even close."

• Lou Nanne

"He was a skilled, competitive guy who hated to lose," said Al MacAdam. "Losing him hurt us because he was a big part of our team at that point."

Naturally, it took time to shake off the rust and regain the form that made No. 4 one of the league's dominant defenders. He rebounded with two more strong seasons and on November 1, 1986, became the first North Stars defenseman to record a hat trick, beating Chicago's Bob Sauve three times in a 6–5 defeat.

A series of unlucky injuries kept him out of the lineup for most of his last two seasons. "When you're a hockey player, you want to play," Hartsburg said. "When you can't because of injuries, you become very frustrated. I tried to come back early and got injured again. It just seemed to get worse over time, and it got to a point where I couldn't perform anymore. I wanted to be around the rink with the guys, but it's not nearly as much fun when you're not playing. You feel like a spare wheel."

An infected right ankle was the malady that eventually led to Hartsburg's retirement in January 1989.

He remained with the North Stars for one more season as an assistant coach and has since held a variety of coaching posts in junior hockey and the NHL.

DENNIS HEXTALL (1971–1976)

Born into a hockey family with long-standing ties to the NHL, left wing Dennis Hextall carved out his own niche as a fiery competitor who agitated players at both ends of the ice.

Hexy's slightly built frame packed a wallop, and he was a willing fighter. He forged a reputation as a tough customer as early as his days skating for Buffalo of the AHL, where he tussled with the likes of Don Cherry, then a veteran roughneck with the Rochester Americans. After one notable bout between the two, Cherry needed seventeen stitches to close a gash above his left eye.

"Hexy was a tough guy," Tom Reid recalled, "and some of the things he did, even as your teammate, would make you cringe."

"Dennis was and still is a fierce competitor," added Fred Barrett. "He was, pound for pound, one of the toughest guys in the league."

The son of Rangers great Bryan Hextall Sr., brother of Bryan Hextall Jr. and the uncle of former Flyers goalie Ron Hextall, Dennis went undrafted after two superb seasons at the University of North Dakota, where he studied predentistry. He completed his degree, declined a scholarship to pursue his masters, and jumped to the pro ranks with the Eastern League's Knoxville Knights.

He muscled his way into the NHL two years later with the Rangers but saw limited duty.

Considered a fourth-line player with marginal talent, Hextall bounced around a bit before landing with the California Golden Seals. It was there that he became a full-time NHLer, pacing the woeful Seals with twenty-one goals and fifty-two points in 1970–71. He also led the club with 217 penalty minutes.

The North Stars acquired him from California in May 1971 for Joey Johnston and Walt McKechnie, and he provided an immediate injection of spunk and skill.

Hextall was Minnesota's leading scorer for three seasons from 1972 to 1975, a period during which he twice led the club in penalty minutes. He also represented the North Stars at the 1974 and 1975 All-Star Games.

"I always tell people the best place I ever lived was the Twin Cities," Hextall said. "I might have played there longer and still be living there if I would have kept my mouth shut."

Ah yes, Hextall's mouth. While he won over the hearts of fans with his determined style of play, he sometimes found himself at odds with teammates. He demanded as much from them as he did from himself, and that was the cause of more than a few heated dressing-room altercations.

> "Some of the things he did, even as your teammate, would make you cringe." • Tom Reid

"Hextall didn't hold back," said Cesare Maniago. "He had the respect of a lot of people but, at the same time, may have aggravated others. Hexy would try to get the best out of anyone, but some guys took it as an offense. Naturally, words were exchanged, and that led to insults."

"Dennis was a little bit abrasive at times and pissed some people off, but a lot of it was because he was such a competitor and expected that from everyone," said Barrett. "We weren't getting that from everyone, so there was a little friction here and there. That was part of his character and what made him successful. It doesn't always work for everybody. Dennis said what he felt and probably wished he hadn't said certain things. When you knew Dennis, you just had to deal with it."

His production on the decline, Hextall was dealt to the Red Wings in February 1976. He remained with Detroit for parts of four seasons before concluding his career with the Washington Capitals.

Hextall continued to live in the Detroit area after his retirement and remained active with the Red Wings Alumni Association, eventually serving as president. He also briefly served as commissioner of the new International Hockey League (formerly the United Hockey League).

AL MACADAM (1978–1984)

Glen Sonmor once said, "Give me a team of Al MacAdams, and I'll give you a championship."

Absent the wonders of cloning technology, the North Stars of the late 1970s and early 1980s had to get by with just one Al MacAdam, a solid all-around player whose rights were transferred to the North Stars in the Cleveland-Minnesota merger.

"I was ready to move at that point," said MacAdam. "After two years in Oakland and two years in Cleveland, I felt I was ready to play for a better team. I was confident in my game, I had good work habits, and I wanted to be in the playoffs."

Like Gilles Meloche, who also played for the Barons, MacAdam couldn't wait to get out of Cleveland, despite having served as team captain. The right wing came to Bloomington and enjoyed a professional rebirth, joining left wing Steve Payne and center Bobby Smith to form the North Stars' highest-scoring line.

A goal scorer by trade, "Spud" proved his worth in other ways by killing penalties and playing rough when games got chippy. He was a fine complement to top-end players like Payne, Smith, or Tim Young but also excelled when cast in a checking role. He displayed a quiet leadership and dedication to the sport that impressed coaches and teammates.

But then none of that came as much surprise to anyone who had watched Reginald Alan MacAdam Jr. since he was drafted by the Flyers in the fourth round of the 1972 draft. Philadelphia traded him to California in 1974, and he never missed a game for the next four seasons.

"He was, pound for pound, maybe the toughest player in the league," said Lou Nanne. "He could fight like you wouldn't believe, and yet he was very quiet and mild-mannered. He was bright too. He was a terrific team player."

37. Al MacAdam.
Courtesy of the
Dallas Stars

"Spud was pretty handy to have over on the right side," said Payne. "I enjoyed playing with him on that line, and we had some good seasons together."

MacAdam was Minnesota's most valuable player during the 1980 playoffs. After leading the North Stars with a career-high forty-two goals and ninety-three points in the regular season, he scored the series-clinching goal in overtime to beat Toronto in the first round. Then he scored a colossal, series-winning goal in Game Seven of the quarterfinals against four-time defending champ Montreal.

Minnesota was eliminated in the following round by Philadelphia, but MacAdam, after just his sixth full NHL season, received the Masterton Trophy for perseverance and dedication to hockey. He was the first player from the Minnesota-Dallas franchise to win the league award named in honor of former North Star Bill Masterton.

The following season, MacAdam averaged a point per game as the team advanced to the Stanley Cup Finals. But his scoring trailed off somewhat in the years that followed, and in 1984 the North Stars traded him to Vancouver for veteran defenseman Harold Snepsts. MacAdam played one final season with the Canucks before calling it quits.

After his retirement, MacAdam was named head hockey coach at St. Thomas University in Fredericton, New Brunswick. He remained in that post for the next decade and then briefly served as the school's assistant athletic director.

He has since worked for the Chicago Blackhawks as an assistant coach and as a scout for the Buffalo Sabres.

CESARE MANIAGO (1967–1976)

Cesare Maniago could have spent his entire career as an understudy to Hall of Fame goalies like Johnny Bower, Jacques Plante, and Ed Giacomin or toiled away in relative obscurity in minor league outposts in Spokane, Omaha, or Baltimore.

Certainly, from 1960 to 1967 it appeared that would be this netminder's fate. In between demotions to the AHL and an assortment of now-defunct leagues, Maniago was a backup in Toronto, Montreal, and New York. He appeared in only fifty-five NHL contests during that stretch, his noteworthy achievements limited to surrendering some milestone goals to Bobby Hull and Bernie (Boom Boom) Geoffrion.

Then came the Great Expansion, and Maniago, claimed by Minnesota from the Rangers, went from backup to franchise building block overnight.

"A class guy," declared Al Shaver. "One of the classiest people I ever met in any sport I ever covered. It was very important to have a guy like Cesare on board. He was absolutely admired by all the players on the team. They thought he was the cat's meow. He was very popular, and he was a leader, which you don't find in a lot of goaltenders."

The Canadian-born son of Italian immigrants, Maniago was just a scrawny kid in his midteens when his goaltending career received a big boost.

Like almost everyone who lived in the small town of Trail, British Columbia, Cesare's father worked in the local mining-smelting industry. Boss Pete McIntyre, a friend of Maple Leafs owner Conn Smythe, called the elder Maniago into his office one day to discuss his son's hockey future. McIntyre had the right connections to place Cesare with some of the best junior teams in Canada. Given the opportunity to continue his

DID YOU KNOW?

Cesare Maniago had the North Stars' longest shutout streak at 188:38, which included three successive shutouts over Los Angeles on December 13, 1967, Los Angeles again on December 15, 1967, and Oakland on December 16, 1967.

development beyond the confines of tiny Trail, the youngster opted for St. Michael's College in Toronto. There he played with future NHLers like Frank Mahovlich and Dave Keon.

Within a few short years Maniago was in the pros and making his dad proud. He recorded his best minor league season in 1964–65 with the Minneapolis Bruins of the old Central Professional Hockey League. That year he was named league MVP by virtue of a 34-26-7 record with six shutouts and a 2.75 goals against average.

In Maniago North Stars GM Wren Blair knew he was getting a well-schooled veteran who understood the values of patience and persever-ance and someone who could bring a calming influence to a fledgling franchise.

The goalie was a scout's dream. His towering, six-feet-three frame cov-ered much of the net, but he also possessed great agility and won over fans and management with his excellent reflexes and acrobatic saves. Even when victories were as difficult to come by as generous general managers, chants of "Hail Cesare!" were a popular refrain at Met Center.

"Cesare was a wonderful teammate and a guy you could always count upon," said Tom Reid. "He'd never let you down." But the North Stars feared a letdown was inevitable. Having played the bulk of Minnesota's games for its first three seasons, Maniago was headed for a burnout.

So in 1970 the club acquired Gump Worsley to split time with Maniago. The duo was dubbed "Mutt and Jeff" after a pair of comic strip characters that appeared in daily newspapers. Mutt was tall and lanky, while Jeff resembled the Monopoly man after a rough night. It was a description that fit the six-feet-three Maniago and the five-feet-seven Worsley perfectly.

"He was very popular and he was a leader, which you don't find in a lot of goaltenders."
• Al Shaver

After nine seasons with the North Stars, Maniago was dealt to the Vancouver Canucks in 1976 for the aptly named Gary (Suitcase) Smith, a fellow goaltender who would go on to play in nine different NHL cities.

Maniago departed as Minnesota's all-time leader in every signifi-cant goaltending category and still holds the franchise record for games played with 420.

After retiring in 1978 he stayed in the Vancouver area and ran a thriv-ing sporting goods distributorship.

BRAD MAXWELL (1977–1985, 1986–1987)

A big, tough rearguard from Western Canada, Bradley Robert Max-well was one of the most coveted defensemen to come out of Canadian juniors in the 1970s.

A first-round draft choice (seventh overall) of the North Stars in 1977, Maxwell had been a defense partner of future New York Rangers star Barry Beck on the New Westminster squad that beat Ottawa for the 1977 Memorial Cup. In fact, it was Maxwell who scored the game winner in the championship match.

The son of former minor leaguer Ron Maxwell, Brad finished fifth in team scoring and first among all North Stars defensemen with eighteen goals and forty-seven points in his rookie campaign. He was an excellent puck carrier and a consistent threat on the power play who could put a shot on net from the point as well as anyone on the team. Perhaps any team.

"Maxy had a great shot," said Al Shaver, "and he loved to use it. Sometimes he took a little long to get it off, though. But when he did, God help the guy who got in front of it."

There was little cause for concern when Maxwell's offensive totals dropped the following season. In fact, some took it as a positive sign that the young blueliner was beginning to address deficiencies in his defensive game. His all-around play showed dramatic improvement, and in 1979 a panel of North Stars media cited Maxwell as the team's most improved player.

"Maxy overstepped his bounds here and there, but you always chalked that off to his youth." • *Fred Barrett*

Added Shaver, "Brad may have been one of the best offensive defensemen the North Stars ever had—certainly the best to come along before Craig Hartsburg."

"He gave us a lot of toughness and skill," said former defense partner Fred Barrett. "He was a bit like Dennis Hextall too, in that you always knew where he stood. Maxy overstepped his bounds here and there, but you always chalked that off to his youth. He became a big part of our hockey team in many ways."

Injuries sidelined Maxwell for most of the 1980–81 season, but he did appear in eighteen of nineteen postseason games as the North Stars advanced to the Stanley Cup Finals. He was most impressive during the opening round series against Boston, standing up to Bruins tough guys like Stan Jonathan and setting a tone that helped Minnesota sweep the Bruins in three games.

In December 1984 the North Stars traded Maxwell and Brent Ashton to the Quebec Nordiques for Tony McKegney and Bo Berglund. Maxy was never in one place for very long after that, hopping from Quebec to Toronto to Vancouver to New York. He was only with the Rangers for about a month when he received an unusual phone call from the team's GM, Phil Esposito.

"I could tell that Phil was someplace far away," Maxwell recalled. "He eventually told me that he'd lost me in a card game to one of my old bosses. I said, 'You what? You lost me in a card game?' Turns out he was down in Florida, where he owned a condo. Lou Nanne had a condo right next door. They'd been out playing golf, maybe having a few drinks, although I can't be sure. Then they started playing cards and gambling with players. Phil lost me to Louie, and that's how I ended up back with the North Stars."

Unable to make the North Stars on a tryout contract in 1987, Maxwell retired and took a sales job with a building supply company in Minneapolis. He later started his own home improvement and remodeling company.

TOM (JUG) MCCARTHY (1979–1986)

The long, strange journey of Thomas Joseph McCarthy began in the suburbs of Toronto, continued through eight-plus seasons in the NHL, and even took an unfortunate detour through the U.S. federal penitentiary at Leavenworth, Kansas.

Nicknamed "Jug," "Juggie," and "Jughead" because of his resemblance to the *Archie* cartoon character, McCarthy was a good skater with quick hands who was tough to beat in one-on-one situations. The Oshawa Generals wanted him badly enough that they selected him first—ahead of Wayne Gretzky—in the 1977 OHA midget draft.

When it came to putting pucks in the net, Jug had the golden touch. Minnesota's first pick (tenth overall) in the 1979 draft was just one more offensive weapon on a team blessed with an abundance of young talent. Bobby Smith, Dino Ciccarelli, Craig Hartsburg, and Neal Broten were all in their prime, but Glen Sonmor, McCarthy's coach for five years, once commented that Jug might have been the best pure talent of the bunch.

If McCarthy had the potential to be the best—333 points in 385 games as a North Star offers a hint of his skills—he might have been the last person to know it. He made the game look so easy sometimes that he was criticized for not pushing himself harder. A bout with substance abuse only further hindered his development.

"He could've been an All-Star," Lou Nanne said. "He was the best backhand passer I've ever seen. He had great vision of the ice and wonderful puck-handling ability. He was big and strong too. But Tommy never worked as hard as he should have, never committed himself fully to being as good as he could be. Had he done that, he might have made the Hall of Fame."

Tired of waiting for McCarthy to kick his drug and alcohol habit, the North Stars shipped the troubled winger to Boston in May 1986 for a pair of draft picks. He played two years for the Bruins before going to

Europe and was out of hockey by 1991. Without the game to keep him occupied, Jug hit rock bottom.

He was arrested by the FBI in 1994 when his name came up in connection with a prominent Minnesota drug dealer. McCarthy pled guilty to driving a truckload of marijuana (150 pounds) from California to Minnesota. Although he was living in Minnesota at the time, he was considered an illegal alien and that led to additional sentencing and his incarceration at Leavenworth.

It was behind bars that McCarthy, who had worked as a hockey school instructor during his offseasons, had a revelation: he would teach hockey to his fellow inmates. To prison officials equipping convicts with hockey sticks sounded crazy. But McCarthy convinced them it could be a positive experience.

"You wouldn't believe what happened," McCarthy recounted years later in an interview with the *Toronto Sun*. "You've never seen hockey until you've seen people from different races playing—the bikers, the natives, the gang members, the Mexicans, the blacks, everyone. I felt like Burt Reynolds in *The Longest Yard*. Every Saturday and Sunday morning we'd get up early before breakfast and have a practice. We had them stickhandling around cones. After breakfast we'd have a game. I was the referee and the coach of both teams. We started with twelve and before long had about one hundred guys. Everybody wanted to play. And you know what? We never had one fight and not a single incident. The whole thing made me feel like this is what I should be doing. Hockey Night in Leavenworth. I thought if I can teach guys who didn't know the game and had never seen it before how to play, I should be coaching."

> If McCarthy had the potential to be the best, he might have been the last person to know it.

And that's just what McCarthy did when his prison term ended in 1998. A year later he was coaching a triple-A team of fifteen-year-old boys in Mississauga, Ontario, passing along his knowledge of hockey and the harsh realities of life.

"I think I have a huge message to pass on," McCarthy said. "None of them, Gretzky, Dionne, Esposito, any of the stars, have what I have to offer. They might have known someone in trouble, but they've never really been in trouble. They can't relate to what I've been through. I've had experiences they'll never know."

BASIL McRAE (1987–1992)

While men like Bobby Smith and Brian Bellows had sealed their North Star legacies by posting big offensive numbers, Basil McRae's on-ice contribution was typically limited to the role of enforcer. But like Clint Eastwood in the *Dirty Harry* films, it was a role McRae filled perfectly.

Among his peers, however, the source of McRae's popularity was his relentless work ethic and willingness to be one of the team's most vocal leaders. In fact, he shared the captaincy with Stew Gavin and Curt Giles during the 1989–90 season.

"Basil had great leadership qualities because he was able to make each game feel as if it was the most important game in the world," said former linemate Dave Gagner. "I looked to him a lot for that motivation. He would do whatever it took. There's nothing you could do to stop him from succeeding."

Signed as a free agent from the Nordiques in June 1987, McRae had yet to play a full season in the NHL. He was twenty-six at the time, a young

39. Razzle Dazzle Basil. Courtesy of the Dallas Stars

ruffian who'd bounced around from Quebec to Toronto to Detroit and back to Quebec without ever really establishing himself.

"Once you get to a level like the National Hockey League," said former NHL tough guy Nick Kypreos, "they're not very patient people. They don't sit and wait for you to develop into a scorer because the pressure to have success right away is large. If a guy like Basil comes up and doesn't put the puck in the net, he's got to find a way to maintain his status in the lineup. If you're not scoring, it's the old 'What else can you do for me?'"

McRae answered that question with his fists. A ready and willing combatant, he turned heads in the spring of 1987 by piling up a mind-boggling ninety-nine minutes in penalties in only thirteen postseason games with the Nordiques.

The North Stars of the late 1980s were no collection of cream puffs. Men like Willi Plett, Dirk Graham, and Keith Acton played a hardnosed style while chipping in timely goals. But there was a need for a legitimate heavyweight—a policeman to send a clear message to opponents that Minnesota's skill players would not be intimidated.

Enter McRae, who averaged over 350 penalty minutes in his first three seasons with the North Stars. By the time the 1989–90 campaign was over, he had already amassed 1,098 PIMs in a Minnesota uniform.

"You can say anything you want about fighting," said Kypreos, "but there's not a guy that doesn't respect someone that has to fill that role. And there's not one guy that won't admit that they feel about two inches taller when a guy like that is in the lineup."

But McRae knew how to score too. He'd done it on the minor league level, topping the twenty-goal mark three times in four seasons. In 1988–89, his second in Minnesota, he scored a career-best twelve goals and thirty-one points.

> "If a guy like Basil comes up and doesn't put the puck in the net, he's got to find a way to maintain his status in the lineup." • Nick Kypreos

Most of those were scored on tip-ins and deflections, since the North Stars liked to position McRae in front of the opposing net on power plays.

"As a kid Basil was a goal-scoring machine," said Gagner. "He was able to score, but when you've got to think about dropping the gloves at any minute, it's not so easy to be skillful. We used to laugh at him in the summers because he'd come down to Minnesota and do toe-drags on guys and waltz around them. He'd say, 'I *told* you I can do it.'"

McRae had a cameo in the 1992 film *The Mighty Ducks*, in which he can be seen wearing a North Stars uniform, but that year he was claimed by Tampa Bay in the expansion draft. He closed out his playing career in 1996 after stints in St. Louis and Chicago.

Eventually settling in the St. Louis area, McRae became active in a Missouri youth hockey program and worked as a financial advisor. He also became co-owner of his former junior club, the OHA's London Knights.

GILLES MELOCHE (1978–1985)

The 1978 Cleveland-Minnesota merger was a boon for the North Stars and a godsend to goaltender Gilles Meloche.

The Montreal native began his NHL career with Chicago but had spent seven depressing seasons as the starting netminder for the bungling California-Cleveland franchise. Be they known as the Golden Seals or the Barons, the club often played in front of sparse crowds and was viewed on most nights as an easy win for stronger opponents.

40. Gilles Meloche. Courtesy of the Dallas Stars

"We'd go on a road trip and play in places like the Montreal Forum and Boston Garden where the atmosphere would be just great," Meloche explained in Dick Irvin's *In the Crease*. "Then we'd go home to Cleveland and it was like being back in the minor leagues."

Meloche did what he could to keep the team competitive, but the nightly onslaught was taking its toll. He approached management and requested a trade, but they wouldn't oblige.

The Barons' precarious financial situation, which had once prompted Meloche and teammates to consider a walkout when paychecks were nearly a month late, would finally work in the goalie's favor.

When the North Stars absorbed Cleveland's roster, it did more than just boost Minnesota's talent level; it made the game fun again for Meloche.

"Gilles was probably an abnormal goalie," said Al MacAdam, a long-time friend and teammate in Cleveland and Minnesota, "in that he thought he could stop *every* puck, and he blamed every goal on himself. Not all goalies do that. He was a quiet guy in addition to being a good goalie, so that's probably why he stayed around for eighteen years."

The North Stars fell just short of a playoff berth in Meloche's first season with the club, but he won twenty games for the first time in his career. Minnesota advanced to the postseason for the next six years, and the goaltender considered them the six most enjoyable years of his career.

Though Meloche is remembered for backstopping Minnesota to its first Stanley Cup Finals appearance in 1981, one of his proudest moments occurred a year earlier during the 1980 quarterfinals against his hometown Canadiens. Recalled Meloche: "They always said about me, 'You're a good goalie, but you've never played with a lot of pressure in the playoffs.' So we came into the Montreal Forum, and I remember the first game when I shut them out, 3-0. Those years you played two games in two nights, and the next night we beat them, 4-1. I was in seventh heaven. We went back to Minnesota, and they won the next two and then beat us again in the fifth game in Montreal. So we were down 3-2 and beat them, 5-2. Then there was a great seventh game in Montreal. We won it, 3-2, when Al MacAdam scored the winner on Denis Herron with about two minutes left in the game. That was the greatest thrill of my life."

> "Gilles was probably an abnormal goalie in that he thought he could stop *every* puck." • *Al MacAdam*

When a veteran rink rat like Dick Irvin rates Meloche's performance in that series as among the best he had ever seen in the playoffs, take it as gospel. It was certainly the best effort by any goalie wearing a North Stars uniform.

Meloche played out his option with the club, but when he could not agree on a new contract with GM Lou Nanne, the North Stars traded him to Edmonton after the 1985 playoffs.

He ended his playing career with Pittsburgh and in 1989 joined the Penguins' management team. Over the next decade he remained with the club as a goaltending coach and scout.

Meloche's son, Eric, was drafted by Pittsburgh and made his NHL debut with the Penguins in 2002.

MIKE MODANO (1988–1993)

When the Dallas Stars won the Stanley Cup in 1999, no player enjoyed a greater feeling of vindication than Mike Modano, who played the entire series with a broken wrist and finally shed the soft, pretty-boy reputation that had plagued him since his earliest days in Bloomington.

As a youngster the future Hall of Famer was said to have been a genuine pain in the butt who excelled in creating mischief, slacking off at school, and mouthing off to grownups. His parents tried a variety of remedies, but nothing seemed to work . . . nothing, that is, until they enrolled Mike in peewee hockey at age nine. He finally had a suitable outlet for all that excess energy, and his skills developed so well and so quickly that by age sixteen, Mike was off to play junior hockey in Prince Albert, Saskatchewan. American college coaches advised him against it, but he was determined to push himself by playing against tougher competition.

41. Mike Modano. Courtesy of the Dallas Stars

"He definitely showed that he wanted to be an NHL hockey player," Lou Nanne said. "You take a kid who, at that young age, goes out to western Canada, not knowing anybody, to play in a really competitive league . . . that tells you this guy is hungry, he wants to make it, and he's willing to pay the price to get there."

In his second year with the Raiders, Modano had 127 points in only sixty-five games. The following year he suffered a broken wrist in the Western Hockey League (WHL) All-Star Game and still managed to lead the team in scoring despite missing twenty-five games because of the injury.

Soon it was being whispered that he was possibly the best American-born prospect *ever*. Which he certainly was . . . when he had the puck. But backchecking? Forechecking? This was alien terminology to Modano, for whom hockey was a release, not yet a profession.

Heading into the 1988 NHL Entry Draft in Montreal, the consensus was that either Modano or Medicine Hat's Trevor Linden would go first overall to the North Stars. Whoever didn't go first was almost definitely going second to the Canucks.

"But there was no real decision yet as to who was going to go one or two that year," Modano recalled. "Neither Minnesota nor Vancouver at the time gave me any indication of what direction they were going to go in. Being an American, I said, 'I'd love to go number one to Minnesota and try to help turn that franchise around.'"

Nanne broke the suspense when he walked up to the stage at the Forum holding a North Stars jersey and announced Modano as that year's top pick.

"Our franchise was in a situation where we had to do something to build a fan base," Nanne explained. "Our people, and myself, were convinced that with the charisma he had and the electrifying way he played the game, Modano would help us in more ways than Linden."

> "It was exciting and fun but at the same time, a lot of pressure to try to help change that organization."
> • Mike Modano

Almost immediately Modano's game-breaking blend of speed and skill made him the face of the North Stars, a struggling franchise in desperate need of a change of fortunes. He found that there's a big difference between saying you want to help be part of the solution and being thrust into the role of savior. That's a hefty weight to drop on any nineteen-year-old's shoulders.

"There was a lot of pressure going into that situation," Modano recalled. "It was exciting and fun but at the same time, a lot of pressure to try to help change that organization. It was a great learning experience. You felt you wanted to come in and really make an impact, and sometimes you felt like you almost tried too hard to change things so fast. It took time."

Nanne always expected Modano to mature into a franchise player. "He's done that and gone beyond our expectations," said Nanne. "We knew he would electrify a crowd, bring them out of their seats. We knew he had great hands and great physical skills. But when we tested him, it showed that he also had great leadership skills. And people weren't looking at him that way because he's somewhat quiet and shy. He's got the ability to lead, and through the work of Bob Gainey and (Dallas coach) Ken Hitchcock, he developed into a phenomenal all-around player."

DID YOU KNOW?

North Stars teammates Mike Modano and Basil McRae had cameos as themselves in the 1992 Disney film *The Mighty Ducks*.

"Mike was fun to be around because he was an upbeat kind of kid," recalled Dave Gagner. "And he was very confident in himself. He knew what he could do, but he wasn't boastful about it. I always said that if my son could grow up to be like that, I'd be pretty happy."

Modano moved with the Stars to Dallas in 1993 and eventually became one of the top two-way players in the game—an almost unimaginable concept in the early days of his career, when he was strictly a point producer.

It was widely believed that the 2009–10 season, Modano's twentieth in the NHL, would be his last. So on April 10, 2010, when the Stars came to St. Paul to play the Wild, the Xcel Center crowd was ready to give Modano a proper sendoff. They got more than they bargained for in what would turn out to be a 4–3 shootout win for the visitors. After Modano was named first star of the game, he emerged from the tunnel sporting the logo and colors he'd worn as a fresh-faced rookie. He waved to the crowd, and they responded with some of the loudest cheers yet heard in that arena. The passage of time had not dulled Minnesota's affection for the former North Star icon.

Modano did decide to play one more season and closed out his career with his hometown Detroit Red Wings. He retired in 2011 as the all-time points leader and goal scorer among U.S.-born players.

LOU NANNE (1967–1978)

Referring to Lou Nanne as a "career North Star" doesn't begin to quantify just how much he meant to the franchise. Nanne represented the club as a player, coach, general manager, and team president . . . not all at once, mind you, but if anyone could've found a way, it would've been Louie.

A native of Sault Sainte Marie, Ontario, Nanne played junior hockey with former Bruins great Phil Esposito, but their careers took different paths when Nanne chose to attend the University of Minnesota. In 1963 he became the first defenseman in history to win the WCHA's scoring title when he paced the Gophers with fourteen goals and forty-three points in twenty-nine games. He also earned All-American honors while winning the league MVP award.

He was drafted by Chicago after graduation but never suited up for the Blackhawks because of a contract dispute. Instead he opted to play for the Rochester (Minnesota) Mustangs of the USHL. He also spent five years coaching the University of Minnesota's freshman hockey team. In 1968, as a naturalized citizen, he captained the U.S. Olympic Team (alongside Herb Brooks) before signing with the North Stars as a free agent.

While "Sweet Lou from the Soo" was a physical, shot-blocking rearguard throughout his collegiate, Olympic, and pro career, the North Stars recognized that he had some good offensive instincts to complement the checking skills he had developed as a defender. So he was moved up to the forward lines and spent a couple of productive seasons at right wing. In 1971–72, at age thirty and a full-time winger for the first time, Nanne popped in a career-best twenty-one goals.

"He'd play wherever you wanted him to play," said Tom Reid, "and he was a hardnosed son-of-a-gun. There are a lot of guys out there who

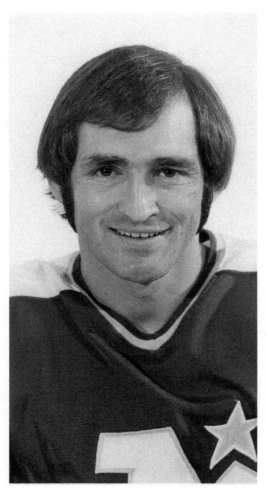

didn't realize how strong he was. He was a hardworking guy who always made his presence felt on the ice."

Nanne might never have made the club were it not for the intervention of team president Walter Bush, who signed the defenseman against Wren Blair's wishes. "Wren did not want Louie on that team for some reason—probably because he wanted too much money," said Bush. "So I signed him to a personal services contract to work in the front office. I felt that as a local guy who could really play, he would be good for the club. He'd come to training camp, and Blair would put him on the B-squad. He had to make the team about three years in a row. Wren must've figured Louie would end up taking his job because he was such a good politician."

Though he never wore the captain's "C," Nanne assumed a leadership role from the very beginning. Ownership took notice and, in the twilight of his playing career, challenged him to lead the last-place North Stars as coach and general manager. His overnight transition from player to executive in the spring of 1978 was easier than one might expect.

"At thirty-six, I was the oldest guy on the team, and I was going to quit at the end of the year anyway," said Nanne. "It wasn't that tough. I'd been in business and been the vice president of the Players' Association. So on the first day I just said to the guys, 'Look, I was your teammate yesterday, and today I'm your boss. I consider you all friends, but I'm not going to let that affect how I do my job. If we're still friends afterwards, and I hope we will be, that's up to you. I have to react differently to you now than I did before.'"

Nanne's turn as coach lasted only twenty-nine games, but he held the manager's post for the next ten years. His first summer on the job may have been his busiest.

As luck would have it, Bobby Smith was available to Minnesota in the 1978 draft, and an unprecedented merger with the Cleveland Barons deepened the North Stars' talent pool. Nanne was charged with the difficult task of handling the player personnel portion of the merger, which included having to cut more than thirty players and $2.5 million in payroll. But he managed to lock up goalie Gilles Meloche and right wing Al MacAdam, as well as the rights to center Mike Eaves, in the process.

Only two years after he joined the front-office ranks, Nanne's North Stars were back in the playoffs and advanced to the semifinals after defeating the defending champion Canadiens. But his proudest managerial moment came the following season, when a team of his own design reached the Stanley Cup Finals for the first time in franchise history.

"We had to make a lot of deals," he said. "I probably made over one hundred trades in my time there."

Not all of Nanne's moves panned out, but he displayed a willingness to take chances. He was crafty too. Trading an injured Mike Fidler to Hartford for Gordie Roberts in 1980 might have been one of his best moves and certainly ranks among his personal favorites.

While Nanne spent much of his time building the North Stars, he was also active at the league level.

"Wren must've figured Louie would end up taking his job because he was such a good politician." • *Walter Bush*

He took a lead role in the NHL's merger negotiations with the WHA and served a term as chairman of the General Managers Committee and as an alternate on the NHL Board of Governors.

A tireless worker, Nanne did everything for the North Stars except sweep Met Center's floors and run the concessions stands. He gave so much of himself to the organization that it began to take its toll.

"He took it so much to heart that it affected his health and that's why he had to get out," said former teammate Cesare Maniago. "I was at some games with him when he was in the managing role, and I would see him age at least ten years in a season. Finally, I said, 'Louie, you've got to get out of this game. It's not good for your health.' Sure enough, when he started to have some health problems, the doctors told him the same thing."

In 1988 Nanne resigned as general manager, though the Gunds convinced him to stay on as team president. In 1990, after more than twenty years of service, he retired from the club for good to pursue other business interests. Later he became involved in trying to bring the Edmonton Oilers to Minneapolis when former owner Peter Pocklington put the team up for sale.

Nanne's ties to Minnesota amateur hockey remained strong throughout his NHL career and beyond. In 2022 he marked his fifty-eighth year providing commentary for TV broadcasts of the Minnesota State High School League boys' hockey tournament.

J. P. PARISE (1967–1975, 1978–1979)

Jean-Paul (J. P.) Parise lacked the eye-popping speed and thunderous shot of contemporaries like Bobby Hull and Guy Lafleur. But the scrappy, undersized left wing garnered acclaim as a dependable and highly coachable checker willing to work hard along the boards and sacrifice statistics when defensive hockey was required.

"He was a workhorse," said Cesare Maniago. "He didn't have the God-given talent that a lot of other guys had, so he had to work to make himself the player that he was. He was probably one of the best cornermen in the league at that time. I played with him in the old Central League, and he showed me then that he was capable of making it just with a strong work ethic."

Wren Blair, who had coached Parise in Kingston of the Eastern Professional Hockey League (EPHL), had his eyes on the winger since the expansion draft. But the Oakland Seals snatched him up just before Minnesota's next pick. Oakland then dealt him to the Maple Leafs, who in turn sent him down to their AHL affiliate in Rochester. When Rochester dropped to last place in December 1967, Blair hatched a scheme to finally get his man.

Murray Hall, Duke Harris, Don Johns, and Len Lunde found out during the North Stars' Christmas skating party that they were being shipped out in an eight-player deal to bring Parise and center Milan Marcetta to Minnesota.

Placed on a line with Bill Goldsworthy and Andre Boudrias, Parise became the heart and soul of the North Stars. "J.P. was a terrific competitor, a tenacious worker, and a great person," said Lou Nanne. "He was totally committed to playing the game once the season started, and he never shortchanged you a nickel the whole year. And he was a great guy to pull pranks on."

Parise's efforts were rewarded with invitations to represent the North Stars at the All-Star Game in 1970 and 1973. And while his unremitting hustle made him a fan favorite in Minnesota, he was a generally unsung hero who went to work each night with a stick in one hand and a lunch pail in the other.

But the spotlight found Parise in 1972, when he joined Goldsworthy, Bobby Clarke, Phil Esposito, and other top players of the day to represent Canada in the classic Summit Series against the Soviet Union. He played in six of the eight games, recording two goals and four points. He was also the tournament's leader in penalty minutes (twenty-eight), though most of those came in the final game in Moscow.

Canada went on to win the hard-fought series, and when Parise returned from Russia, his hometown of Smooth Rock Falls, Ontario, welcomed him with a day in his honor.

About halfway through the 1974–75 season, GM Jack Gordon took a long, hard look at his struggling club and decided that it was time to start phasing out some of the older players from the Wren Blair era. Parise, by then an eight-year-veteran North Star, was terrified that Gordon would dump him on one of the new expansion teams. He even went to Gordon's office one day and pleaded not to be traded to the New York Islanders, who in their infancy were certainly the worst of the lot.

Soon thereafter Parise received an early-morning call telling him to come to the GM's office at Met Center. Because the Bruins had been in Bloomington the night before, and because they had injuries, Parise wondered if Boston would be his next destination. He envisioned

> Parise became the heart and soul of the North Stars.

himself playing alongside Bobby Orr, at last competing for a Stanley Cup. Instead, when he arrived at Met Center, Gordon informed him that he had been traded to the Islanders.

"I wanted to jump over the desk and strangle him," Parise later recalled. But Parise's Long Island experience turned out far better than he could have imagined. Later that season he scored a colossal overtime goal in the opening round of the Wales Conference playoffs, defeating the Rangers and giving the Islanders their first-ever playoff series victory.

Three years later the Islanders traded Parise to the Cleveland Barons. When the Barons merged with Parise's old team, the North Stars, he found himself back in familiar territory. He played the last season of his career in Minnesota.

After retiring as a player, Parise spent eight seasons as an assistant coach with the North Stars before embarking on a career selling commercial insurance. He later became director of hockey at Shattuck-St. Mary's High School in Faribault, Minnesota, where he coached sons Zach and Jordan. Both brothers eventually turned pro in the New Jersey Devils system. Parise died in January 2015 at age seventy-three.

STEVE PAYNE (1978–1988)

It was the summer of 1978, and North Stars GM Lou Nanne had just selected Steve Payne in the second round (nineteenth overall) of the NHL Entry Draft.

Jim Devellano, chief scout for the Islanders, reportedly turned to Nanne and said, "Last year we got the sleeper in the draft when we took Mike Bossy. This year I think you got the same caliber of player in Payne. We would have taken him if you didn't."

In fact, Payne fully expected to be the Islanders' first-round pick. He was at the draft with his parents, waiting to hear his name called

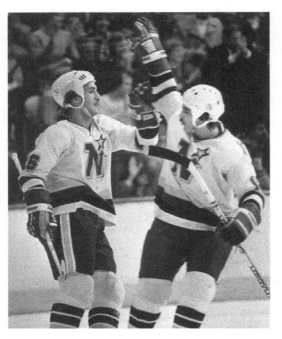

when New York's turn came up at No. 15. Instead they selected center Steve Tambellini.

Bobby Smith, his buddy and Minnesota's top pick that year, walked over to a perplexed Payne and said, "Surprised you didn't go? Well, when the North Stars pick again, they're picking you."

Though some believed he had the size, strength, and skill to be the best left wing in hockey, Payne's goal-scoring prowess would never be on par with that of the immortal Bossy. But the Toronto native accomplished what few star players in the modern era have before or since, spending his entire ten-year NHL career with the team that drafted him.

A linemate of Smith during his junior days with the Ottawa 67's, Payne was reunited with the playmaker in Minnesota and partnered with right wing Al MacAdam. Together the trio formed one of the most prolific lines in the history of the franchise.

Payne was a two-time All-Star whose first seven years were among the most productive ever recorded by a North Stars player. Among current NHLers, Payne feels his style most closely resembles that of Todd Bertuzzi.

"He probably dukes it out a little bit more than I did," said Payne, "but physically, he seems like the same kind of guy—crashing the net, crashing the corners, and overpowering his opponents. They used to joke that the best strategy against me was just not to bump into me. But if you decided to knock me down, and I was in a slumber, that woke me up. I liked that part of the game. I liked the physical challenge of seeing who'd be the last man standing."

Payne could not escape comparisons to Bossy during the 1981 play-offs, a period during which he played the best hockey of his career. His game-winning goal in Game Four of the Stanley Cup Finals was his fourth of the postseason and drew the kind of praise usually reserved for superstars.

"If we should win the Stanley Cup," said Nanne, "Payne should be awarded the Conn Smythe Trophy as the most valuable player. The guy has scored twenty-nine points (seventeen goals and twelve assists) in eighteen games of the playoffs. Only Bossy has more (thirty-four points in seventeen games). You can't play any better hockey than what Payne has done for us in the playoffs. He has been a dominating player game after game."

But even Payne's heroics in the clutch weren't enough to hold off the Islanders, who took Game Five and the series, ending Minnesota's dream season.

After years of consistency, injuries began to limit Payne's effectiveness. He missed most of the 1985–86 and 1986–87 seasons while recovering from an assortment of knee and back surgeries, including one to repair a ruptured disc.

On November 14, 1987, the North Stars visited Landover, Maryland, for a game against the Capitals. A cross-check from behind by Washington center Dale Hunter caused Payne's head to snap back, aggravating an earlier injury. That caused bone spurs to develop, and those spurs grew into Payne's spinal cord.

> "They used to joke that the best strategy against me was just not to bump into me."
> • *Steve Payne*

By December doctors had determined that if Payne continued playing he would need career-ending spinal fusion surgery. He retired rather than risk further damage.

It's probably no coincidence that the North Stars failed to qualify for the playoffs during Payne's final three seasons.

Payne had an opportunity to join the North Stars coaching staff as an assistant under Herb Brooks. But the day he accepted the job, Brooks was fired.

Rather than pursue other jobs in hockey, Payne dabbled in commercial real estate and video production. He still gets his hockey fix by participating in charity games with fellow North Stars alums like Reed Larson, Brad Maxwell, and Gordie Roberts.

TOM REID (1968–1978)

The North Stars of the early 1970s might have lived in constant fear of Wren Blair were it not for amateur comedians like Tom Reid, who reminded teammates that hockey is a game and games are meant to be fun.

"He was the jokester in the room," recalled Cesare Maniago. "He was the guy who'd cut the laces in our skates or saw someone's stick about halfway through the shaft so as soon as the player went for warm-ups, it would snap in half on his first shot. He did a lot of things prior to the game just to keep the guys loose."

One of Reid's favorite gags—an oldie but a goodie—was to attach a thin black string to a one-dollar bill and place it in the middle of an airport concourse. When someone bent down to pick it up, he would give the tether a yank. What bewildered travelers never knew was that the other end of that string was in Reid's hand.

"There were a number of guys who did things; it wasn't just me," said Reid. "Charlie Burns was one of the worst pranksters also. We always seemed to find a way to have fun. It was important for the guys to relax a little bit. Everything was so uptight all the time. And being relaxed, it made them play a little bit better."

As a young man Reid never imagined he would have a chance to play in the NHL. Until 1967 there were only six teams, and most of them carried only five defensemen.

The University of Michigan rejected his application for an athletic scholarship because coaches didn't think he could make the squad. So Reid played junior hockey with St. Catharines of the OHA, which at the time was operated by the Chicago Blackhawks. In unfamiliar surroundings and unsure of his abilities, he soldiered through a tough first year.

"My style was so unorthodox, and I was so uncoordinated," he said. "But then my body started to catch up to my feet. I started to think, 'Jeez, maybe I do have a chance to play in the NHL.'"

A good final year in St. Catharines, combined with expansion and an increase in the number of NHL jobs, led to Reid signing his first pro contract. He made his NHL debut with the Blackhawks in 1967 but could not earn a full-time job on a defense corps crowded with veterans like Doug Mohns, Pat Stapleton, and Pierre Pilote. A big, stay-at-home defenseman, Reid split time between the Blackhawks and their minor league affiliate in Dallas until February 1969, when opportunity knocked again in the form of a multiplayer deal with the North Stars.

"When I got traded to Minnesota," he said, "it really gave me an opportunity to get a lot of ice time and develop as a player."

And develop he did, becoming a mainstay on the North Stars blueline for a decade. He retired in 1978 after a decade in the green and gold but returned to the club a short time later when team president Walter Bush asked him to join play-by-play man Al Shaver as a radio analyst.

> "I started to think, 'Jeez, maybe I do have a chance to play in the NHL.'" • *Tom Reid*

Reid quit when Norm Green purchased the team in 1990 but continued working as a television analyst for the University of Minnesota hockey team. When the NHL returned to Minnesota in 2000, he worked telecasts for the Wild.

Reid remained a popular figure in the Twin Cities and his sports bar, Tom Reid's Hockey City Pub in downtown St. Paul, became a favorite destination for postgame crowds.

Tom Reid was one of only three North Stars to successfully score on a penalty shot during the regular season (October 14, 1971, against Montreal's Ken Dryden). The others were Bo Berglund (October 10, 1985, against Detroit's Corrado Micalef) and Dennis Hextall (March 8, 1975, against Toronto's Gord McRae).

GORDIE ROBERTS (1980–1988)

A mainstay on the Minnesota blue line for nearly a decade, Gordie Roberts broke into professional hockey as a highly touted seventeen-year-old with the WHA's New England Whalers. In 1977–78 and 1978–79, he led all WHA defensemen in scoring and remained with the Whalers after the WHA-NHL merger in 1979.

Born in Detroit and named for Red Wings legend Gordie Howe—his folks were big fans—Roberts came from a strong hockey-playing family. He was the younger brother of former college hockey player Jack Roberts, ex-Bruins winger Doug Roberts, and former minor leaguer Dave Roberts.

Young Gordie was a star on Detroit-area youth programs and one of the first American kids ever drafted by a Canadian Major Junior team. As such, pro scouts were watching him before he could shave.

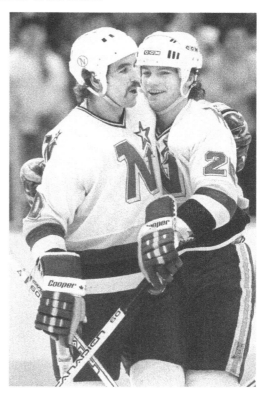

44. Gordie Roberts (left) and Dino Ciccarelli celebrate a North Stars goal. Courtesy of the Dallas Stars

He jumped to the Whalers after only one season with Victoria of the Western Canadian Hockey League (WCHL) and, ironically, made his NHL debut in 1979 against the North Stars. Later, while playing alongside his namesake in Hartford, Roberts earned the distinction of assisting on Howe's last NHL goal.

The December 1980 trade that brought him to Minnesota is considered one of the biggest steals in the history of the organization and certainly the most notable from Lou Nanne's term as general manager. In exchange for Roberts the Whalers received oft-injured left wing Mike Fidler, a two-time twenty-goal scorer on the downside of his career.

Over the next seven-plus seasons, Roberts became one of Minnesota's top defenders. He was a self-motivator who took pride in his work, and his rugged style of play and dependability made him a favorite among fans and teammates. Although he appeared impatient early on, Gordie turned into a solid offensive defenseman on the NHL level.

Believing him to be on the decline, the North Stars sent Roberts to the Philadelphia Flyers for future considerations in February 1988. But his career was far from over. A three-year stint in St. Louis was followed by a trade to Pittsburgh, where Roberts, now a steady, stay-at-home type, won Stanley Cups with the Penguins in 1991 and 1992.

The following year, as a member of the Boston Bruins, he became the first U.S.-born player to play one thousand games. He retired as a player in 1996 after one season with the IHL's Minnesota Moose.

Roberts was inducted into the U.S. Hockey Hall of Fame in 1999. He continued to work in the sport as an NHL executive, assistant coach, and pro scout. He also coached at the collegiate and high school levels.

BOBBY SMITH (1978–1983, 1990–1993)

A self-motivated and gifted offensive player, Bobby Smith drew frequent comparisons to another tall and graceful centerman of the past.

"People compared me to Jean Beliveau," said the four-time All-Star, whose superb stickhandling and long, striding skating style reminded many observers of the former Canadiens legend. "Our size and styles were similar, but it reminds me of the quote Sparky Anderson once had about comparing Thurman Munson to Johnny Bench. He said, 'Let's not go embarrassing anybody by comparing them to Bench.' I guess that's how I feel about people comparing me to big Jean. He was one of the greatest ever to play."

Smith was accustomed to flattery during a brilliant junior career with the OHA's Ottawa 67's in which he played left wing before becoming a full-time center in 1977–78. That year he set an OHA single-season record of 192 points, was named Canadian Major Junior Player of the Year, then set his sights on becoming the world's top-rated prospect.

But there was no drama in being selected first overall in the 1978 draft because Smith, who had very seriously considered abandoning hockey to pursue a career in medicine, had already signed a contract to play for the North Stars. Before the draft he went to Minnesota and met with GM Lou Nanne and members of the original ownership group, including Gordon Ritz and Walter Bush. They made it abundantly clear to Smith that he was in their future plans.

He was envisioned as a cornerstone—a player around whom Nanne could rebuild a floundering franchise. Smith could have suffocated beneath the weight of those expectations, but he responded by scoring thirty goals and seventy-four points and winning the 1979 Calder Trophy as rookie of the year.

A mature twenty, the kid oozed confidence (as evidenced by his team-leading 244 shots on goal) and was well received by veteran teammates like Fred Barrett, Al MacAdam, Gilles Meloche, and J. P. Parise, who realized Smith was there to work hard and play winning hockey.

"They were terrific to me," said Smith, "and later on in my career, I tried to help young players the way those guys helped me. When I came in, they saw me as confident, not cocky. They did all the little things that gave me the sense they were genuinely pulling for me, not hoping I'd get smacked down a few times to learn things the hard way."

Deceptively quick and able to burn defenders with crafty one-on-one maneuvers, Smith used a long, thirty-seven-inch stick to evade opposing checkers and could find his wingers with tape-to-tape passes. The most common criticism levied at Smith was his tendency to hold on to the puck too long. But a playmaker of his ability rewarded linemates for their patience more often than not. MacAdam and Steve Payne each topped the forty-goal mark for the first and only time in their careers in their first year flanking Smith.

45. Bobby Smith led the North Stars in scoring in 1978–79, 1980–81, and 1981–82. Courtesy of the Dallas Stars

Smith's point totals increased in each of his first three seasons. In 1980–81 he finished with twenty-nine goals and ninety-three points but considered his performance "mediocre." He didn't like the fact that so many of his points had been scored at home, and that despite his best efforts, he was unable to adapt to a change in tactics by other teams.

The summer following Minnesota's defeat at the hands of the New York Islanders, Smith went to training camp for the Canada Cup. He was among the first to be cut.

A rededicated, reinvigorated Smith came back to North Stars training camp determined to play the best hockey of his still-young career. He hit the weight room and added some much-needed muscle to strengthen his tall, slender frame. The "new" Bobby Smith answered his own challenge with career highs in goals (43), assists (71) and points (114).

But the good times turned sour with the hiring of Bill Mahoney as coach in June 1983. Under Glen Sonmor, Smith had been given carte blanche to utilize his considerable talents and creativity. But Mahoney had different plans and cut Smith's ice time dramatically.

Smith still scored at a point-per-game pace, but tensions mounted when it became clear that their personalities would never mesh well. It wasn't long before coach and player were locking horns.

Young and impatient, Smith announced that if he wasn't traded to a team that appreciated him, he would quit hockey and go back to school.

The North Stars must have believed their superstar center wasn't bluffing. Only ten games into the 1983–84 season, they traded Smith to Montreal in exchange for forwards Keith Acton and Mark Napier and a draft choice (Ken Hodge Jr.).

Smith played some of his best hockey with the Habs, winning a Stanley Cup in 1986. But it became clear as the eighties drew to a close that his most productive seasons were behind him. After slumping through an injury-plagued 1989–90 campaign, the Canadiens traded Smith back to Minnesota for a draft choice.

It was a bittersweet homecoming for Smith since the North Stars had never really been the same since the day they traded him. Slowed by age and injury, the former All-Star struggled during his final three seasons, especially when coach and former Montreal teammate Bob Gainey cast him in a defensive role.

And yet there was still some magic left in Smith's oversized stick. In the 1991 playoffs he helped power the North Stars back to the Stanley Cup Finals before bowing out to Mario Lemieux and the Pittsburgh Penguins. He scored eight goals and sixteen points in twenty-three postseason games, reminding fans of his glory days a decade earlier.

Smith enrolled at the University of Minnesota full-time after his retirement in 1993 to complete his business degree. A few years later he was named executive vice president of hockey operations for the Winnipeg Jets and relocated with the team after it moved to Phoenix. He held a number of executive posts with the club until 2001. In 2003 he became majority owner of the QMJHL's Halifax Mooseheads.

MARK TINORDI (1988–1993)

He may have been guilty of dragging his feet through a morning practice or two, but hulking Mark Tinordi never gave less than 100 percent once the puck dropped.

The six feet four, 205-pounder struck an imposing form on the North Stars blue line for five seasons and left a trail of bruised bodies in his wake. In an age when big power forwards like Cam Neely and Rick Tocchet were muscling their way past average-sized defenders, Tinordi was the perfect countermeasure.

Born in Red Deer, Alberta, Tinordi didn't start playing serious, organized hockey until he was thirteen. After peewee he moved in with his aunt and uncle in Lethbridge and joined the WHL team there. Beginning in 1982–83 he played four seasons with the Broncos before getting traded to the Calgary Wranglers.

Undrafted at age twenty, he thought about going back to school. Then he received a visit from Rangers scout (and future North Stars GM) Jack Ferreira, trawling the junior ranks for some much-needed muscle to beef up the Blueshirts. It wasn't long before Tinordi's signature was on his first professional contract.

Two fight-filled seasons in the Rangers' system convinced most of the hockey world that Tinordi was just another one-dimensional thug. But the big guy's career really took off after he was part of a multiplayer deal with Minnesota in October 1988.

"That tickled me to no end," Tinordi revealed in *Hockey Stars Speak*. "I didn't like New York too much for a whole bunch of reasons, starting with the fact that I'm a defenseman—played my whole life as a defenseman—but the Rangers played me at left wing. Not only that, but [coach] Michel Bergeron put me in the role of a fighter and I'd fight. Trouble was, I didn't want to get tagged in that role because I felt I was capable of being a regular defenseman, not a left wing who would go out fighting."

The North Stars saw great potential in Tinordi and paired him with defensive stalwart Curt Giles. The two had played together briefly when Giles was in New York, so it was an ideal fit.

Like so many Minnesota players of that era, Tinordi rose to stardom during the 1991 playoffs. "He was known as a very reliable and tough defensive guy that nobody wanted to play against because he was so mean," said Dave Gagner. "But then, all of a sudden, after we traded Larry Murphy to Pittsburgh, Mark was given an opportunity to play on the power play and add some offensive flair to his game. It was unbelievable how he emerged. Mark just became a force in all areas of the ice. The maturation process must've happened in about a week. He shocked a lot of guys that year."

The goon was gone. In his place emerged a Norris Trophy–caliber defender who barely resembled the awkward roughneck who broke into the league with the Rangers. He never lost his affinity for the big hit, however, and still duked it out when challenged.

Tinordi took over from Giles as team captain in 1991–92 and remained with the franchise when it relocated to Dallas the next season.

46. Mark Tinordi. Courtesy of the Dallas Stars

But his rough-and-tumble style wasn't conducive to longevity. He missed seventeen games from a bout with foot palsy in 1991–92—the result of nerve damage suffered when he was hit by a puck behind his knee during an October game at Calgary. Tinordi couldn't move his foot for three months, and doctors feared that his career might be over. Eventually feeling slowly returned to Tinordi's leg, but it would be a full year before he would be completely over the effects of the injury. The next season he was sidelined for fifteen games with a broken collarbone.

> "It was unbelievable how he emerged. Mark just became a force in all areas of the ice."
> • *Dave Gagner*

Tinordi moved with the team to Dallas, but his injury problems continued. He was eventually traded to the Washington Capitals, with whom he spent the final five seasons of his career.

His son Jarred, a 2010 first-round pick of the Montreal Canadiens, made his NHL debut in 2013.

LORNE (GUMP) WORSLEY (1969–1974)

History best remembers the maskless, roly-poly goaltender with the tightly cropped haircut and self-deprecating sense of humor from his sometimes depressing decade in Manhattan and his storied reign as a Stanley Cup champion in Montreal.

But some people forget that Gump Worsley's Hall of Fame career concluded with a four-year stay in the Twin Cities, helping bring credibility to Minnesota's fledgling hockey team.

Worsley had over fifteen NHL seasons under his rather capacious belt when the Canadiens demoted him to the minors in 1969. He never reported and decided to hang up his skates instead. A member of four Stanley Cup winners with the Habs and a two-time winner of the Vezina Trophy, his legacy was secured. Worsley had nothing left to prove, and in truth, the rigors of the game were catching up to the forty-one-year-old netminder.

Expansion not only doubled the number of teams from six to twelve but also dramatically altered the schedule. The addition of teams in California, St. Louis, and elsewhere meant longer flights, an aspect of the job that Worsley hated.

Legend had it that Worsley's fear of flying dated back to his days with the minor league New York Rovers. The Rovers were flying east after a game in Milwaukee when one of the plane's engines caught fire and the pilot had to make an emergency landing in Pittsburgh.

"Gump would polish off a coffee or two," chuckled one former teammate, "but when it was time for takeoff, all of a sudden, he'd hang on for dear life to those armrests. He'd white-knuckle it all the way and break into a sweat. Once we were at a cruising speed it wasn't bad, but as soon as they'd announce that we were coming in for a landing, he'd go through the same routine again. It was pure hell for him."

Wren Blair, badly in need of a backup for starter Cesare Maniago, phoned Canadiens GM Sam Pollock to work out a deal for Worsley. "Gump is telling everyone that he's retiring and not going to play anymore," Pollock told Blair. "You pay the Montreal Canadiens forty thousand dollars for Worsley's rights, whether he plays or not. It becomes totally your responsibility to get him to play. If you agree to that, we'll sell him to Minnesota."

So Blair made the deal. Now all he had to do was coax the goalie out of semiretirement. Resistant at first, Worsley finally agreed to discuss the matter over dinner at the Mount Royal Hotel in Montreal. Blair promised to pick up the tab.

None of the GM's persuasive strategies worked until he offered to pay the stubborn netminder 35 percent more than he had been making in his last year with the Canadiens. "Are you nuts?" Worsley gasped. "I don't think anybody on the Montreal team, including Maurice Richard or Jean Beliveau, make that much." By the end of dinner, the North Stars had themselves a new goalie.

Worsley joined the club in February 1970, while it was in the midst of a twenty-game winless streak. Even though he hadn't been on skates for over a month, Gump's presence had an immediate impact. The North Stars went 9-5-4 over their final eighteen games and qualified for the playoffs.

Maniago welcomed Worsley with open arms because he knew that the veteran, ten years his senior, could offer insights into the craft that a coach could not. He also knew that Worsley had no aspirations to steal his job.

In fact, Maniago noticed that Worsley sometimes came down with a mysterious ailment on days when he was scheduled to start against a tough Eastern Division foe like the Bruins or the Rangers. Come game time Gump would go to the coach or the trainer and say that he couldn't play because he had a "flu bug," a "groin pull," or some other phantom malady.

"I knew what was going on, but I respected him," Maniago said. "I knew that at his age, the stress was tough enough." So the pair devised a system in which Worsley would give Maniago advance warning on days he didn't want to play. It worked like a charm, and the two not only became an effective tandem but also great friends.

One of hockey's best big-game goalies, Gump's girth didn't prevent him from performing catlike maneuvers in the crease. He rarely surrendered big rebounds and was adept at handling the puck. Knowing which teammates were left or right handed, Worsley could place the puck at just the right spot for skaters to retrieve it without breaking stride.

"Gump was an amazing angle goalie who knew exactly where he was in the net," said Fred Barrett. "He didn't have to move much because the puck just hit him. He was a great goaltender to play in front of because he'd give you directions when the puck was shot so you knew exactly what to do. As a young defenseman I benefited from that kind of help."

Worsley was also one of the last goalies to play without a face mask, donning one only in his last season. He had spent his entire career maligning those inclined to wear facial protection and was fond of saying that his face *was* his mask. His sense of humor helped keep the dressing room loose.

> "Everybody used to say that he had a beer belly, but he didn't drink beer. He liked his whiskey." • *Fred Barrett*

"He could stand up and tell the mayor to shove it up his ass, and everybody would just laugh," said Barrett. "Everybody used to say that he had a beer belly, but he didn't drink beer. He liked his whiskey."

Gump's biting wit and comical exploits were known in dressing rooms throughout the league. Players heard all the stories about his late-night cavorting and fondness for scotch, but by the time he landed in Bloomington, Worsley was taking slightly better care of himself and appeared to have left his truly wild days behind.

In 1974 Blair persuaded Worsley to come back for one last season by offering a five-year contract: one as a player and four as a scout. He agreed, and when that deal expired, he ended up scouting for the club for another ten years.

He finished with 335 wins in 861 games, which ranked fourth on the all-time list behind Terry Sawchuk, Jacques Plante, and Glenn Hall.

Worsley was inducted into the Hockey Hall of Fame in 1980, the first North Stars player so honored. He passed away in 2007 at age seventy-seven.

TIM YOUNG (1975–1983)

Tim Young was an offensive-minded center with great skill—the kind of player who made things look effortless. But midway through the 1978-79 season, nothing was coming easily for the Scarborough, Ontario, native. He was stuck in an awful rut and had only ten goals on the season when the North Stars came to Madison Square Garden on January 15, 1979. That night Young would find the perfect medicine for what ailed him: Rangers goalies Wayne Thomas and Doug Soetaert.

Forty-nine seconds after assisting on the opening goal by Jimmy Roberts, Young scored his first of the night against Soetaert on a power-play

47. Tim Young.
Courtesy of the
Dallas Stars

slap shot. In the second period he scored Minnesota's next two goals on a breakaway—scored after falling at the blue line—followed by a sixty-foot slap shot. The Rangers pulled Soetaert for the final period, and Thomas surrendered Young's fourth and fifth goals, the last of which came on a wrist shot preceded by a breakaway. By scoring five goals on five shots, Young had tied an NHL record set two years earlier by the Maple Leafs' Ian Turnbull.

"I have no book on Young," said a shell-shocked Soetaert after the North Stars rolled to an 8–1 win. "He usually doesn't do that well against us."

Young's special night was one highlight in a career that also included five consecutive seasons with twenty or more goals and an appearance in the 1981 Stanley Cup Finals, though a knee injury limited the center to only two games in that series.

Nicknamed "Blade," Young was selected by Los Angeles in the first round of the 1975 draft after a highly successful junior career with the Ottawa 67's. But shortly after the draft, the Kings signed legendary center Marcel Dionne, recently acquired from Detroit. Young worried that Dionne's presence would jeopardize his chances of cracking the LA roster, so he approached Kings management about a trade. Less than two months later, the six feet one, 190-pound Ontario native was dealt to Minnesota.

By his second NHL season, Young recorded career highs in assists (sixty-six) and points (ninety-five) and also made an appearance in the 1977 All-Star Game.

"Tim Young has more talent in his little finger," Glen Sonmor said, "than a lot of hockey players have in their entire body."

"He was highly skilled," Al MacAdam said. "But as a person? You must remember that it takes all kinds to make a team, and Tim was one of those 'all kinds' guys."

Young missed the beginning of the 1981–82 season while recovering from a broken ankle, an injury he suffered during an off-season neighborhood softball game. He rebounded with an eighteen-goal, fifty-three-point effort the following year, his last in Minnesota.

By the time he was traded to Winnipeg for a pair of prospects in August 1983, Young ranked among the franchise's all-time leaders in goals, assists, points, and game-winning goals.

He retired in 1985 as a member of the Philadelphia Flyers.

6

BEST OF THE REST

You might call this our "honorable mention" chapter—a place to acknowledge the efforts of fifty more notable North Stars. Most of the names will be familiar to you, though some will not. But know that all these players wore the green and gold with distinction, however briefly.

Kent-Erik Andersson (1977–1982) was Swedish Player of the Year in 1977, the same year he came to North America as an undrafted free agent. A right wing, Andersson had spent six seasons in the Swedish Elite League and was already an accomplished defensive forward when he signed with the North Stars. He was a gifted penalty killer who was especially dangerous in shorthanded situations. His best offensive season came in 1980–81, when he had career-highs in goals (seventeen), assists (twenty-four), and points (forty-one).

Fred Barrett (1970–1983) suffered a cracked kneecap when he was still in juniors, an injury that set the stage for a career marked by frequent stints on the IR list. Broken bones in Barrett's hand, jaw, knee, thigh, and ankle were either evidence of his hard-hitting style or a testament to the defenseman's lack of good fortune. However, he had a knack for recovering quickly from what could generally be described as freak injuries and managed to play 745 NHL games, 730 of them with the North Stars. Barrett, who briefly held the team record for most games played, returned to his hometown of Gloucester, Ontario, and became a firefighter after his retirement. Today there is an arena in Gloucester named in his honor.

Scott Bjugstad (1983–1988) was named a Hobey Baker Award finalist in 1983 after recording ninety-one points in forty-four games in his senior year at the University

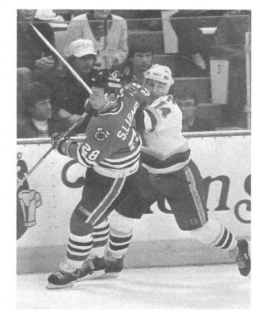

48. Scott Bjugstad gets tangled up with Chicago's Steve Larmer. Courtesy of the Dallas Stars

of Minnesota. He wasn't nearly as prolific a scorer in the pros, but in 1985–86 Bjugstad (pronounced "BEWG-STAD") set a North Stars single-season record (since broken) for goals by a left wing with forty-three, playing alongside Neal Broten and Dino Ciccarelli. Retiring as a player in 1993, he went on to coach high school hockey and opened a hockey school in Lake Elmo, Minnesota. His son Nick broke into the NHL in 2010 with the Florida Panthers.

Per-Olov Brasar (1977–1979) had been considered one of the best two-way players in his native Sweden, and he wore the blue and gold of the Tre Kronor (Three Crowns) with distinction at numerous international tournaments. It was countryman and good friend Roland Eriksson who convinced Brasar to join him in Minnesota, and he signed with the North Stars as a free agent in August 1977. Playing left wing on an all-Swedish line with Eriksson at center and Kent-Erik Andersson on the right, Brasar collected a slew of North Stars club awards in his first NHL season, including most valuable player, most popular player, and top rookie. He'd made a splendid first impression, playing solidly in all three zones of the ice while scoring a respectable twenty goals and fifty-seven points. When Brasar's goal total plummeted to six the following season, observers chalked it up to the absence of Eriksson, who had since moved on to the Vancouver Canucks. Brasar's scoring woes continued into the first half of the 1979–80 season, prompting the North Stars to trade him to Vancouver.

Charlie Burns (1969–1973) suffered a fractured skull while playing junior hockey in Toronto, an injury that required a metal plate be inserted into his head. Burns, who wore a heavily padded helmet for the rest of his career, was an outstanding defensive forward and an excellent skater respected for his experience and leadership skills. In 1969–70 the North Stars briefly utilized the Detroit native as a player/coach. Burns's fourteen-year NHL career also included stints with the Red Wings, the Bruins, the Seals, and the Penguins.

Steve Christoff (1980–1982) was such a good college player that his likeness was used as a model for the sculpture that became the Hobey Baker Award. This member of the "Miracle on Ice" squad was the first to turn pro, signing with the North Stars only four days after winning the gold medal in Lake Placid. During the 1981 playoffs the talented forward played on a line with Brad Palmer and fellow Olympian Neal Broten. Christoff's NHL career spanned only five seasons, but he posted back-to-back twenty-goal efforts in 1980–81 and 1981–82. He became an airline pilot after his retirement

Shane Churla (1989–1993) was one the toughest hockey players teammate Bobby Smith had ever seen—one who refused to take himself out of the lineup, even when injured. "I have a ton of admiration for him," Smith said. "Whether it was a separated shoulder or a broken hand, Shane played hard. He was also pretty vocal in the dressing room. You knew he gave everything he had, every game." In his heyday this power puncher with the menacing nickname "Chainsaw" took on all comers—he broke Chicago defenseman Bob McGill's jaw during a notable 1989 bout—and holds the distinction of having the highest penalty minutes-per-game average ever (4.71) among seasoned enforcers. As he matured, Churla learned how to play "smart tough," that is, knowing when *not* to fight in order to draw a less experienced or less disciplined player into taking a dumb penalty. After eight years with the Minnesota-Dallas franchise, plus three more split between the Kings and the Rangers, Churla retired to begin a new career as a scout.

Bill Collins (1967–1970) already knew his way around the Twin Cities when he was claimed by the North Stars from the Rangers in the 1967 Expansion Draft. The right winger spent two seasons playing for the Rangers' minor league club in St. Paul, hoping to one day get a chance to star on Broadway. As it did for so many fringe players previously unable to crack an Original Six roster, expansion offered Collins the opportunity of a lifetime: the chance to compete at hockey's highest level. Primarily a defensive forward, Collins was among the North Stars' best penalty killers. He scored nine goals in each of his first two years with the team before breaking out with a career-high twenty-nine goals in 1969–70. That performance may have helped earn Collins his ticket out of town. In May 1970 he was traded to Montreal to complete transaction that sent Jude Drouin to Minnesota.

Wayne Connelly (1967–1969) led the North Stars in scoring in their inaugural season. A gritty right wing with a blistering slap shot, he holds the distinction of being the first North Star to score a hat trick (versus Philadelphia, January 10, 1968) and the first player to score on a penalty shot in the playoffs, beating Terry Sawchuk of the Kings on April 27, 1968. Connelly was also one of the first NHL players to defect to the WHA in 1972 when the Fighting Saints gave him a five-year contract, three years of which was payable in advance. Years later Connelly would recall that it was impossible to turn down a deal that sweet. "I had all of that money in the bank," he said, "before I even went to training camp."

Russ Courtnall (1992–1993) was an electrifying right winger with terrific skating ability and puck-handling skills. At five feet eleven and 180 pounds, he didn't have the size to barrel through defenders to get his goals, but he did enjoy pulling the puck through their legs while motoring past them en route to the net, a trick he executed on more than a few occasions throughout his seventeen NHL seasons. Acquired from the Canadiens for Brian Bellows in September 1992, Courtnall was coming off a season shortened due to shoulder and hand injuries. But Minnesota coach and GM Bob Gainey, who had played with Courtnall in Montreal, was confident that his former teammate would be rejuvenated by the trade. Gainey's instincts were correct. Courtnall went on to enjoy a career year in his lone season as a North Star, pacing the club with thirty-six goals.

Ray Cullen (1967–1970) didn't get the chance to be a full-time NHLer until he was claimed by the North Stars from Detroit in the 1967 Expansion Draft. From that point forward, he was a bubble player no longer. In fact, Cullen anchored the North Stars' top line in their inaugural season, finishing second on the team with twenty-eight goals and fifty three points. After his retirement from hockey, Cullen became a car salesman and eventually opened his own dealership in London, Ontario.

Gaetan Duchesne (1989–1993) contributed in subtle ways that were not always appreciated by media and spectators but were greatly valued by his coaches and teammates. A speedy left winger, "Gator" was often assigned to shadow opposing teams' top scorers. He and linemate Stew Gavin were the North Stars' tight-checking shutdown duo, snuffing out power plays by handling the puck down low and then getting it out of their zone quickly. Although he possessed excellent speed and vision, Duchesne didn't have great hands. He was reminded of his offensive shortcomings after Game One of the 1991 Stanley Cup Finals, when he was slammed in the press for missing some quality scoring opportunities. He took the criticism in stride, saying, "I don't need to score, as long as we win. And you just watch—when I do score, it's going to be a huge goal, one everybody will remember." Sure enough, in Game Three, Duchesne scored a third-period goal to regain a two-goal lead lost forty-six seconds earlier, knocking in a rebound off a shot by Gavin. In all, Gaetan appeared in over one thousand NHL games with the Capitals, Nordiques, North Stars, Sharks, and Panthers. In 2007 Duchesne suffered a fatal heart attack while working out at a gym in his native Quebec. He was forty-four.

Mike Eaves (1978–1983) was among the players whose rights were absorbed by Minnesota when the team merged with Cleveland in 1978. A former two-time All-American at the University of Wisconsin, Eaves was an intelligent, unselfish, and highly competitive center who scored a career-high eighteen goals for the North Stars in 1979–80. Although a member of the 1981 team that advanced to the Stanley Cup Finals, Eaves missed the series due to a concussion. He joined the coaching ranks after his playing days, serving as an assistant for the Penguins and the Flyers before returning to his alma mater to become head coach. In 2006 he guided the Badgers to an NCAA title. Mike's son, Patrick, made his NHL debut in 2005 with the Ottawa Senators.

Roland Eriksson (1976–1978) joined the wave of skilled Swedish players—Anders Hedberg, Ulf Nilsson, and Borje Salming, most notably—who came to North America in the 1970s following the siren song of big NHL paychecks. The talent drain decimated the once-powerful Swedish national team but greatly benefited clubs like the North Stars, one of the pioneering franchises when it came to giving Europeans a chance to star in the NHL. Eriksson was the first Swede ever drafted by the North Stars, selected in the eighth round (131st overall) in 1974. The tall, playmaking center made his North American pro debut in 1976, tying a league record by recording four assists

49. Mike Eaves's career was cut short by a head injury suffered during preseason in 1985. Courtesy of the Dallas Stars

in his first game. He set a North Stars rookie record (eventually broken) with twenty-five goals, forty-four assists, and sixty-nine points. Although Eriksson was among the rookie scoring leaders, he finished third in Calder Trophy voting as the league's top freshman (the award went to Atlanta's Willi Plett). In 1977–78 Eriksson continued to be one of the few drawing cards on a dreadful North Stars team, pacing the club with sixty points and playing in his first NHL All-Star Game. Despite Eriksson's obvious value to the North Stars, the team let him walk when he became a free agent that offseason. GM Lou Nanne had to cut millions in payroll and shed dozens of contracts after the merger with the Cleveland Barons, making Eriksson expendable.

Mike Gartner (1989–1990) combined great speed and a blistering slap shot to become one of the game's most prolific and consistent goal scorers. The Hall of Fame right wing came to Minnesota from Washington with Larry Murphy in a 1989 deadline trade for Dino Ciccarelli and Bob Rouse, a swap of players with similar skills but very different personalities. "We needed an ambassador for the organization and the Twin Cities," North Stars coach Pierre Page said of Gartner. "He's unbelievable. We got him, in part, because he's a good example for our younger players. He was the most popular player in Washington. This guy has class over class over class." (Translation: Unlike Ciccarelli, Gartner wasn't going to get caught in public without his pants.) Rather than try to replace Dino in the hearts of fans—an impossibility—Gartner focused on his play and establishing himself as a positive presence in the community. Page paired him with Brian Bellows and Neal Broten on a line that quickly became one of the most potent in the NHL, and he scored forty-one goals in eighty regular season games as a North Star. Off the ice, as he had in Washington, Gartner spearheaded a fundraising program to benefit a local children's hospital. Although there was a brief but testy contract dispute with management, Gartner seemed to be happy in Minnesota—happy enough to build a house in Edina. But con-

50. Mike Gartner. Courtesy of the Dallas Stars

cerns over Gartner's age (thirty) and expiring contract prompted GM Jack Ferreira to trade the veteran right winger to the Rangers in March 1990 for twenty-three-year-old Ulf Dahlen. It was a deal that fans and even Ferreira's successor, Bob Clarke, considered a major blunder because of the gap in skill exchanged. Gartner played another eight years in the NHL, retiring in 1998 with 708 career goals.

Stew Gavin (1988–1993) was an excellent checker and penalty killer claimed off waivers from the Whalers in October 1988. Playing, as he did, for weak teams in Toronto and Hartford, the speedy right winger tended not to watch the Stanley Cup Finals on TV because he could barely stomach the sight of other players getting to compete for the silver chalice. He finally got his turn in the spring of 1991, thanks in large measure to the suffocating defensive blanket he and linemate Gaetan Duchesne threw over some of the game's top scorers: Steve Larmer and Jeremy Roenick of Chicago, Brett Hull and Adam Oates of St. Louis, and even Mark Messier of Edmonton. Along the way Gavin also chipped in thirteen points in twenty-one playoff games—an unexpected bonus from someone who'd missed most of the 1990–91 season with a torn MCL in his left knee. He remained one of Minnesota's unsung heroes until additional knee injuries forced him to retire in 1993. Gavin later worked as a scout for the team before making a brief comeback bid in the IHL. He settled in Toronto after his retirement and became a financial advisor.

Barry Gibbs (1969–1975) did not perform on the soundtrack to *Saturday Night Fever*, but thanks to Internet search engines, he'll forever be linked to Bee Gees founder Barry Gibb. A former first overall pick of the Bruins in the 1966 Amateur Draft, Gibbs couldn't crack a deep Boston defense corps, so he was traded to the North Stars for draft picks in May 1969. He became one of Minnesota's best two-way defenders and later represented the North Stars at the 1973 All-Star Game. Gibbs wasn't afraid to get his nose dirty, either, leading the club in penalty minutes for three consecutive seasons. In 1975 he was traded to the Atlanta Flames for Dean Talafous and Dwight Bialowas.

Dirk Graham (1983–1988) was a hardworking checker, team leader, and underrated scorer who spent parts of five seasons with the North Stars. Although a dominant offensive player in juniors and on the minor league level, Graham developed into one of the NHL's best defensive forwards. His best season with Minnesota came in 1985–86, when he scored twenty-two goals and fifty-five points. In the playoffs that year, he set a franchise record (since broken) for shots in one playoff game with ten during the division semifinals against St. Louis. The Blues won the best-of-five series, but Graham scored the game-winning goals in each North Stars victory. In January 1988 Minnesota traded Dirk to the

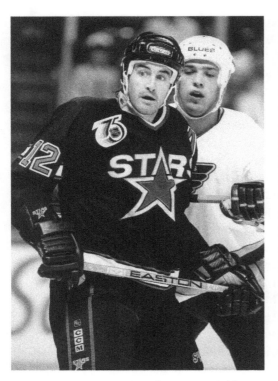

51. Stew Gavin.
Courtesy of the
Dallas Stars

rival Blackhawks for Curt Fraser. Graham later held coaching posts in Chicago and with the AHL's Springfield Falcons.

Ted Harris (1970–1973) served as captain in Montreal, and brought his "C" with him to Minnesota when Wren Blair plucked him from the Canadiens in the 1970 Intra-League Draft. A four-time Stanley Cup winner and a respected leader, Harris bolstered a blue-line corps that already featured Tom Reid, Fred Barrett, and Lou Nanne. He represented the North Stars at the 1971 and 1972 All-Star Games, and in 1972–73 he scored a career-high seven goals and thirty points—not bad for a defensive defenseman. In November 1973 the North Stars traded Harris to the Red Wings for defenseman Gary Bergman. But even as he was shown the door, it was expected Harris would one day return to Minnesota. A year earlier Blair had signed Harris to a special long-term deal that guaranteed him a job with the club whenever he decided to retire as an active player. Sure enough, in 1975, after Harris added a fifth Stanley Cup ring to his collection as a member of the Philadelphia Flyers, he was back in Bloomington to replace interim coach Charlie Burns behind the North Stars bench.

Fred (Buster) Harvey (1970–1974) was Minnesota's first pick (seventeenth overall) in the 1970 Amateur Draft and made his NHL debut in October of that year. Although he played defense for much of his junior career, Harvey broke into the pro ranks as a right wing. He spent most of the 1971–72 season with the North Stars' AHL affiliate in Cleveland but was back in Minnesota full time the following year, when he had his best NHL point totals with twenty-one goals and thirty-four assists. Traded to the Flames in 1974, Harvey also played for the Scouts and the Red Wings before closing out his career in the minors. He passed away in November 2007 after a battle with cancer. The following year it was announced that a new sports and leisure complex in his hometown of Fredericton, New Brunswick, would be called the Grant-Harvey Centre, an honor to be shared with Harvey's former North Stars teammate (and fellow Fredericton native) Danny Grant.

Derian Hatcher (1991–1993) got a tip at the 1990 Entry Draft that the North Stars were going to select him with the eighth overall pick. The source of the leak was none other than Shawn Chambers, the

North Stars defenseman who grew up in Sterling Heights, Michigan, only five houses away from Hatcher. What Chambers might not have known was that Minnesota GM Bob Clarke and his scouts had debated long and hard about whether to take Hatcher or goalie Trevor Kidd, who ended up going eleventh overall to Calgary. At six feet five, 204 pounds, Derian was the biggest player available in the draft. Unlike his older brother, Washington's Kevin Hatcher, Derian was not a pure offensive defenseman but a defense-first blueliner capable of moving the puck out of his zone quickly. It was somewhat surprising when he was cut from the U.S. Olympic Team in September 1991, forcing the North Stars to decide whether to return Hatcher to junior hockey for the entire season or give the towering teen a chance to start his NHL career. Coach Bob Gainey saw enough potential in Hatcher to give him a shot, and within months, he was a regular on the Minnesota blueline. He seemed to make a strong impression on everyone: coaches appreciated his willingness to work on facets of his game that needed improvement; teammates were impressed by his poise, confidence, and positive attitude; and opponents got a taste of the nasty streak that would become one of his trademarks. In late 1991, Hatcher earned the first of numerous suspensions after high-sticking ex–North Star Dino

52. Derian Hatcher. Courtesy of the Dallas Stars

Ciccarelli in the face during a game against the Capitals. But the North Stars (and later, Dallas Stars) were willing to live with Hatcher's occasional use of excessive force because he was destined to become a cornerstone of the franchise. When Dallas won its first championship in 1999, Hatcher became the first American-born captain to hoist the Stanley Cup. In 2010, a year after retiring as a member of the Flyers, he was elected to the U.S. Hockey Hall of Fame.

Doug Hicks (1974–1978) was selected sixth overall by Minnesota in the 1974 draft. At one time, Hicks held the team record for being the youngest person to play for the North Stars when he made his NHL debut on October 9, 1974, at age nineteen years, four months, eleven days. Hicks was a durable and reliable blueliner who missed only one regular-season game in three years with the team, but his numbers suffered considerably because he played on some of the worst Minnesota teams ever. In 1978 the North Stars were in rebuilding mode and traded Hicks and a draft pick to Chicago for goalie Eddie Mio and right wing Pierre Plante, neither of whom ever played for Minnesota. After retiring from the NHL, Hicks opened a wine store in Edmonton.

Jim Johnson (1990–1993) honed his skills as a stay-at-home defenseman at the University of Minnesota–Duluth, where he briefly played with a freshman named Brett Hull. After graduation Johnson signed with Pittsburgh as an undrafted free agent. Six years later the New Hope, Minnesota, native was traded to his home state North Stars. Tough enough not to be intimidated but smart enough not to go looking for trouble, Johnson relied on good skating and sound positional play to neutralize attackers. His commitment to playing well in his own end freed up defense partners like Mark Tinordi and Brian Glynn to get more involved offensively. Johnson retired as a player in 1998 but has since worked as an assistant coach with Tampa Bay, Washington, and San Jose. He also served as interim head coach of the Coyotes in 1999–2000.

Claude Larose (1968–1970) earned five Stanley Cup rings in Montreal but was treasured in Minnesota, albeit briefly, for his fine two-way play and skating ability. Acquired from the Canadiens with Danny Grant for the North Stars' first round pick in the 1972 draft, cash, and future considerations, Larose scored a career-best twenty-five goals and sixty-two points in 1968–69. A two-time All-Star with Minnesota, Larose served as captain in his second and final season with the North Stars before heading back to Montreal in a trade for Bobby Rousseau. "The two years I spent in Minnesota helped me," Larose said. "I learned so many things about hockey because the players, being strangers in town, were together all the time. We were always giving each other tips and discussing hockey." Larose later worked as a pro scout for the Carolina Hurricanes.

Brian Lawton (1983–1988) garnered national acclaim during his prep school years in Rhode Island and was projected to be the jewel of the 1983 draft. As further proof of his blue-chip status, the night before the draft Lawton received a phone call from Wayne Gretzky. An invitation to dinner followed, and The Great One, who'd been following Lawton's rising star with interest, recommended his agent to guide Lawton's career. The North Stars, owners of the No. 1 pick, were smitten with Lawton, and not merely because he possessed enormous talent. Like all the best playmakers, he also had an uncanny awareness of the players surrounding him and the ability to see things others couldn't. However, the problem with "can't-miss" prospects is

53. Claude Larose. Graphic Artists/ Hockey Hall of Fame

that they really can't miss. Fans and media expected the world from Lawton as an eighteen-year-old, and it likely hampered his development. And choosing to wear jersey No. 98—one digit shy of Gretzky's famous 99—was a misstep that some observers misinterpreted as cockiness on Lawton's part. Ultimately, Lawton never lived up to the hype preceding his NHL debut, but he did post respectable numbers in five seasons as a North Star. Some of his more productive nights were spent skating on "The Crisis Line" alongside Dennis Maruk and Brian Bellows. In 1988 Lawton was traded to the Rangers in a multiplayer deal that fetched the North Stars Mark Tinordi. After his retirement as a player, Lawton became a very successful agent, listing Sergei Fedorov, Steve Yzerman, and ex-linemate Bellows among his notable clients. From 2008 to 2010 he served as general manager of the Tampa Bay Lightning.

Craig Ludwig (1991–1993) could never completely shake the reputation of a hard-partying, motorcycle-riding, barroom brawler who cared more about softball—he'd play in as many as five leagues during the summer—than he did about hockey. But Ludwig cared enough about his winter sport to put his body in harm's way on a nightly basis. At six feet three, 220 pounds, the big defenseman was not an easy man to skate around, and his patented nosedive, belly flop maneuver presented opposing shooters with a significant obstacle. Worn-out shin pads held together by duct tape gave Ludwig extra courage to throw himself in front of the hardest slapper, but he still spent most of the season covered in welts and black and blue marks. The Hall of Fame asked for those pads three times, but Ludwig wouldn't give them up—not unless they took him too. So they stopped asking. Ludwig moved with the team to Dallas and remained a fixture on the Stars' blue line until his retirement in 1999.

Dennis Maruk (1978, 1983–1989) measured a mere five feet eight and weighed 165 pounds, but he decided early on that he wouldn't be intimidated by bigger players. Immediately recognizable thanks to his trademark Fu Manchu mustache, what really set the pint-sized playmaker apart was his ability to steal pucks and explode down the ice on breakaways. The 1978 Cleveland-Minnesota merger made Maruk a North Star, but he was soon told by North Stars GM Lou Nanne that with centers Bobby Smith and Tim Young already in the fold, Maruk would be dealt. After failing to trade Maruk during the offseason, Minnesota dressed Maruk for two games in October 1978 before sending him to the struggling Washington Capitals for a draft pick. The North Stars got him back five years later, although by then his best offensive seasons were behind him. Maruk continued to be a reliable playmaker and was particularly effective during the 1986 playoffs, pacing the North Stars with thirteen points in only five games. It turned out to be his last shot at winning a Stanley Cup, as Minnesota was bounced in the first round by St. Louis. A serious knee injury suffered in February 1988 forced Maruk to miss the rest of the season and eventually led to his retirement. **Brian MacLellan (1986–1989)** overcame some significant obstacles to become a pro-

54. Dennis Maruk. Courtesy of the Dallas Stars

fessional athlete. A childhood condition affecting the hip joint kept MacLellan in a leg brace, but doctors recommended hockey as a way to alleviate the malady. A few short years later, he was an All-American at Bowling Green State University. Then, at nineteen he broke two vertebrae in his neck when he was hit headfirst into the boards. The towering left winger fully recovered and went on to play ten years in the NHL, including three with the North Stars. Traded by the Rangers to Minnesota in 1986, MacLellan joined a North Stars team lacking in depth on the left side, due to Steve Payne's rehab from knee surgery. The club leaned on "Big Mac" in a big way, and he responded with a career-high thirty-two goals. Although not the best skater, MacLellan had good hands and was tough to move out of position, especially when he parked his massive, 220-pound frame in front of the crease. Throughout his career he encountered criticism that he was a poor defensive player, and a league-worst plus-minus rating of -44 in 1987–88 didn't help his case. MacLellan's production dropped to sixteen goals in each of the next two seasons, and in March 1989 he was traded to Calgary to shore up the Flames' playoff drive. In recent years he has held a number of high-level positions in the Washington Capitals front office.

Doug Mohns (1971–1973) played defense and left wing throughout his career and was still playing forward when the North Stars acquired him from Chicago with Terry Caffery for Danny O'Shea in February 1971. But with the team's defense corps depleted due to injury, "Diesel" was soon asked to move back to the blue line. Mohns's experience, versatility, and presence were a tremendous lift to the North Stars, and these qualities helped carry his new team into the playoffs that year. At thirty-seven he was still a strong skater. For much of his time in Minnesota, Mohns was partnered with former Chicago teammate Tom Reid, and the two formed a tough and reliable defense pairing. Mohns represented the North Stars at the 1972 All-Star Game.

Larry Murphy (1989–1990) was one of the top rushing defensemen of the eighties and nineties—an agile skater prized for his puck-handling skills and dangerous shot from the point. Acquired from Washington in the Dino Ciccarelli trade, Murphy lived up to his billing as one of the game's better power-play performers, but he had only a passing interest in playing defensive hockey. That the physical game wasn't Murphy's cup of tea didn't much matter to the North Stars, at least in the short term. In his only full season with the club, he led all blue-liners on the team with ten goals and 68 points. In all, Murphy spent parts of three seasons in Minnesota before being traded in 1990 to Pittsburgh. Months later he helped the Penguins beat Minnesota in the Stanley Cup Finals. During his career Murphy was never a real threat to challenge perennial Norris Trophy candidates like Ray Bourque or Paul Coffey for consideration as the best at his position, but statistics (1,216 points) and longevity (1,616 games over twenty seasons) helped earn him election to the Hockey Hall of Fame.

Kent Nilsson (1985–1987) went by "Kenta" in his native Sweden but was known as "The Magic Man" on the other side of the Atlantic. In the first half of the 1980s, there were few players in the world who could mystify a crowd the way Nilsson could. Called "the purest, most talented player in the league" by none other than Edmonton's Wayne Gretzky, Nilsson was at once dynamic *and* versatile: a brilliant playmaker with a big-time shot, blazing speed, and the ability to play any forward position. In 1980–81, while starring for the Flames, he finished third in the NHL scoring race behind only Gretzky and LA's Marcel Dionne. But that wasn't the player the North Stars were getting when they acquired Nilsson in 1985 for a draft pick that the Flames would eventually use to draft Joe Nieuwendyk. Although he was only twenty-nine, Nilsson's forty-goal, one-hundred-point days were over, but the North Stars hoped he had enough magic left in his stick to help propel the team back to the top of the Norris Division. The results were mixed. Nilsson averaged a point per game in two seasons with the club, yet spent much of that time falling short of people's expectations. Ironically, the onetime superstar who claimed to have spent his formative years rifling shots at his father's garage until he was exhausted now seemed to lack the confidence to unleash that shot with any consistency; he was criticized for neglecting defense to make the fancy offensive play; and by his own admission, Nilsson was incapable of getting angry or depressed after a loss, contributing to the perception that he didn't care one way or another. "I care," he once told a *Star Tribune* scribe, "but life is not that long so why not be happy? I might be a lot better hockey player, though, if I could get really upset." Coach Lorne Henning was constantly looking for new ways to keep Nilsson motivated, and that's how the enigmatic Swede ended up on a line with Dino Ciccarelli and Dennis Maruk, neither of whom would tolerate playing with a slacker. Nilsson responded positively to that healthy dose of peer pressure, playing some of his best hockey as a North Star. But the experiment may have come too late. In March 1987, as the team was sliding out of playoff contention, the North Stars traded Nilsson to Edmonton, where he promptly won his first Stanley Cup. Inducted into the International Ice Hockey Hall of Fame in 2006, Nilsson would eventually rejoin the Oilers as their European scout.

Dennis O'Brien (1970–1977) was among the defensemen (along with Fred Barrett, Lou Nanne, and Tom Reid) retained when management gutted the North Stars roster in the mid-1970s. "Swoop" was a big, tough, stay-at-home defender who excelled at clearing away traffic in front of his goalie. But he could also contribute offense, scoring 102 of his 122 career points in a Minnesota uniform. In 1977–78 O'Brien became the first NHL player to play for four teams in the same season. Beginning the year with Minnesota, he also saw action with the Colorado Rockies, the Cleveland Barons, and the Boston Bruins. Dennis's nephew, defenseman Shane O'Brien, made his NHL debut in 2006 with the Anaheim Ducks.

55. Kent Nilsson. Courtesy of the Dallas Stars

Murray (Muzz) Oliver (1970–1975) was a crafty playmaker adept at killing penalties or generating offense on the power play. Traded to the North Stars by Toronto late in his career, Oliver's productivity never skipped a beat. He was especially useful in the postseason, scoring seven goals when the upstart North Stars extended Montreal to six games in the 1971 semifinals. In 1971–72, while centering a line with Lou Nanne and Dean Prentice, Oliver scored a career-high twenty-seven goals. He held a number of positions with the North Stars after his retirement, including assistant coach under Glen Sonmor.

Danny O'Shea (1968–1971) had been property of the Canadiens until North Stars GM Wren Blair coughed up Minnesota's first-round draft choices in 1970 (Chuck Lefley) *and* 1971 (Chuck Arnason) to get him. Initially, it looked as if Blair got the better end of the deal. Occupying the center ice spot behind Ray Cullen on the early North Stars teams, O'Shea was a good playmaker and face-off specialist who didn't shy away from the rough stuff. He and linemates Danny Grant and Claude Larose represented Minnesota at the 1969 and 1970 All-Star Games. O'Shea's production began to slip, however, and he was traded to the Blackhawks in February 1971.

Willi Plett (1982–1987) was a lacrosse player who didn't take up organized hockey until age twelve. A former rookie of the year with the Calgary Flames, Plett was traded to the North Stars on his twenty-seventh birthday in 1982 and was immediately sworn in as Met Center's resi-

56. Willi Plett.
Courtesy of the
Dallas Stars

dent brawler. He led the team with 170 penalty minutes in 1982–83, and the following year he punched his way to a career-high 316 penalty minutes (Curt Fraser and Al Secord were two of his favorite dance partners). Plett had some offensive skills too, scoring twenty-five goals in his first season with the club, including four in one game against St. Louis. Although immensely popular with fans, the blond-haired, helmetless power forward saw his goal production decline each season with the team, and with it, his ice time. It became harder and harder for Plett to earn a regular spot in the lineup with right wingers like Brian Bellows, Dino Ciccarelli, and Dirk Graham ahead of him on the depth chart. The transition from top-six star to bottom-six role player didn't sit well with Plett, who felt he needed to play physical every shift, every night, to avoid banishment to the press box. He spent much of his five years with the North Stars wondering how much more he could be doing for the team if only given the chance, whereas his coaches grappled over how best to use an aging power forward losing his scoring touch. The issue was resolved just before the start of the 1987–88 season when the North Stars, tired of his complaints about playing time and worried that his negativity was rubbing off on younger teammates, traded Plett to the Rangers for Pat Price. A month later he was scooped up by Boston in the waiver draft. Plett, who'd never had the opportunity to play in a Stanley Cup Final, was about to get his chance. Although Edmonton would sweep the series, a somewhat vindicated Plett closed out his twelve-year NHL career knowing that he could still play for a Stanley Cup contender.

Mike Polich (1978–1981) starred at Hibbing High School and the University of Minnesota, where he won a national championship in 1974, before breaking into the NHL with Montreal. Signed by the North Stars as a free agent in September 1978, Polich was a smallish center known for his hustle and smothering defensive play. This earned him the nickname "The Shadow," and he was routinely matched up against the opposition's top scorer. He was a finalist for the 1979 Selke Trophy, an award for the top defensive forward in the league, but he lost out to Montreal's Bob Gainey. Polich retired from hockey in 1981 and became a real estate agent in the Twin Cities.

Dean Prentice (1971–1974) has been called one of the best players not enshrined in the Hockey Hall of Fame, and it's easy to understand why. The durable and consistent left winger played twenty-two seasons in the NHL—a remarkable feat in any era—compiling 860 points over 1,378 games for the Rangers, Bruins, Red Wings, Penguins, and North Stars. Although those numbers compare favorably with many players already in the hall, the four-time All-Star spent much of his career playing for weak teams and being overshadowed by the likes of Andy Bathgate, his longtime linemate in New York, Johnny Bucyk in Boston, or Gordie Howe in Detroit. Being underrated didn't seem to faze Prentice. With a quiet, unassuming demeanor, he just focused on being the best two-way player he could be, killing penalties, backchecking, and chipping in the odd power-play goal. A year after almost retiring to spend more time with his family in Guelph, Ontario, Prentice was traded by Pittsburgh to Minnesota. Had the Penguins known how much hockey Dean had left in his tank, they might have demanded more than just cash in return. In 1971–72, at age thirty-nine, he recorded the eighth twenty-goal season of his career. He scored twenty-six more the following season as the North Stars finished third in the West Division before falling to Philadelphia in the quarterfinals. Prentice called it quits following the 1973–74 season and immediately accepted an offer to coach the North Stars' AHL affiliate in New Haven (the Nighthawks

57. Brian Propp. Courtesy of the Dallas Stars

advanced to the Calder Cup Finals in his one season behind the bench).

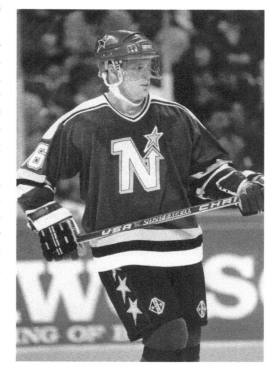

Brian Propp (1990–1993) turned down an offer from the Blackhawks to ink a free agent deal with the North Stars in July 1990. It was Propp's former linemate on the Philadelphia Flyers, Bob Clarke, who got his name on the contract. Propp had been one of the top left wings in hockey throughout the 1980s, widely respected for his consistent goal scoring, willingness to play in the corners, passing ability, and penalty killing. Although he'd lost a step or two by the time he arrived in Minnesota, Propp brought leadership and character and could still be used in any game situation. His first season in green and gold, 1990–91, was by far his most productive, when he scored twenty-six goals, then added eight more (including three game-winners) during the playoffs as the North Stars advanced to the Stanley Cup Finals. In fact, all eight of Propp's postseason goals were scored on the power play, a North Stars record. His play began to decline, however, and after clearing waivers in November 1992, he was assigned to a team in Lugano, Switzerland. The North Stars brought Propp back in the closing weeks of the 1992–93 campaign, and he played his final ten games with the club that spring. He signed with Hartford as a free agent the following season, his last in the NHL.

Dave Richter (1982–1985) played in a very different NHL from the one we know today. For better or worse, there was still a role for the one-dimensional enforcer whose sole purpose was to fight. Richter didn't have the skill or mobility to be an everyday defenseman, but his menacing size—he stood six feet five and weighed over two hundred pounds—and willingness to insert himself into hostile situations prompted the North Stars to select the University of Michigan grad with their tenth round pick at the 1980 Entry Draft. Because he rarely if ever instigated a fight, Richter isn't remembered as one of the eminent heavyweights of his time, but he was a dangerous man when he needed to be. In Bob Duff's *The Bruise Brothers*, former Red Wing Joey Kocur recalled a bout against Minnesota's mustached behemoth in 1985, Kocur's first year in the league. "I remember Dave Richter well," Kocur said. "I guess he'd probably heard about me, so he didn't give me a chance to get prepared. He dropped the gloves. I tried to drop the gloves, but couldn't get them off. I went to grab his right arm, not knowing he was a lefty. He must've hit me five times right square on the yapper." Richter continued to fight (literally) for playing time until November 1985, when he and Bo Berglund were traded to Philadelphia for Todd Bergen and Ed (Boxcar) Hospodar.

Bob Rouse (1983–1989) was the defensive defenseman that every team needs and wants, quietly doing his job and letting flashier performers (i.e., Craig Hartsburg) get top billing. Although he was one of three team captains during the 1988–89 season, Rouse had trouble meeting the expectations of a string of North Stars coaches who saw him as a big, tough defenseman who didn't use his six-feet-two, 225-pound frame to full advantage (an affliction later termed Hal Gill's Disease). When the gloves came off, Rouse could hold his own against the league's heavyweights, but he rarely initiated a conflict. The young defenseman became expendable when it became obvious he wasn't going to be the blue-line terror his coaches were hoping for. Rouse was included in the 1989 deadline deal that sent Dino Ciccarelli to the Washington Capitals. He would go on to play over one thousand games in the NHL before retiring in 1999.

58. Gary Sargent is pursued by a Montreal Canadien. Courtesy of the Dallas Stars

Gary Sargent (1978–1983) was one of the league's top puck-moving defenseman in the late 1970s. He possessed a hard, accurate shot, fine passing skills, and the skating ability to rush the puck. At the same time, he had the muscle to move opposing players away from the Minnesota net. Growing up in Bemidji, "Sarge" was a great all-around athlete in high school who turned down several college football scholarships as well as an offer to sign with the Minnesota Twins as a third baseman. Like his cousin, Henry Boucha, Sargent was a full-blooded Ojibwa. A 1974 draft pick of the Kings, he played three seasons in Los Angeles before signing with the North Stars. In 1978–79 he led all Minnesota blueliners in scoring with twelve goals and forty-four points. Chronic back problems and a nagging knee injury shortened what should have been a much longer career.

Glen Sharpley (1976–1980) scored twenty-five goals in his rookie season and continued to produce for the North Stars, thanks to his quickness, accurate shot, and proficiency in the face-off circle. The speedy center also proved he could handle the responsibility of killing penalties. During the 1978–79 season "Sharps" teamed with left wing Mike Fidler and right wing Kris Manery to form one of the club's most effective lines. A highlight of Sharpley's four-plus seasons in Minnesota occurred when his team upset the reigning Stanley Cup champion Montreal Canadiens in the 1980 playoffs. On the mend from a knee injury suffered earlier that season, Sharpley didn't dress for the first four games of the quarterfinals. But when the North Stars trailed 3–2 in the series, Sharpley scored three points in a 5–2 victory in what was one of the best games of his career, and probably his biggest as a North Star. Minnesota went on to eliminate the Habs in a decisive Game Seven. There should have been many more memorable moments from Sharpley's tenure with the North Stars, but he had a rocky relationship with Glen Sonmor and a falling-out with the coach led to Sharpley demanding a trade. GM Lou Nanne complied and dealt Sharpley to Chicago for left wing Ken Solheim and a draft pick in December 1980. After his career was cut short by a serious eye injury, Sharpley operated a sporting goods business in Haliburton, Ontario.

Paul Shmyr (1979–1981) was twice named the WHA's most outstanding defenseman after beginning his NHL career with Chicago. When the WHA folded in 1979, the North Stars claimed Shmyr (pronounced "SHMEER") from Edmonton in the expansion draft. Already a twelve-year veteran, his reputation as a good leader preceded him, and he was named the ninth captain of the North Stars. Shmyr brought experience and toughness to a young Minnesota team that advanced to the Stanley Cup Finals in 1981, although he missed most of the playoffs that year due to injury and subsequent benching by coach Glen Sonmor. After two seasons with the North Stars, he closed out his career with the Hartford Whalers. Shmyr passed away in 2004 at the age of fifty-eight after a bout with cancer.

Greg Smith (1978–1981) so impressed North Stars beat writers and broadcasters in his first season with the team that they voted him the Tom Dill Cup as the team's top defenseman. Smith's rights were transferred to Minnesota following the merger with Cleveland, and he brought with him a nice blend of skills: intelligence, toughness, and a heavy shot. Smith proved to be such a valuable asset that he was included in the August 1981 deal to acquire Detroit's first-round pick in 1982, a pick used to select Brian Bellows.

Dean Talafous (1975–1978) had been a collegiate hockey legend at the University of Wisconsin, where he scored the 1973 NCAA Championship winning goal and was named the tournament's MVP. That performance helped get the tall, almost gangly centerman from Duluth drafted by the Atlanta Flames the next year. He played in Atlanta only briefly before coming home to Minnesota. The three and a half seasons Talafous spent as a North Star were the best of his career, and he enjoyed some success playing on a line with Blake Dunlop and Ernie Hicke. He scored a career-high twenty-two goals and forty-nine points in 1976–77, but dependable two-way play, not flashy offensive totals, are what kept him in the league. Traded to the Rangers in 1978, Talafous played a few more seasons, then retired rather than accept a trade to Quebec. After his playing days he embarked on a long and successful career in coaching on the college level.

Elmer (Moose) Vasko (1967–1970) broke into the NHL during the Original Six era—not an easy task for a defenseman, when you consider the limited number of jobs available. But the assets Vasko brought to the game—size, speed, and physicality—would have made him a star in any era. In fact, at six feet three and between 215 and 220 pounds, he was at one time the biggest player in the league. Chicago fans would yell "Mooooose!" as Vasko, a fast but ungraceful skater, rushed down the ice, and the nickname stuck. In 1966, after a decade with the Blackhawks, Vasko called it quits. He had been out of the game for a year when he met the determined Wren Blair, who was looking to bolster the expansion North Stars' blue line with some veteran leadership. Vasko declared himself unretired and gave the North Stars two-plus seasons of service. A former team captain in Chicago, Vasko wore the "C" for Minnesota in 1968–69, his last full season in the league. That year, despite getting into trouble with coach John Muckler for occasional pedestrian play, he also played in his fourth and final All-Star Game. The following year he played only a few games for the North Stars before closing out his career with Salt Lake City of the WHL. Vasko died of cancer in 1998. He was sixty-two.

Tommy Williams (1969–1971) won a gold medal with the 1960 U.S. Olympic Team and was among the first Americans to become regular skaters in the NHL. The North Stars acquired Williams and defenseman Barry Gibbs from the Bruins for a draft pick and future considerations in May 1969. A versatile forward from Duluth, Williams was a local boy whom Minnesotans followed with heightened interest. In 1969–70 he finished second on the North Stars with sixty-seven points, including a team-leading (and career-high) fifty-two assists. Williams's play declined following the tragic death of his wife in November 1970, and he was traded to the California Seals the following spring. He died in 1992 at the age of fifty-one.

59. Personal troubles cast a dark shadow over Tommy Williams's career. Graphic Artists/Hockey Hall of Fame

Ron Wilson (1985–1988) has coached over 1,400 games with the Anaheim Ducks, Washington Capitals, San Jose Sharks, and Toronto Maple Leafs. At least some of the wisdom he imparted to his players was gleaned during his brief turn as a Minnesota North Star. Born in Canada but raised in Rhode Island, Wilson had been an All-American at Providence College, leading the Friars in scoring for all four years—an amazing feat for a defenseman. Drafted by the Maple Leafs, he spent the first few years of his pro career bouncing between Toronto and the minor leagues. Tired of that routine, he moved to Europe and became the Bobby Orr of Switzerland (no, really). Wilson won two championships with HC Davos and even became the first defenseman to lead the Swiss league in scoring. Despite these accomplishments, in the back of Wilson's mind he always wondered about the NHL career he had left behind. He also feared that if he spent his entire career in Europe, it would be difficult for him to get a coaching job in North America after his retirement. At the same time, the struggling North Stars were in desperate need of a puck-moving defenseman. In March 1985, after Davos's season wrapped up, Lou Nanne convinced Wilson to sign a free-agent contract to play for Minnesota for the remainder of the regular season and the playoffs. It was a bit of an adjustment. At just five feet ten and 165 pounds, Wilson was too small to play the same style as other NHL defensemen. To be effective he needed to play the way he did in college and in Europe: darting this way and that, using his quickness and agility to maximize his offensive skills. He spent parts of four seasons with the North Stars before retiring in 1988 to begin his long-desired second career as an NHL coach.

Tom Younghans (1976–1981) is best remembered for scoring a huge, game-winning goal against Montreal in the 1979 playoffs, but a knack for good defensive hockey is what kept him in the NHL. Undrafted, the St. Paul native turned down an offer to play for the WHA's Calgary Cowboys to sign with the North Stars as a free agent in June 1976 after winning a national championship under Herb Brooks at the University of Minnesota. As a pro he was a reliable penalty killer whose versatility allowed him to play all three forward positions. In 1981, after playing parts of six seasons for the green and gold, Younghans was traded to the Rangers for cash.

Ron Zanussi (1977–1981) played a spirited brand of hockey that earned him respect from teammates and coaches alike. The hardworking, hard-hitting right winger finished his checks and fought when sufficiently provoked. Minnesota's third-round pick in 1976, "Zoo" was a capable depth forward, scoring fifteen goals in his rookie season while playing on a line with Tim Young and Per-Olov Brasar. That marked the offensive ceiling for a player who once scored fifty-three goals with the IHL's Fort Wayne Komets. The North Stars traded Zanussi to the Maple Leafs for a draft pick at the trade deadline in March 1981, a deal believed to have been a favor by Leafs GM Punch Imlach to his son, Brent Imlach, Zanussi's agent at the time.

7

BEHIND THE BENCH AND OVER THE AIR

WREN BLAIR

The first coach and general manager of the North Stars, Wren Blair was a wall-punching, bench-kicking, expletive-shouting firebrand who wore his emotions on his sleeve. After games he had to be bathed in towels because he'd worked up such a tremendous sweat.

"One night," Blair recounted in his 2002 memoir *The Bird*, "a fan came to me and said, 'I don't know much about hockey, but I only come to the games to watch you. I can't believe how hard you work up and down the bench. You're talking to your players all the time, you're yelling at the referees. The energy you display during the game is endless.'"

Blair may have been at his most animated during the 1967 division finals against St. Louis, once angrily hurling a towel onto the ice after disagreeing with a referee's call. Blair said later that he had intended to throw the towel onto the floor and insisted that a mysterious "blast of air" caught it at the last second and carried it out onto the ice. Nevertheless, it resulted in a bench penalty, and the Blues used the subsequent power play to score the tying goal.

If there was a method to Blair's madness, it was his belief that players would feed off his energy and carry it out onto the ice. "That's why I was on the referees so much," he said. "To let the players know I was on their side."

Born in Lindsay, Ontario, a small mill town about two hundred miles west of Ottawa, Wren quit school at sixteen and took a job delivering milk for Beaton's Dairy. A year later he decided to enlist in the Canadian Army. His parents were dead set against the idea but finally consented when he told them that if he didn't have their blessing, he would simply run away from home.

After a brief but enlightening stint in the military—he was once locked up for shooting craps in the barracks—Blair took a manufacturing job with General Motors in Oshawa. In his spare time he played softball with coworkers . . . not the usual launching pad for a thirty-year career as a hockey executive. But within a few years he was running several softball teams in the area, which led to him managing and coaching hockey teams.

In 1957, at just thirty-two years old, he coached the senior league Whitby Dunlops to an Allan Cup title as the top amateur team in Canada. The following year, as defending Allan Cup champs, Blair and the Dunlops were in Oslo, Norway, as Canada's representative to the World Hockey Championships (Blair had traveled to Europe by boat, since he refused to get on an airplane). The stakes were high. Canada was still reeling from its loss in the 1956 Olympics and then boycotted the worlds in 1957 to protest the Soviets' invasion of Hungary. In the finals the Dunlops defeated the Soviet Union to reestablish Canada's hockey hegemony.

Blair's meteoric rise from milk truck driver to hockey hotshot hadn't gone unnoticed. The very next morning after the Dunnies' gold medal victory, he received a phone call in his hotel room from Toronto Maple Leafs chairman Stafford Smythe. Characteristically curt, Smythe kept the pleasantries brief, then got down to business: he wanted Blair to promise him that he wouldn't talk to any other NHL clubs about a job without talking to him first.

When Blair got back home, he met with Smythe in Toronto. The Leafs, Blair learned, were interested in giving him an unspecified job in the organization. The salary was more than he was making as a housing appraiser, and there was the possibility—but no guarantee—that he'd be in line for the general manager's post. It was a tempting offer, but the uncertainty of it worried Blair. He needed time to mull it over.

Wren very quickly received another offer to run the Eastern Hockey League's Clinton Comets. The money was better, *and* Blair would be allowed to continue running the Whitby Dunlops (who, with Blair at the helm, would win a second Allan Cup in 1959).

When Blair met with Smythe to tell him he'd decided to take the Clinton job, Smythe thanked him for his time and informed him that he'd never work for the Toronto Maple Leafs. Wren wasn't losing any sleep over it. He was finally a full-time hockey man.

In 1960, the same year the Dunlops folded, Blair met with Boston Bruins GM Lynn Patrick to discuss a job running the Bruins' EPHL team, the Kingston Frontenacs. Blair had one condition: that he be allowed to continue to run the Clinton Comets. Patrick had a condition too: that this Bird finally get over his fear of flying. "You certainly can't work for the Boston Bruins," Patrick told Blair, "if you don't fly." Blair agreed, albeit reluctantly.

When the entire EPHL moved to the United States in 1963, the Kingston Frontenacs became the Minneapolis Bruins. The Boston Bruins would own 51 percent of the club, and the remaining 49 percent would be owned by three local investors: Walter Bush, Gordon Ritz, and Bob McNulty, the trio who would eventually form the core of the Minnesota North Stars ownership group.

By now Bird was running not only the Minneapolis Bruins but the Clinton Comets and the OHL's Oshawa Generals, too. He was also doing some scouting for the folks in Boston, which is how he met, befriended, and schmoozed a hot prospect from Parry Sound, Ontario, named Bobby Orr. Blair never accepted credit for "discovering" Orr—there were plenty of other folks who'd seen the kid play in peewee and bantam and suspected he had the makings of a superstar—but he did manage to get Bobby to sign a contract to play for the Oshawa Generals, which Blair co-owned with the Bruins. If not for Blair, then, Orr might very well have ended up a Detroit Red Wing or a Toronto Maple Leaf.

In early 1966 Blair learned that Minnesota had been granted an NHL expansion franchise and that his friends Bush, McNulty, and Ritz were behind the winning bid. And there was more good news: they wanted to talk to Blair about running the team. Fueled by a seemingly insatiable ambition that had seen him juggle managerial duties of multiple teams simultaneously, there was no way he was going to pass up this opportunity.

Strict tampering rules dictated that any meeting with Bush and company be held on the down-low, since Bird was still employed by the Bruins. They convened in frigid Fargo, North Dakota, on a Saturday, and by the end of the weekend, Blair had agreed to be the new general manager of the North Stars. His four-year contract included an option to coach.

Like the other expansion GMs, Blair was faced with the challenge of molding a rag-tag group of players that other teams didn't want into a cohesive unit. In his own unique way the demonstrative manager-coach proved to be a galvanizing force.

"To me," said Tom Reid, "Wren Blair was a really good guy but not a very good coach. The problem with Wren was that he didn't understand the game, and he would scream and holler at you in front of the other players. So players rallied around each other."

"It was us versus him," said Cesare Maniago. "We said, 'Let's show that SOB what we're capable of doing.' He belittled us constantly and said that we weren't good enough. He was kind of a control freak who tried a variety of methods to get us going. In training camp, during our very first exhibition game, we were losing 2–0 after the first period. He told me, 'Take off your stuff. You're not good enough.' And it happened with a variety of players."

Bird flipped out again during the team's second regular-season game, played in Oakland. The North Stars carried a 1–0 deficit into the first intermission when a furious Blair tore through the visitors' dressing room, assailing his players with a barrage of criticism as if they trailed 4–0 or 5–0. Maniago received an especially vigorous tongue-lashing.

When Blair's tirade was over, a seething Maniago asked to continue the conversation in private.

"We went outside the dressing room, and boy, I just went at him," Maniago recalled. "I told him, 'If you ever do that again, I literally will shove my fist down your throat.' From that day on, we were the best of friends. I guess it's like calling someone's bluff."

"Wren was tough with everybody and it didn't matter who you were," said Lou Nanne. "Because he'd do such wild and crazy things, it gave us something to joke and laugh about. One day, he tried to be real tough by throwing a stick at the boards. Well, it bounced off the boards and hit him right between the eyes. Another time he was going to show Leo Boivin, of all people, how to bodycheck. He thought Leo didn't bodycheck right, and Leo had been in the league for almost twenty years. So Bird stood on the blue line and called for Bill Collins to come down the wing. He wanted to show Leo how to eliminate the man. Well, Billy couldn't wait. So he came down and knocked Wren ass-over-tea-kettle. His stick and gloves went flying. Bird was so mad he started swearing at us and then called off practice."

Blair's unpredictable behavior and outspoken nature helped get the North Stars some press—no easy feat in a market dominated by the Vikings, the Twins, and the Gophers—but he was probably a better front-office man than coach, as evidenced by acquisitions like Jude Drouin, Barry Gibbs, Danny Grant, Dennis Hextall, J. P. Parise, and Gump Worsley. There can be no denying that his cunning and zeal as an executive helped win the North Stars their fair share of respect in the years immediately following expansion. In *Hockey: The Story of the World's Fastest Sport*, Gordon Ritz lauds Blair's managerial skills, comparing him to the shrewd merchant who sees that a certain product isn't selling: "So he marks the goods down for a quick sale, in order to at least get some of his investment out of it."

When Blair realized that the North Stars were vulnerable to poaching by the WHA, he successfully lobbied a frugal ownership group to increase his salary budget. With the owners' blessing he met individually with every player on the roster before they left for the summer in 1972 and was successful in inking most to new long-term contracts.

The North Stars were chugging along nicely with Blair entrenched in the GM's chair and Jack Gordon now handling the coaching duties, finishing with a winning record and making the playoffs in 1971–72 and 1972–73.

But a seventh-place finish in 1973–74, stemming at least in part from Gordon's sudden resignation, cost Blair his dream job. He'd heard rumors throughout the season that ownership might let him go, but when the end came, it still came as a shock.

In *The Bird* Blair recalls how a local sportswriter asked him what it felt like to be fired by the North Stars. "Perhaps I should've seen it coming," he said. "I feel like a parent who adopts a child, and after nine years and you've pretty well raised them through their formative years, someone comes along and says, 'I'll take that child now.' You know how that would feel. That's how I feel about being fired because the North Stars, for over nine years, were certainly my baby."

Blair wasn't out of the game for very long. Less than a year after leaving Minnesota, he became one of the owners of the Pittsburgh Penguins. That was followed by a six-year stint as director of player personnel for the Los Angeles Kings.

He died at his home in Whitby, Ontario, in January 2013. He was eighty-seven.

GLEN SONMOR

Glen Sonmor was a battler. The fighting spirit that helped make him the winningest coach in the history of the North Stars probably also saved his life.

Born in Moose Jaw, Saskatchewan, Glen moved with his family to Toronto at the onset of the Great Depression. His father, a heavy gambler and drinker, wasn't around much, and when he was, he'd leave a trail of misery in his wake.

Glen found the perfect escape in sports. Here was the competition, companionship, and structure he craved, along with a mentor and father figure in Bob Abate, the youth sports coach and playground director who achieved some celebrity in Canada for his great success with the Elizabeth Playground sports teams. Abate's teams, the "Lizzies," were the pride of Toronto, winning more than 150 titles at the city, provincial, and national levels in baseball, basketball, football, and hockey. A good all-around athlete, Glen played 'em all.

Hockey became his passion and as a teen, Glen was good enough to make the Junior-B Hamilton Lloyds and then the Junior-A Guelph Biltmores. This was the top of the line as far as amateur hockey in Canada was concerned. Although he'd always planned to attend college on an athletic scholarship and get a degree in physical education, the opportunity to sign a pro contract with the AHL's Cleveland Barons was just too good to pass up. He set a goal for himself to one day play in the NHL, and if it didn't work out, well, he could always go back to school.

At twenty Sonmor found himself in Minnesota playing for the Minneapolis Millers of the USHL, a league two notches below the NHL. It was there that he met someone who would change his life forever: John Mariucci. Once a feared enforcer for the Chicago Blackhawks, now the elder statesman on a team of NHL hopefuls and career minor leaguers, Mariucci taught Sonmor the value of sticking up for oneself and for one's teammates. It was also Mariucci who urged (nay, commanded) Sonmor to start taking classes at the University of Minnesota to get his degree. Glen acquiesced, squeezing in as many courses as he could during the summers.

Sonmor was eventually called up to play for the Barons. He'd earned a reputation for being a tough little SOB who wouldn't back down from a fight, and that gritty, agitating style is what helped get him noticed by the New York Rangers. Halfway through the 1953–54 season, the Barons traded Sonmor to the Rangers for future Hall of Famer Andy Bathgate and cash . . . but this "trade" was really just an arrangement between the teams to get Bathgate, a rapidly rising star for the Blueshirts, some extra ice time in the minors. That didn't matter much to Glen—he was just tickled that he'd finally get a chance to play in the NHL. That summer there was another reason to celebrate when he married his long-time girlfriend, Margaret Mitchell. Life was good.

And then, in an instant, everything changed. On February 27, 1955, only four days after celebrating the birth of his daughter, Sonmor was back with the Barons to play the Pittsburgh Hornets. Midway through the game, as he was trying to screen the Hornets' goalie, a teammate's slap shot from the point struck him square in the left eye. He was rushed to a Pittsburgh hospital, but doctors were unable to save his eye. At twenty-five Glen had to accept the painful truth that his career as a player was over.

While recuperating from his injury, Glen received a call from his old pal John Mariucci, who was now head hockey coach at the U of M. He'd arranged for Sonmor to come back to Minnesota to coach the Gophers' freshman team. It's no wonder Glen has often called Mariucci one of his guardian angels. He would meet another one soon enough.

Working at the U of M allowed Sonmor to complete his studies, and he eventually succeeded Mariucci as head coach of the Gophers. It was around this time that Sonmor met Lou Nanne, the former Gophers captain who had been hired to coach the freshman team. The two forged a strong friendship and remained close even after Nanne left the school in 1968 to play for the North Stars.

Sonmor was named WCHA Coach of the Year in 1970 after leading the Gophers to a 21-12 record and a WCHA regular season title. From the U of M he went on to coach the Minnesota Fighting Saints and the Birmingham Bulls of the WHA. With its wild, brawling image, the rebel league was the perfect backdrop for someone who had been such a pugnacious character during his playing days.

By 1978 Lou Nanne was general manager of a North Stars team in rebuilding mode, and one of his first tasks was to hire a coach. After Herb Brooks turned him down, Nanne offered the job to Sonmor. At first ownership wanted no part of him—not after he had worked for the Saints, a team that only a few years earlier nearly put the North Stars out of business. Nanne held firm, threatening to walk if the board didn't support his decision. They relented, and the North Stars had themselves a new coach.

Sonmor was everything the club needed at that critical moment in its checkered history: he was demanding but fair, keen on the fundamentals, expected everyone to buy into his team-first concept, and had an innate ability to identify a player's greatest strengths and then use him in situations where he would be most effective. Above all he was an impeccable motivator who encouraged his teams to play with emotion rather than adhere to some strict, disciplined system. At times his enthusiasm bordered on outrageousness, but it helped make him one of the better coaches of his time and certainly one of its most colorful.

"Glen understood that there was an entertainment component to the game," said Bobby Smith, whose considerable offensive skills were nurtured under Sonmor. "We were a fun team to watch because of that."

"He was a hell of a coach," added Al MacAdam. "He was very upbeat. There were no down days with him. He had a passion that carried over to the players, and his emotion was just contagious. Players just liked getting on the ice with him. I loved that about Glen."

"Glen was a great cheerleader who got you pumped up to play," said Brad Maxwell. "He was not a great tactician like, say, Herb Brooks, who I also played for. But when you think about it, there's not a lot of real coaching to be done at that level. Most of the guys are pretty talented players."

Maxwell still laughs when he remembers how, just moments before the North Stars were set to take the ice against Montreal in the 1980 quarterfinals, Sonmor's glass eye popped out . . . on the bench. "They had just lowered the lights before the National Anthem," he said, "and the next thing I know, Glen comes down to the defensemen's end of the bench and says, 'Maxy, help me find my eye. I lost my eye.' Well, he must've gotten so excited that he whipped around, and his glass eye popped out. Here we are, right before a big playoff game, and three or four of us are down on our hands and knees feeling around in the dark for his eye. So we found it, he popped it back in, and as soon as the lights came back on, he was like, 'Okay, boys, let's go!'"

Sonmor's illimitable zeal masked a drinking problem that threatened to ruin his career just as it would ultimately ruin his marriage. One early sign of trouble occurred in 1970 when he was busted for drunk driving, an incident that wouldn't have been big news had he been a barber or a plumber instead of the coach of the Gophers. Only out of concern for his high-profile job did he take steps to get his drinking under control, but he still wasn't convinced he had a problem.

Not long after the North Stars made it to their first Stanley Cup Final, Glen caught wind of rumors in the press that the team was thinking about replacing him. The stress caused him to fall back into bad habits, and in 1982 he lost his license following another drunk-driving arrest.

Thank goodness for loyal friends, because no matter how badly or how often Sonmor fell off the wagon, Nanne refused to give up on him. There were interventions and a trip to rehab—Louie even put a clause in Glen's contract stating that the team could terminate him on the spot if he started drinking again—but nothing was going to change for Glen until he found the strength within himself to get help and beat his addiction once and for all.

On January 12, 1983, after the North Stars beat the Penguins 7–0 in Pittsburgh, Sonmor sneaked off to a local bar to throw back a few. Once sufficiently tanked, he stumbled out into the night to head back to the team's hotel and was jumped by a couple of thugs. They dragged Sonmor into an alley and beat the tar out of him. The next day he tried to hide his broken nose and black eyes behind a pair of dark sunglasses, hoping players and other team staff wouldn't notice. But he knew he wasn't fooling anyone . . . and he finally realized that he'd hit rock bottom.

The next night he was behind the bench for a 2–1 win over the Maple Leafs at Met Center. Immediately after the game a press conference was held in which Sonmor announced he was stepping down as coach to get some much-needed rest. In truth Nanne had arranged for Sonmor to check back into a rehab facility in California.

There were more relapses in the days that followed; he even drank on the flight out to Los Angeles, but those drinks turned out to be his last. Glen went through the rehab program with a renewed sense of purpose and emerged better equipped to deal with the inevitable temptations life was going to throw at him.

Nanne welcomed Sonmor back into the North Stars fold by giving him a job in player development. This wasn't charity. It was a smart hockey decision, for Glen was still one of the best evaluators of talent around.

Early in the 1984–85 season, after the North Stars fired coach Bill Mahoney, Glen was asked to fill in for the remainder of the year. The team continued to struggle, finishing eighteen games under .500, but Sonmor managed to guide the North Stars into the postseason, where they upset St. Louis in the first round. A second-round loss to Chicago was tough to stomach, but Sonmor was thrilled to have been given the opportunity to coach again. He went back to player development and scouting but stepped behind the bench one last time in February 1987 as a temporary replacement for the just-fired Lorne Henning. His final record: 174-161-81.

Sonmor's career in hockey also included many years broadcasting Gophers games on the radio and a stint working for the Minnesota Wild as a scout. He died in 2015 at age eighty-six.

AL SHAVER

From the moment the North Stars took the ice against the St. Louis Blues on October 11, 1967, to their last road game at Detroit's Joe Louis Arena on April 15, 1993, legendary radio play-by-play man Al Shaver chronicled their every exploit over the airwaves.

When Shaver called a game, you didn't need a TV. You could see everything—every hit, every save, and every goal.

"I remember listening to him with my dad," said John Walton, play-by-play announcer for the Washington Capitals and a childhood fan of the North Stars. "The two men who most influenced me from a hockey standpoint were Al and TV announcer Bob Kurtz. Being able to listen to them as a kid and growing up was such a joy. Al's style was what hockey should be—very rapid fire and pronounced. He had a real presence. It was almost beyond description. I'd be a rich man if I had some old clips of games that he did."

Prior to his award-winning work with the North Stars, Shaver spent nineteen years broadcasting an array of sports in Canada, including thirteen seasons of Canadian Football League action. He also handled play-by-play duties for junior and minor-pro hockey, minor league baseball, high school and college basketball, curling, golf, and soccer.

Born in London, Ontario, but raised about twenty-eight miles south in Tillsonburg, a small town in tobacco country, this Canadian import became synonymous with Minnesota hockey.

"In my last year of high school, I had no idea what I wanted to do after graduation," he said. "I really didn't want to spend any more time going to university, so one of my teachers suggested I take a look at broadcasting. A few days later I was in the school library, and there was a pamphlet advertising the Lorne Greene Academy of Radio Arts. So I enrolled there, and that got me my first job in Guelph, Ontario."

With the first wave of NHL expansion on the horizon, Shaver wanted a play-by-play job with one of the new clubs. Family friend Harold Ballard, former owner of the Maple Leafs, invited him to record a demo tape during a 1967 Stanley Cup Finals game between Toronto and Montreal.

On his way out of Maple Leaf Gardens that night, Shaver ran into Wren Blair, newly appointed coach and general manager of the North Stars. "I asked Wren, 'What should I do with this tape I just made?' and he told me to send it to the North Stars since they'd forward it to whichever radio station they'd end up making a deal with. So I did, and two weeks later I

60. Al Shaver, by
Terrence Fogarty.
© 2002 Used
with permission
of the artist

got a call from the general manager of WCCO. He said, 'Come on down, we want to talk to you.' That's how it all happened."

Throughout his nearly thirty years of play-by-play work with the North Stars, the University of Minnesota Golden Gophers, and the state's high school tournament, Shaver painted a verbal picture of the game that still remains with Minnesota hockey fans.

Although the North Stars' two appearances in the Stanley Cup Finals are among Shaver's favorite hockey memories, the inaugural season of 1967–68 holds a really special place in his heart. "That first year in Minnesota was very exciting," he said. "It was a new thing for the players and also for those of us who worked in broadcasting because we finally got a chance to be on the air. When I was living up in Canada, there was only the Maple Leafs and the Canadiens. There were no opportunities to broadcast NHL games, so it was a wonderful opportunity for me."

It wasn't until the North Stars' final home game in 1993 that Shaver and son Wally realized a lifelong dream of working together on air. Both men called it the only enjoyable aspect of an inexorably gloomy and tearful affair.

"I wasn't sure how I'd sign off that night," Al recalled. "I was worried about it. I thought I'd break up. I didn't make a lengthy sign-off, I'll tell you that. All I could do was say, 'Thank you for all your support over the years, for both myself and the team.' I got it over with as soon as possible."

Later that year the NHL Broadcasters Association presented Shaver with the prestigious Foster Hewitt Award for excellence in hockey broadcasting. He also was an eleven-time selection as Sportscaster of the Year by the Minnesota chapter of the National Association of Sportswriters and Sportscasters of the United States of America.

And in 2000 the former voice of the North Stars was recognized for his many years of service to hockey in Minnesota when the expansion Minnesota Wild unveiled a permanent tribute in his honor inside Xcel Energy Center: the Al Shaver Press Box.

"I will be eternally grateful for that," he said. "There have been a couple of great honors—the kinds of things that you treasure for the rest of your life."

8

BRAWN OVER BEAUTY

Because the area was without a facility suitable for NHL hockey when Minnesota was granted an expansion team in 1966, one had to be built. And quickly.

Team owners wanted the support of all Minnesotans but feared that by placing the arena in either St. Paul or Minneapolis, they risked alienating fans from the other city. Divided by the Mississippi River, the municipalities could trace their rivalry back to the days after the Civil War. In fact, it was alleged that each city padded the 1890 Census report in an attempt to appear bigger than the other. Bloomington, a suburb of Minneapolis, was more or less considered neutral ground.

Metropolitan Sports Center, or Met Center as it became known, was built within sight of Metropolitan Stadium on Cedar Avenue and opened just in time for the North Stars' first home game on October 21, 1967, against the Oakland Seals.

Architecturally, the Met was no Louvre. Developed by Bob McNulty, one of the team's original co-owners, and constructed at a cost of $6 million (about $40 million in 2012 dollars), it was utilitarian in appearance—rectangular in shape, white exterior, no windows—and never boasted fancy amenities, but it was widely regarded by fans and players as a great building for hockey. The ice was fast, the lighting was good, and the player locker rooms and facilities were top-notch. Sightlines were among the best in the league. There was not a bad seat to be found.

"The site was perfect," said Walter Bush, who, along with his fellow investors, funded construction for Met Center out of their own pockets. "We had this huge parking lot and we took care of customers by having a service crew on hand to start your car if it wouldn't start."

"For what it cost to build," said Cesare Maniago, "it was one of the better arenas for its value. I found it a little hilarious with those different-colored chairs they had in there, though. That was unique."

Ah yes, the seats. They added to the building's character and were still being installed in the hours leading up to the team's first home game. Original plans called for sections to be divided by color: yellow, green, black, and white.

"But because they were tight on the schedule," Wally Shaver explained, "workers started installing the seats haphazardly because the supervisors were gone. And once they got back, and saw that a whole bunch of seats had been put in that way, they just decided to continue with that arrangement. It was always a unique stadium because of that random pattern of seat coloring."

JIM BOWERS

A fixture at Met Center for two decades, Jim Bowers was the official anthem singer of the North Stars.

A former opera singer with a deep baritone, Bowers was one of the best in the business. His stirring renditions of "The Star-Spangled Banner," "God Bless America," and other arena standards became as much a Met Center tradition as, say, grabbing a beer at the Blue Line Club, shouting obscenities at Al Secord, or the organist playing the theme music from *Jaws* whenever Jack Carlson took the ice.

Bowers had a reverence for the songs he performed, and in those few minutes before the opening face-off, when the spotlight belonged to him and him alone, he tried to strike an emotional chord with the fans. "I don't want to sound arrogant," Bowers said in a 1990 interview, "but every time I sing [the anthem], I want it to be an event. I want to see tears in peoples' eyes."

Before he became the area's most popular and sought-after anthem singer, Bowers performed in nightclubs and at church functions. Then, in the late 1960s, wcco Radio's Charlie Boone suggested that Bowers sing the national anthem before a Twins game. He did, and the positive response gave Bowers the confidence to sing at other sporting events. He eventually became the official anthem singer for the Fighting Saints.

In the mid-70s, around the time the Saints were going under, Bowers was approached by Gordon Ritz about singing the anthem at Met Center. The rest is history.

The North Stars drew well in their first few seasons and attendance climbed every year from 1968–69 to 1971–72, when the team averaged 15,319 per game—the most ever during its Minnesota years. In January 1972 Met Center hosted the NHL's twenty-fifth All-Star Game (the East beat the West, 3–2, and Boston's Bobby Orr was named MVP).

When the rival WHA was formed, it brazenly placed teams in some of the NHL's oldest strongholds, places like New York, Chicago, and Boston. But Minnesota had also proven itself as a big-time hockey market, and the WHA designated the Twin Cities for one of its inaugural franchises. After opening the 1972–73 season at the St. Paul Auditorium, the Minnesota Fighting Saints moved into the new sixteen-thousand-seat St. Paul Civic Center. Not coincidentally North Stars attendance dropped every year from 1972–73 to 1977–78.

"It pretty much split the pro hockey crowd," said Shaver. "If you threw 'em all in one building, you'd be selling out. I think that if people had an issue with the NHL or the North Stars, they started going to Saints games as an alternative."

By 1978–79, however, the WHA was on the brink of extinction, and the North Stars were poised for a comeback. In 1981 the team shocked the NHL and its fans by advancing to its first Stanley Cup Finals and repeated the feat a decade later.

In addition to the North Stars, Met Center hosted scores of non-hockey events like rock concerts, circuses, rodeos, a Vietnam War rally, and numerous family shows. Frank Sinatra, Elvis Presley, Michael Jackson, Bill Cosby, Diana Ross, and opera star Luciano Pavarotti were some of the major celebrities to perform there.

Some scenes for the 1978 film *Ice Castles*, starring Lynn-Holly Johnson and Robby Benson, were filmed at Met Center. In the film Benson's character tries out for the North Stars but is assigned to their fictional farm team in Lincoln (likely Nebraska, though the state is never mentioned).

When the team moved to Dallas in 1993, civic leaders grappled over what to do with their now-vacant hockey arena. Initially Bloomington's Metropolitan Sports Facilities Commission, which owned Met Center and the land it occupied, preferred to keep the building to attract another NHL club. But since there were already too many arenas in too small a market, it was more likely that owners of an expansion or existing team would be drawn to the newer, bigger Target Center in Minneapolis or construct a facility of their own.

In December 1994 the commission scheduled Met Center for demolition, but it would not fall easily. The demolition crew was unsuccessful in its first attempt to bring the building down. Much of the structure was still standing even after explosives were detonated inside. Mobile demolition equipment had to be brought in later to finish the job. In the end Bloomington's beloved hockey arena had proven more resilient than handsome.

The barren site, once the state's most valuable undeveloped parcel because of its close proximity to the huge Mall of America and the Min-

HOLLYWOOD STARS 8, NORTH STARS 6

On January 10, 1987, just prior to a game between the North Stars and the Hartford Whalers, Met Center was the scene of an exhibition match between a group of hockey-playing celebrities and a collection of former North Stars and local media. Michael J. Fox (*Back to the Future*) paced the celebrity squad with a hat trick. Other star attractions included Michael Keaton (*Mr. Mom, Batman*), and Richard Dean Anderson (TV's MacGyver), a onetime youth hockey star in his native Roseville. Glen Sonmor coached the North Stars alumni/media team, stepping behind the bench clad head to toe in black leather and sporting a black patch over his eye.

neapolis-St. Paul International Airport, remained empty until 2004, when an IKEA furniture store opened on the west side of the property.

Bush remembered watching Met Center's demolition in person. "When I retired in 1984," he said, "the North Stars gave me four lifetime tickets. Then Norm Green bought the team and moved it. I thought, 'I guess I can take my tickets and go sit in the parking lot.'"

"I was very fortunate to acquire two seats from Met Center along with one of the upper deck section signs," said Matt Myer of Crystal, Minnesota. "The Met was really special to me, and it's still painful to look at that area next to the Mall of America where it used to stand. It might sound cheesy, but I still get choked up when I look over that way and don't see it."

9

BLOOD FEUD

The best rivalries are the ones you know by heart. Think Coke versus Pepsi, Superman versus Lex Luthor, or Godzilla versus King Kong. Heck, even David Letterman versus Jay Leno held our attention for a spell.

Rivalries in sports elevate the intensity of any competition, and the NHL has had some great ones over the years. It didn't have the history of Canadiens-Maple Leafs, but what the North Stars-Blackhawks rivalry lacked in longevity it more than made up for in mutual animosity. These teams *hated* each other, and that hatred provided blood-thirsty spectators on both sides with countless hours of entertainment.

Prior to 1967 the Blackhawks could lay claim to the entire Midwest as their turf. Expansion ended that monopoly. The first shots of the hockey border war between the Twin Cities and the Windy City were fired sometime after realignment in 1970–71, when the Hawks—a league powerhouse boasting stars like Bobby Hull, Stan Mikita, and Tony Esposito—moved out of the East Division and into the West. The gap in talent was glaring at first, but as the North Stars improved, so did the rivalry.

NORTH STARS VERSUS BLACKHAWKS ALL-TIME RECORD

In 169 regular season meetings between the clubs, Chicago held a 92-56-21 advantage over Minnesota.

"The rivalry really picked up after I became GM (in 1978) because it seemed that it was us and Chicago playing each other in the playoffs all the time," Lou Nanne said. "We had some very physical games and really tough guys on each side, and that just drove the rivalry. It really started around 1980, and from then on, it just went berserk. It was nasty. Chicago became our best rival."

The teams' postseason duels became an annual rite of passage. Minnesota and Chicago met six times overall, including four years in a row. The Blackhawks held a 4-2 advantage in series wins.

Personalities drove the rivalry too. Denis Savard, Steve Larmer, and Jeremy Roenick were among the "most wanted" in Bloomington but none more so than Al Secord, a big left winger who loved being the target of Met Center's venom. "I was a 'fan-favorite' there," Secord recalled, tongue planted firmly in cheek. "The North Stars fans were always chanting the 'Secord sucks' thing, and it kept on going for several minutes. Actually, it was great. It gave me a boost every time to play even harder."

"For three or four years [in juniors], I had to defend myself against Tim Coulis and Al Secord," Dino Ciccarelli remembered. "Then I go to Minnesota and we have a rivalry with Chicago, so who do I line up against for twelve or thirteen more years? Secord!"

Because he played with a snarl and refused to be intimidated, Ciccarelli was as despised in Chicago as Secord was in Bloomington. It wasn't uncommon to see little green "Dino" dinosaurs dangling from homemade nooses at Chicago Stadium.

And yet even with all that bad blood, Gordie Roberts said, "There's always a level of mutual respect. It's like I try to tell young players that I coach now: when you're at the rink and the puck drops, your personality may change a bit, but it's still just business."

Mutual respect? Just business? Judge for yourself as you review this timeline of turmoil:

October 28, 1967: In the first-ever regular-season meeting between the clubs, the Blackhawks snap the North Stars' first winning streak. Final score: Chicago 4, Minnesota 2.

November 21, 1981: The two premier antagonists of the Minnesota-Chicago rivalry, Dino Ciccarelli and Al Secord, exchange blows for the first time as pros in the closing minutes of a 6–4 Blackhawks win.

April 4, 1982: To conclude the regular season, the Blackhawks face the North Stars in a seemingly unimportant game. Psychologically, however, it would prove crucial. Not only does Chicago rally from a three-goal deficit to win 4–3, but afterward Glen Sonmor is so upset with the intimidating tactics of Secord that he calls the Hawks big man an "idiot" and vows that his team will retaliate. "In the playoffs we won't go after Secord," Sonmor growls, "we'll go right up to Savard and wring his neck." Not coincidentally Savard is the Hawks' leading scorer and, at five feet ten and 167 pounds, their smallest player.

Norris Division Semifinals, April 7–11, 1982: In the riotous first period of Game One, referee Bob Myers doles out 125 penalty minutes. The chaos begins when Hawks defenseman Dave Hutchison butt-ends Ciccarelli in the face. Dino requires four stitches to close the gash in his head, and Hutchison is assessed a five-minute major penalty. A minute after stepping out of the penalty box, he is attacked by Jack Carlson, who delivers a beating so severe that Hutchison is unable to return for the remainder of the game and the next. Carlson mangles his knuckles on Hutchison's teeth and misses the next three games. The Blackhawks win 3–2 in overtime, despite being outshot 47–22. The heroes for Chicago are goalie Murray Bannerman (forty-five saves) and center Tom Lysiak, who has two goals and two assists plus twelve stitches, courtesy of the stick of Curt Giles. The North Stars win Game Three, 7–1, which includes a hat trick from Ciccarelli. The Hawks, trailing after two periods and resigned to their fate, decide to let elbows and sticks fly in the third. Savard gets into a shouting match with Sonmor, then spits at the North Stars coach, drawing a gross misconduct penalty. Multiple fights break out in the Chicago Stadium crowd that halt play, and someone hurls a bottle that shatters near Gilles Meloche. Afterward Lou Nanne remarks, "I don't remember ever wanting to beat a team as bad as I want to beat these guys. Tonight's game was sickening." The Blackhawks go on to win the best-of-five series, three games to one.

February 12, 1983: Did Chicago's Jack O'Callahan actually *bite* Minnesota's Ron Friest on the nose during the first of their two fights? Would it surprise you if he did? Final score: Minnesota 5, Chicago 4.

March 21, 1983: At Met Center a third-period fight between Savard and Ciccarelli escalates into a bench-clearing brawl that lasts for twenty minutes and halts the action for almost an hour. Five players from each team receive game misconducts. Ron Friest is assessed a match penalty for bouncing Steve Larmer's head off the ice. Final score: Minnesota 4, Chicago 3.

Norris Division Finals, April 14–20, 1983: Chicago finishes ahead of Minnesota by eight points in the division, and both teams win their first-round matchups to force a rematch of the '82 semis. The Blackhawks defeat the North Stars for the second straight year, four games to one.

THE OTHER RIVALRY

Minnesota-St. Louis was almost—but not quite—as nasty a rivalry as Minnesota-Chicago, which is a bit surprising, since the teams occupied the same division for all twenty-six years of the North Stars' existence. In fact, Minnesota played more games against St. Louis than any other team.

In 181 regular season meetings, the Blues went 82-64-35 against the North Stars and won five of nine playoff series: 1968, 1970, 1972, 1986, and 1989. The North Stars advanced in 1971, 1984, 1985, and 1991.

In the early years, the Blues had the edge in goal with Hall of Famers Glenn Hall and Jacques Plante and a solid defense anchored by brothers Bob and Barclay Plager. Scotty Bowman was their coach, and capitalizing on a playoff format that required an expansion team to make the Stanley Cup Finals, he led the team to the final round in each of its first three seasons.

But no matter the era, St. Louis always seemed to have players who could beat the North Stars with their skill (Garry Unger, Bernie Federko, Brett Hull), their fists (Kelly Chase, Bob Gassoff, Dwight Schofield), or both (Brian Sutter, Perry Turnbull, Brendan Shanahan).

Norris Division Semifinals, April 4–10, 1984: Hostilities are renewed with Al Secord when he chops Dino Ciccarelli down with his stick in Game Four. The North Stars, coming off just their second division title, win the best-of-five series, three games to two. Gordie Roberts sums up the mood of the victors: "It was a good feeling to shake their hands with a smile on our faces and not hear them say, 'Have a nice summer.'"

Norris Division Finals, April 18–30, 1985: Chicago coach and GM Bob Pulford admits to being "nervous and scared" about facing the North Stars in the postseason for the fourth straight year. After sweeping first-place St. Louis in the semifinals, the North Stars open this series with an 8–5 win at Chicago. The Hawks answer with three consecutive wins and eventually take the series, four games to two. The last three games end in overtime, with Chicago's Darryl Sutter scoring two of the game winners. Willi Plett spends much of the series throwing hooks and jabs at Curt Fraser, Al Secord, and Behn Wilson.

December 3, 1985: A very appreciative Met Center crowd watches their team humiliate the Blackhawks, 9–2. Tony McKegney leads the North Stars with a hat trick. "This was embarrassing," a dejected Hawks defenseman Doug Wilson tells reporters afterward. "They beat us at every aspect of the game. They outworked us and beat us . . . more than beat us, actually."

61. Keith Acton and Keith Brown. Courtesy of the Dallas Stars

February 19, 1986: A rowdy Chicago Stadium crowd is treated to a first-period scrap between old pals Ciccarelli and Secord. It begins with the pair exchanging pushes and shoves at one end of the rink, far from the game action. Secord gets in an extra stick and punch to Ciccarelli's head before officials realize what's happening. Ciccarelli's ill-timed retaliatory high-stick at Secord is dangerously close to referee Dave Newell's face, and results in a ten-minute misconduct plus a two-minute minor for high-sticking. Secord gets only two minutes for high-sticking. Final score: Minnesota 6, Chicago 5.

January 4, 1988: The Blackhawks, battered by injuries to their right side, do the unthinkable by trading popular left wing Curt Fraser to the North Stars for right wing Dirk Graham. It is the first trade between the clubs in seven years, and initially teammates and fans have a tough time adjusting to the swap. Graham makes the mistake of wearing Fraser's old No. 8 in his first game at Chicago, and is booed. All is forgiven after he scores three goals and two assists in his first five games and changes to No. 33. He goes on to become one of the most popular Hawks of all time, while Fraser plays only fifty-three games over the next three years before retiring due to chronic back problems.

March 23, 1988: In a penalty-filled second period, Hawks defenseman Gary Nylund crosschecks Dino Ciccarelli from behind, sending the North Star winger sliding headfirst into the end boards. Dino charges Nylund, and fists start flying. Bob Rouse rushes to Ciccarelli's defense but is ejected for being the third man into a fight. Dirk Graham scores twice against his former mates. Final score: Minnesota 5, Chicago 4.

December 28, 1989: The North Stars and the Blackhawks square off in a bloody and wild brawl *twenty-five minutes* before the start of their scheduled game. As the teams skate in their respective zones as part of the pregame warm-ups, Chicago's Wayne Van Dorp and Minnesota's Shane Churla fight on Chicago's side of center ice. With the referees apparently still in their dressing room, North Stars coach Pierre Page and his assistant, Doug Jarvis, come out and try to get their players off the ice. Churla and Van Dorp slug it out until Van Dorp, his jersey ripped off and face covered in blood, skates off into the Hawks' locker room. The fighting continues as skirmishes break out all over the ice. At one point Denis Savard retrieves a stick and skates toward someone to chop when he's confronted by Jon Casey, who has a stick of his own. Officials finally arrive to restore order, and the teams skate to a 1–1 tie. Churla and Van Dorp are each suspended ten games for their roles in the melee, Basil McRae (match penalty for kneeing Mike Peluso after their second-period fight) is suspended for five games, and both teams are fined twenty-five thousand dollars.

April 1, 1990: In their final meeting of the regular season, the North Stars and the Blackhawks combine for 243 minutes in penalties from an eye-popping forty-eight infractions. Knowing they will play each other when the postseason begins in a matter of days, both teams treat this as a "statement game." This is especially true of Shane Churla, whose hands are taped up like a boxer's. He is ejected when referee Ron Hoggarth spots the illegal tape after Churla fights Dave Manson. Later Hoggarth throws out three more players after another fight: Mark Tinordi from the North Stars and Wayne Presley and Adam Creighton from the Hawks. Final score: Chicago 4, Minnesota 1.

Norris Division Semifinals, April 4–16, 1990: Steve Konroyd finds out the hard way why Shane Churla is called "Chainsaw." Their fight in Game Four looks evenly matched until Churla unleashes a flurry of hard right jabs, pounding Konroyd to the ice. In Game Seven, Keith Brown and Denis Savard are each ejected for stick fouls, but the North Stars can't build on their 1–0 lead on the ensuing five-on-three power play. Wayne Presley (two goals, assist) and Jeremy Roenick (two goals) dominate the second period, putting the game and the series out of reach for the North Stars. Final score: Chicago 5, Minnesota 1.

Norris Division Semifinals, April 4–14, 1991: Minnesota finishes fourth in the division and thirty-eight points behind Chicago. No one gives the North Stars a chance to win the series, making their colossal, six-game upset over the Presidents' Trophy winners that much sweeter. In the past, the North Stars' strategy had been to match the Blackhawks blow for blow. But coach Bob Gainey breaks with tradition by urging his players to turn the other cheek, suspecting the Hawks could be goaded into taking penalties. Gainey's plan works like a charm, and the North Stars get eleven power plays in the first game, scoring on three of them. In Game Five, a 6–0 Minnesota win, the North Stars score five power-play goals on twelve chances, inciting the Chicago Stadium crowd to litter the ice with debris. A frustrated Chris Chelios attacks Brian Bellows at center ice, gouging at his right eye and scratching his cornea.

December 31, 1991: Mark Tinordi crushes Jeremy Roenick with a clean but devastating shoulder hit behind the Minnesota net (Didn't see it? Picture a Hummer slamming into a Toyota Prius). The usual North Star-Blackhawk shenanigans ensue. Final score: Minnesota 6, Chicago 2.

March 19, 1992: The Blackhawks lock up a playoff spot on home ice in a 4–1 win over the North Stars. A relatively uneventful contest becomes eventful with just under nine minutes to play when Mike Craig collides with Jeremy Roenick, drawing the ire of Stephane Matteau, who then challenges Craig to a fight. Roenick squares off with Derian Hatcher and drops the rookie defenseman with a punch that is somehow overlooked since Roenick isn't penalized.

April 13, 1993: The North Stars' last home game before moving to Dallas. It isn't enough that Minnesotans are about to lose their team—they also have to sit through one more loss to the Blackhawks. Final score: Chicago 3, Minnesota 2.

10

A WILD NEW BEGINNING

Gordon Gund was right. Minnesota could live without the North Stars . . . but it couldn't live without the NHL, not after it had a taste of hockey played at its highest level. That's why when the league announced its intentions to grow from twenty-six to thirty teams by the year 2000, it was a given that any application from the Twin Cities region would receive special consideration.

But which of the twins stood a better chance of getting a team? Minneapolis had the advantage of already being a home for major league sports teams and, as Walter Bush recalled from his days with the North Stars, the reputation of showing stronger support for the NHL: "Ticket sales were very disproportionate to Hennepin County [Minneapolis] versus Ramsey County [St. Paul]. We sold many, many more tickets from Hennepin County. It was probably about 80:20 in favor of the Minneapolis side."

On the other hand, St. Paul had Mayor Norm Coleman, who envisioned an NHL franchise as the centerpiece of a revitalized downtown. Having previously failed to woo the Hartford Whalers and the Winnipeg Jets to his city, Coleman rested his hopes on expansion.

In 1996 he was introduced to local businessman Bob Naegele Jr. Naegele was like a lot of Minnesotans: he had played hockey in high school, enjoyed watching the pro game, and hoped it would one day return to the area. Unlike most fans, however, Naegele had the resources to make it happen. He was sitting on a fortune built on the Twin Cities billboard company founded by his father and was a former chairman of Rollerblade. Realizing he'd found a kindred spirit, Coleman convinced Naegele that the political climate was ripe for St. Paul to get an NHL expansion team.

Naegele set out to assemble an investor group and pitch the NHL on the dream of bringing hockey back to Minnesota. He would need to convince the league that the state had an adequate fan base—understandable, given the North Stars' well-documented struggles filling the Met—and that financing for construction of a new arena could be secured. The

NHL, which had already deemed the aging St. Paul Civic Center inadequate, was clear on this point: no arena, no franchise.

Although Governor Arne Carlson was on board with a plan for the state to split the projected $130 million cost of arena construction with St. Paul, the legislature was not. So Coleman, up against a league deadline and not inclined to go door-to-door to debate the merits of using taxpayer dollars to build arenas for privately owned sports teams, made a commitment to the Naegele group and the NHL that St. Paul would back the *entire* $130 million with the hope that the state would eventually vote to split the cost with the city . . . which it did, two years later.

Naegele and his fellow investors put up the full $80 million franchise fee, and the NHL gave its final approval for a St. Paul franchise in June 1997. Within an hour of the announcement, six thousand hockey fans put down one hundred dollars each to reserve season tickets.

The Wild played their first home game before a standing-room-only crowd in the new Xcel Energy Center three years later. Fans were excited that NHL hockey was back . . . and looking forward to proving to the league and all of North America that it should never have left.

Where the Wild organization has really distinguished itself from the rest of the expansion pack is in its commitment to a robust business plan that has helped make the club a perennial attendance leader (the team's consecutive sellout streak of 409 games began in its inaugural season and wasn't broken until September 2010). Naegele and his fellow investors laid the groundwork by building a veteran management team that concentrated its efforts on employing marketing experts and establishing community ties to drum up fan interest throughout the state. They made it a point to target youth, high school, and collegiate hockey organizations and built excitement by tapping into something primal: Minnesotans' pride in the contributions their state has made to hockey in the United States.

"I really feel like we've connected with the heart and soul of the fans here," said Matt Majka, the Wild's chief operating officer. "We had the curse and the blessing of three full years from the time we were granted the franchise until we played our first game. So we had nothing better to do than talk with our fans. We listened and learned, and what they told us was that there was a tradition and a heritage they wanted honored. We were the beneficiaries of that pride. They made it clear to us that they wanted us, as their NHL representatives, to honor the past—from the North Stars to youth hockey to the U.S. Olympic teams."

The Wild settled on the "State of Hockey" branding position, which celebrates the contributions Minnesota has made over the years to the sport. It works because it's a message that rings true with fans. "They believe it and they've lived it," Majka said. "We've tried to be stewards of that tradition, and it's worked out really well for us."

The team has artfully struck a balance between establishing its own identity and honoring the state's NHL past. You see it in the team logo, which blends the rugged Minnesota wilderness with the silhouette of a wild animal. The "eye" of the beast is the North Star—a subtle, tasteful homage to the team whisked off to Texas in 1993.

The Wild had another advantage that few expansion teams do: they followed a team that had already been in that market and failed. There were lessons to be learned, the first of which was to listen to your fans. Lesson No. 2? See Lesson No. 1.

"It's tough to nail down exactly why the North Stars left," Majka said, "and you could debate why they left or even if they should've left. A lot of fans would like to weigh in on that. But what we learned, ultimately, is that fans were really proud of what the North Stars were and they felt cheated that the North Stars left. We felt that we had to honor their passion for the game, for the North Stars, and for all hockey in Minnesota, from the peewees to the pros. And that's what we've tried to do every day."

PASSING THE TORCH

In 2008 Bob Naegele sold his majority stake in the Wild to Craig Leipold, a Wisconsin entrepreneur and former owner of the Nashville Predators. Naegele is still a minority investor.

Recent years have seen a spike in the frequency and visibility of North Stars alumni events. The Wild haven't turned their backs on this phenomenon. They've embraced it.

"We love what the former North Stars players represent and know how much they mean to our fans," said Majka, himself a former North Stars season-ticket holder during his college days at the U of M. "We have a lounge at our arena for the Minnesota NHL Alumni Association, and we give season tickets to that organization for its members to share. We're proud to have a special place for them here where they can congregate and share stories and take in a Wild game. We have a very close relationship with them."

On the ice the Wild have followed the standard trajectory of most expansion teams: endure a few seasons of mediocrity, shock everyone by winning a playoff round or two, then slide back into the herd with the rest of the also-rans. That tedious cycle repeats itself until the club acquires some A-list talent, typically through the draft or free agency.

On July 4, 2012, the Wild took a bold step to break that cycle by opening the vault for the two most prized free agents on the market: left wing Zach Parise and defenseman Ryan Suter.

Parise, who was captain of a New Jersey Devils team that just lost in the Stanley Cup Final, and Suter, a stalwart on the Nashville Predators blue line for seven seasons, were friends from their days in the U.S. hockey program and had talked throughout the year about how great it would be to continue their NHL careers in the same place. At the time only a few teams had the salary cap space to sign both players. That each had ties to Minnesota—Zach was born and raised there, attended Shattuck-St. Mary's, and is son of North Stars great J. P. Parise, while Ryan grew up in neighboring Wisconsin and his wife, Becky, is from Bloomington—gave the Wild an advantage over perennial Stanley Cup contenders like Detroit and Pittsburgh. Each player signed a thirteen-year contract worth $98 million, and just in time, since another owner-imposed lockout would soon make megadeals like theirs a thing of the past.

Having flown beneath the radar for much of its first dozen seasons, the Wild were suddenly on everyone's scopes. When the signings were announced, even Mike Modano tweeted, "Can I come back and play there?"

"The Wild organization is top-notch," said Bloomington's Brian Scott, "from the president all the way down to the janitor. I have grown to really love this team, and I know management will bring us a Stanley Cup one day in my lifetime."

APPENDIX 1: Season Summaries

Summary by season, record, results

1967–1968: 27-32-15, 69 Points (Fourth in West Division)

COACH

Wren Blair

SKATERS

Dave Balon, Andre Boudrias, Bob Charlebois, Bill Collins, Wayne Connelly, Ray Cullen, Sandy Fitzpatrick, Pete Goegan, Bill Goldsworthy, Murray Hall, Duke Harris, Bronco Horvath, Don Johns, Marshall Johnston, Len Lunde, Parker MacDonald, Milan Marcetta, Bill Masterton, Ted McCaskill, Bob McCord, Walt McKechnie, Mike McMahon, Barrie Meissner, Lou Nanne, J. P. Parise, Bill Plager, Andre Pronovost, George Standing, Jean-Guy Talbot, Ted Taylor, Moose Vasko, Bob Woytowich

GOALTENDERS

Garry Bauman, Cesare Maniago, Carl Wetzel

1968 PLAYOFF RESULTS

Quarterfinals

April 4: Minnesota 1 at Los Angeles 2
April 6: Minnesota 0 at Los Angeles 2
April 9: Los Angeles 5 at Minnesota 7
April 11: Los Angeles 2 at Minnesota 3
April 13: Minnesota 2 at Los Angeles 3
April 16: Los Angeles 3 at Minnesota 4 (OT)
April 18: Minnesota 9 at Los Angeles 4

Minnesota wins best-of-seven series, 4-3.

Semifinals

April 21: Minnesota 3 at St. Louis 5
April 22: St. Louis 2 at Minnesota 3 (OT)
April 25: Minnesota 5 at St. Louis 1
April 27: Minnesota 3 at St. Louis 4 (OT)
April 29: Minnesota 2 at St. Louis 3 (OT)
May 1: St. Louis 1 at Minnesota 5
May 3: Minnesota 1 at St. Louis 2 (2OT)

St. Louis wins best-of-seven series, 4-3.

1968–1969: 18-43-15, 51 Points (Sixth in West Division)

COACH

Wren Blair (12-20-9), John Muckler (6-23-6)

SKATERS

Leo Boivin, Andre Boudrias, Mike Chernoff, Bill Collins, Wayne Connelly, Ray Cullen, Gary Dineen, Bill Goldsworthy, Danny Grant, Larry Hillman, Wayne Hillman, Joey Johnston, Marshall Johnston, Claude Larose, Danny Lawson, Parker MacDonald, Barry MacKenzie, Milan Marcetta, Bob McCord, Walt McKechnie, Mike McMahon, Barrie Meissner, Lou Nanne, Bill Orban, Danny O'Shea, J. P. Parise, Tom Reid, Duane Rupp, Brian Smith, Moose Vasko

GOALTENDERS

Garry Bauman, Cesare Maniago, Fern Rivard

1969 PLAYOFF RESULTS

Did not qualify

1969–1970: 19-35-22, 60 Points
(Third in West Division)

COACH

Wren Blair (9-13-10), Charlie Burns (10-22-12)

SKATERS

Bob Barlow, Leo Boivin, Charlie Burns, Bill Collins, Ray Cullen, Grant Erickson, Barry Gibbs, Gilles Gilbert, Bill Goldsworthy, Danny Grant, Marshall Johnston, Claude Larose, Danny Lawson, Walt McKechnie, John Miszuk, Lou Nanne, Bill Orban, Danny O'Shea, J. P. Parise, Tom Polanic, Dick Redmond, Tom Reid, Darryl Sly, Moose Vasko, Bob Whitlock, Tommy Williams

GOALTENDERS

Ken Broderick, Cesare Maniago, Fern Rivard, Gump Worsley

1970 PLAYOFF RESULTS

Quarterfinals
April 8: Minnesota 2 at St. Louis 6
April 9: Minnesota 1 at St. Louis 2
April 11: St. Louis 2 at Minnesota 4
April 12: St. Louis 0 at Minnesota 4
April 14: Minnesota 3 at St. Louis 6
April 16: St. Louis 4 at Minnesota 2

St. Louis wins best-of-seven series, 4-2

1970–1971: 28-34-16, 72 Points
(Fourth in West Division)

COACH

Jack Gordon

SKATERS

Bob Barlow, Fred Barrett, Norm Beaudin, Charlie Burns, Terry Caffery, Jude Drouin, Gary Geldart, Barry Gibbs, Bill Goldsworthy, Danny Grant, Ted Hampson, Ted Harris, Buster Harvey, Bill Heindl, Marshall Johnston, Gord Labossiere, Danny Lawson, Walt McKechnie, Doug Mohns, Wayne Muloin, Lou Nanne, Dennis O'Brien, Murray Oliver, Danny O'Shea, J. P. Parise, Tom Polanic, Dick

62. Barry Gibbs played nearly half of the 1971–72 season recovering from a fractured jaw. The break was wired shut, and he was restricted to a liquid diet for nearly two months. Courtesy of the Dallas Stars

Redmond, Tom Reid, Bobby Rousseau, Dan Seguin, Tommy Williams

GOALTENDERS

Gilles Gilbert, Cesare Maniago, Gump Worsley

1971 PLAYOFF RESULTS

Quarterfinals
April 7: Minnesota 3 at St. Louis 2
April 8: Minnesota 2 at St. Louis 4
April 10: St. Louis 3 at Minnesota 0
April 11: St. Louis 1 at Minnesota 2
April 13: Minnesota 4 at St. Louis 3
April 15: St. Louis 2 at Minnesota 5

Minnesota wins best-of-seven series, 4-2.

Semifinals

April 20: Minnesota 2 at Montreal 7
April 22: Minnesota 6 at Montreal 3
April 24: Montreal 6 at Minnesota 3
April 25: Montreal 2 at Minnesota 5

April 27: Minnesota 1 at Montreal 6
April 29: Montreal 3 at Minnesota 2
Montreal wins best-of-seven series, 4-3.

1971–1972: 37-29-12, 86 Points
(Second in West Division)

COACH

Jack Gordon

SKATERS

Charlie Burns, Craig Cameron, Jude Drouin, Gary Gambucci, Barry Gibbs, Bill Goldsworthy, Danny Grant, Ted Hampson, Ted Harris, Bill Heindl, Dennis Hextall, Gord Labossiere, Doug Mohns, Lou Nanne, Bob Nevin, Dennis O'Brien, Murray Oliver, Bob Paradise, J. P. Parise, Dean Prentice, Tom Reid

GOALTENDERS

Gilles Gilbert, Cesare Maniago, Gump Worsley

1972 PLAYOFF RESULTS

Quarterfinals
April 5: St. Louis 0 at Minnesota 3
April 6: St. Louis 5 at Minnesota 6 (OT)
April 8: Minnesota 1 at St. Louis 2
April 9: Minnesota 2 at St. Louis 3
April 11: St. Louis 3 at Minnesota 4
April 13: Minnesota 2 at St. Louis 4
April 16: St. Louis 2 at Minnesota 1 (OT)

St. Louis wins best-of-seven series, 4-3

1972–1973: 37-30-11, 85 Points
(Third in West Division)

COACH

Jack Gordon

SKATERS

Fred Barrett, Don Blackburn, Charlie Burns, Jerry Byers, Jude Drouin, Barry Gibbs, Bill Goldsworthy, Danny Grant, Ted Harris, Buster Harvey, Dennis Hextall, Terry Holbrook, Jim McElmury, Bruce McIntosh, Doug Mohns, Lou Nanne, Bob Nevin, Dennis O'Brien, Murray Oliver, J. P. Parise, Dean Prentice, Tom Reid

GOALTENDERS

Gilles Gilbert, Cesare Maniago, Gump Worsley

1973 PLAYOFF RESULTS

Quarterfinals
April 4: Minnesota 3 at Philadelphia 0
April 5: Minnesota 1 at Philadelphia 4
April 7: Philadelphia 0 at Minnesota 5
April 8: Philadelphia 3 at Minnesota 0
April 10: Minnesota 2 at Philadelphia 3 (OT)
April 12: Philadelphia 4 at Minnesota 1

Philadelphia wins best-of-seven series, 4-2

1973–1974: 23-38-17, 63 Points
(Seventh in West Division)

COACH

Jack Gordon (3-8-6), Parker MacDonald (20-30-11)

SKATERS

Chris Ahrens, Fred Barrett, Gary Bergman, Jerry Byers, Rick Chinnick, Jude Drouin, Blake Dunlop, Tony Featherstone, Gary Gambucci, Barry Gibbs, Bill Goldsworthy, Danny Grant, Ted Harris, Buster Harvey, Dennis Hextall, Terry Holbrook, Alain Langlais, Lou Nanne, Rod Norrish, Dennis O'Brien, Murray Oliver, J.P. Parise, Bill Plager, Dean Prentice, Tom Reid, John Rogers, Fred Stanfield

GOALTENDERS

Cesare Maniago, Fern Rivard, Gump Worsley

1974 PLAYOFF RESULTS
Did not qualify

1974–1975: 23-50-7, 53 Points
(Fourth in Smythe Division)

COACH

Jack Gordon (11-22-5), Charlie Burns (12-28-2)

SKATERS

Chris Ahrens, Fred Barrett, Dwight Bialowas, Henry Boucha, Craig Cameron, Rick Chinnick, Tom Colley, Bob Cook, Dave Cressman, Jude

Drouin, Blake Dunlop, John Flesch, Barry
Gibbs, Bill Goldsworthy, Norm Gratton,
Dennis Hextall, Ernie Hicke, Doug Hicks,
Alain Langlais, Kim MacDougall, Don
Martineau, Lou Nanne, Rich Nantais, Rod
Norrish, Dennis O'Brien, Murray Oliver, J. P.
Parise, Bill Plager, Tom Reid, John Rogers,
Doug Rombough, Fred Stanfield, Dean
Talafous

GOALTENDERS

Pete LoPresti, Cesare Maniago, Fern Rivard

1975 PLAYOFF RESULTS

Did not qualify

1975–1976: 20-53-7, 47 Points
(Fourth in Smythe Division)

COACH

Ted Harris

SKATERS

Chris Ahrens, Mike Antonovich, Fred Barrett,
Dwight Bialowas, Craig Cameron, Dave
Cressman, Blake Dunlop, Jerry Engele, John
Flesch, Bill Goldsworthy, Norm Gratton,
Bryan Hextall, Dennis Hextall, Ernie Hicke,
Doug Hicks, Bill Hogaboam, Pierre Jarry,
Steve Jensen, Lou Nanne, Rich Nantais,
Dennis O'Brien, Bill Plager, Tom Reid, Doug
Rombough, Glen Sather, Dean Talafous, Tim
Young

GOALTENDERS

Paul Harrison, Pete LoPresti, Cesare Maniago

1976 PLAYOFF RESULTS

Did not qualify

1976–1977: 23-39-18, 64 Points
(Second in Smythe Division)

COACH

Ted Harris

SKATERS

Chris Ahrens, Fred Barrett, Nick Beverley,
Dwight Bialowas, Blake Dunlop, Jerry

63. Fred Barrett, four times voted the North Stars' top
defenseman. Courtesy of the Dallas Stars

Engele, Roland Eriksson, Bill Fairbairn, Bill
Goldsworthy, Ernie Hicke, Doug Hicks, Bill
Hogaboam, Pierre Jarry, Steve Jensen, Lou
Nanne, Rich Nantais, Dennis O'Brien, Alex
Pirus, Tom Reid, Jim Roberts, Glen Sharpley,
Dean Talafous, Tim Young, Tom Younghans

GOALTENDERS

Paul Harrison, Pete LoPresti, Gary Smith

1977 PLAYOFF RESULTS

Preliminary Round
April 5: Minnesota 2 at Buffalo 4
April 7: Buffalo 7 at Minnesota 1

Buffalo wins best-of-three series, 2-0.

1977–1978: 18-53-9, 45 Points
(Fifth in Smythe Division)

COACH

Ted Harris (5-12-2), Andre Beaulieu (6-23-3), Lou Nanne (7-18-4)

SKATERS

Chris Ahrens, Kent-Erik Andersson, Fred Barrett, Harvey Bennett, Nick Beverley, Jim Boo, Per-Olov Brasar, Bill Butters, Jerry Engele, Roland Eriksson, Bill Fairbairn, Jamie Gallimore, Doug Hicks, Bill Hogaboam, Don Jackson, Pierre Jarry, Steve Jensen, Dean Magee, Brad Maxwell, Bryan Maxwell, Lou Nanne, Dennis O'Brien, Alex Pirus, Tom Reid, Jim Roberts, Glen Sharpley, Dean Talafous, Tim Young, Tom Younghans, Ron Zanussi

GOALTENDERS

Paul Harrison, Pete LoPresti, Gary Smith

1978 PLAYOFF RESULTS

Did not qualify

1978–1979: 28-40-12, 68 Points
(Fourth in Adams Division)

COACH

Harry Howell (3-6-2), Glen Sonmor (25-34-10)

SKATERS

Kent-Erik Andersson, Chuck Arnason, John Baby, Fred Barrett, Per-Olov Brasar, Bill Butters, Jack Carlson, Dan Chicoine, Mike Eaves, Mike Fidler, Bill Hogaboam, Don Jackson, Al MacAdam, Kris Manery, Dennis Maruk, Brad Maxwell, Bryan Maxwell, Jim McKenny, J. P. Parise, Steve Payne, Alex Pirus, Mike Polich, Jean Potvin, Jim Roberts, Gary Sargent, Glen Sharpley, Bobby Smith, Greg Smith, Tim Young, Tom Younghans, Ron Zanussi

GOALTENDERS

Gary Edwards, Pete LoPresti, Gilles Meloche

1979 PLAYOFF RESULTS

Did not qualify

1979–1980: 36-28-16, 88 Points
(Third in Adams Division)

COACH

Glen Sonmor

SKATERS

Kent-Erik Andersson, Fred Barrett, Per-Olov Brasar, Dan Chicoine, Steve Christoff, Jim Dobson, Mike Eaves, Mike Fidler, Rob Flockhart, Jon Fontas, Curt Giles, Dave Hanson, Craig Hartsburg, Don Jackson, Robbie Laird, Al MacAdam, Kris Manery, Brad Maxwell, Tom McCarthy, Steve Payne, Mike Polich, Gary Sargent, Glen Sharpley, Paul Shmyr, Bobby Smith, Greg Smith, Tony White, Tim Young, Tom Younghans, Ron Zanussi

GOALTENDERS

Gary Edwards, Steve Janaszak, Jean-Louis Levasseur, Gilles Meloche

1980 PLAYOFF RESULTS

Preliminary Round
April 8: Toronto 3 at Minnesota 6
April 9: Toronto 2 at Minnesota 7
April 11: Minnesota 4 at Toronto 3 (OT)

Minnesota wins best-of-five series, 3-0

Quarterfinals
April 16: Minnesota 3 at Montreal 0
April 17: Minnesota 4 at Montreal 1
April 19: Montreal 5 at Minnesota 0
April 20: Montreal 5 at Minnesota 1
April 22: Minnesota 2 at Montreal 6
April 24: Montreal 2 at Minnesota 5
April 27: Minnesota 3 at Montreal 2

Minnesota wins best-of-seven series, 4-3

Semifinals
April 29: Minnesota 6 at Philadelphia 5
May 1: Minnesota 0 at Philadelphia 7
May 4: Philadelphia 5 at Minnesota 3
May 6: Philadelphia 3 at Minnesota 2
May 8: Minnesota 3 at Philadelphia 7

Philadelphia wins best-of-seven series, 4-1

64. Craig Hartsburg. Courtesy of the Dallas Stars

1980–1981: 35-28-17, 87 Points
(Third in Adams Division)

COACH

Glen Sonmor

SKATERS

Kent-Erik Andersson, Fred Barrett, Neal Broten, Murray Brumwell, Jack Carlson, Steve Christoff, Dino Ciccarelli, Joe Contini, Jim Dobson, Mike Eaves, Mike Fidler, Rob Flockhart, Jon Fontas, Ron Friest, Curt Giles, Craig Hartsburg, Don Jackson, Al MacAdam, Brad Maxwell, Kevin Maxwell, Tom McCarthy, Roger Melin, Brad Palmer, Steve Payne, Mike Polich, Gordie Roberts, Gary Sargent, Glen Sharpley, Paul Shmyr, Bobby Smith, Greg Smith, Ken Solheim, Tim Young, Tom Younghans, Ron Zanussi

GOALTENDERS

Don Beaupre, Gilles Meloche

1981 PLAYOFF RESULTS

Preliminary Round
April 8: Minnesota 5 at Boston 4 (OT)
April 9: Minnesota 9 at Boston 6
April 11: Boston 3 at Minnesota 6

Minnesota wins best-of-five series, 3-0.

Quarterfinals
April 16: Minnesota 4 at Buffalo 3 (OT)
April 17: Minnesota 5 at Buffalo 2
April 19: Buffalo 4 at Minnesota 6
April 20: Buffalo 5 at Minnesota 4 (OT)
April 22: Minnesota 4 at Buffalo 3

Minnesota wins best-of-seven series, 4-1.

Semifinals
April 28: Minnesota 4 at Calgary 1
April 30: Minnesota 2 at Calgary 3
May 3: Calgary 4 at Minnesota 6
May 5: Calgary 4 at Minnesota 7
May 7: Minnesota 1 at Calgary 3
May 9: Calgary 3 at Minnesota 5

Minnesota wins best-of-seven series, 4-2.

Stanley Cup Finals
May 12: Minnesota 3 at NY Islanders 6
May 14: Minnesota 3 at NY Islanders 6
May 17: NY Islanders 7 at Minnesota 5
May 19: NY Islanders 2 at Minnesota 4
May 21: Minnesota 1 at NY Islanders 5

NY Islanders win best-of-seven series, 4-1.

1981–1982: 37-23-20, 94 Points
(First in Norris Division)

COACH

Glen Sonmor

SKATERS

Kent-Erik Andersson, Mike Antonovich, Fred Barrett, Neal Broten, Murray Brumwell, Jack Carlson, Steve Christoff, Dino Ciccarelli, Jim Dobson, Mike Eaves, Ron Friest, Curt Giles, Anders Hakansson, Craig Hartsburg, Peter Hayek, Archie Henderson, Mark Johnson, Udo Kiessling, Al MacAdam, Brad Maxwell, Kevin Maxwell, Tom McCarthy, Ron Meighan, Roger Melin, Bill Nyrop, Brad Palmer, Daniel Poulin, Dave Richter, Gordie Roberts, Gary Sargent, Bobby Smith, Ken Solheim, Tim Young, Warren Young, Tom Younghans

GOALTENDERS

Don Beaupre, Gilles Meloche, Lindsay Middlebrook

1982 PLAYOFF RESULTS

Division Semifinals
April 7: Chicago 3 at Minnesota 2 (OT)
April 8: Chicago 5 at Minnesota 3
April 10: Minnesota 7 at Chicago 1
April 11: Minnesota 2 at Chicago 5

Chicago wins best-of-five series, 3-1

1982–1983: 40-24-16, 96 Points
(Second in Norris Division)

COACHES

Glen Sonmor (22-12-9), Murray Oliver (18-12-7)

SKATERS

Fred Barrett, Brian Bellows, Bob Bergloff, Neal Broten, Dino Ciccarelli, Jordy Douglas, Mike Eaves, George Ferguson, Ron Friest, Curt Giles, Anders Hakansson, Craig Hartsburg, Wes Jarvis, Al MacAdam, Dan Mandich, Brad Maxwell, Tom McCarthy, Steve Payne, Willi Plett, Dave Richter, Gordie Roberts, Gary Sargent, Bobby Smith, Ken Solheim, Randy Velischek, Tim Young, Warren Young

GOALTENDERS

Don Beaupre, Markus Mattsson, Gilles Meloche

1983 PLAYOFF RESULTS

Division Semifinals
April 6: Toronto 4 at Minnesota 5
April 7: Toronto 4 at Minnesota 5 (OT)
April 9: Minnesota 3 at Toronto 6
April 10: Minnesota 5 at Toronto 4 (OT)

Minnesota wins best-of-five series, 3-1.

Division Finals

April 14: Minnesota 2 at Chicago 5
April 15: Minnesota 4 at Chicago 7
April 17: Chicago 1 at Minnesota 5
April 18: Chicago 4 at Minnesota 3 (OT)
April 20: Minnesota 2 at Chicago 5

Chicago wins best-of-seven series, 4-1.

1983–1984: 39-31-10, 88 Points (First in Norris Division)

COACH

Bill Mahoney

SKATERS

Keith Acton, Brent Ashton, Brian Bellows, Scott Bjugstad, Neal Broten, Dino Ciccarelli, Tim Coulis, Jordy Douglas, George Ferguson, Curt Giles, Dirk Graham, Craig Hartsburg, Tom Hirsch, Paul Holmgren, David Jensen, Brian Lawton, Craig Levie, Lars Lindgren, Al MacAdam, Dan Mandich, Dennis Maruk, Brad Maxwell, Tom McCarthy, Mark Napier,

Steve Payne, Willi Plett, Dave Richter, Gordie Roberts, Bob Rouse, Bobby Smith, Randy Velischek

GOALTENDERS

Don Beaupre, Jon Casey, Jim Craig, Gilles Meloche

1984 PLAYOFF RESULTS

Division Semifinals
April 4: Chicago 3 at Minnesota 1
April 5: Chicago 5 at Minnesota 6
April 7: Minnesota 4 at Chicago 1
April 8: Minnesota 3 at Chicago 4
April 10: Chicago 1 at Minnesota 4

Minnesota wins best-of-five series, 3-2.

Division Finals

April 12: St. Louis 1 at Minnesota 2
April 13: St. Louis 4 at Minnesota 3 (OT)
April 15: Minnesota 1 at St. Louis 3
April 16: Minnesota 3 at St. Louis 2
April 18: St. Louis 0 at Minnesota 6
April 20: Minnesota 0 at St. Louis 4
April 22: St. Louis 3 at Minnesota 4 (OT)

Minnesota wins best-of-seven series, 4-3.

Conference Finals

April 24: Minnesota 1 at Edmonton 7
April 26: Minnesota 3 at Edmonton 4
April 28: Edmonton 8 at Minnesota 5
May 1: Edmonton 3 at Minnesota 1

Edmonton wins best-of-seven series, 4-0.

1984–1985: 25-43-12, 62 Points (Fourth in Norris Division)

COACH

Bill Mahoney (3-8-2), Glen Sonmor (22-35-10)

SKATERS

Keith Acton, Brent Ashton, Brian Bellows, Bo Berglund, Don Biggs, Scott Bjugstad, Neal Broten, Dino Ciccarelli, Tim Coulis, Curt Giles, Dirk Graham, Craig Hartsburg, Tom Hirsch, Paul Holmgren, David Jensen, Brian

Lawton, Dan Mandich, John Markell, Terry Martin, Dennis Maruk, Brad Maxwell, Tom McCarthy, Tony McKegney, Mark Napier, Steve Payne, Willi Plett, Chris Pryor, Dave Richter, Gordie Roberts, Bob Rouse, Gord Sherven, Harold Snepsts, Ken Solheim, Tim Trimper, Randy Velischek, Ron Wilson

GOALTENDERS

Don Beaupre, Roland Melanson, Gilles Meloche, Mike Sands

1985 PLAYOFF RESULTS

Division Semifinals
April 10: Minnesota 3 at St. Louis 2
April 11: Minnesota 4 at St. Louis 3
April 13: St. Louis 0 at Minnesota 2

Minnesota wins best-of-five series, 3-0

Division Finals

April 18: Minnesota 8 at Chicago 5
April 21: Minnesota 2 at Chicago 6
April 23: Chicago 5 at Minnesota 3
April 25: Chicago 7 at Minnesota 6 (2OT)
April 28: Minnesota 5 at Chicago 4 (OT)
April 30: Chicago 6 at Minnesota 5 (OT)

Chicago wins best-of-seven series, 4-2

1985–1986: 38-33-9, 85 Points (Second in Norris Division)

COACH

Lorne Henning

SKATERS

Keith Acton, Jim Archibald, Brian Bellows, Bo Berglund, Scott Bjugstad, Neal Broten, Dino Ciccarelli, Tim Coulis, Larry DePalma, Curt Giles, Dirk Graham, Marc Habscheid, Mats Hallin, Craig Hartsburg, Ed Hospodar, Paul Houck, David Jensen, Dave Langevin, Brian Lawton, Craig Levie, Dan Mandich, Dennis Maruk, Tom McCarthy, Tony McKegney, Kent Nilsson, Steve Payne, Willi Plett, Chris Pryor, Dave Richter, Gordie Roberts, Bob Rouse, Gord Sherven, Randy Smith, Bill Stewart, Emanuel Viveiros, Ron Wilson

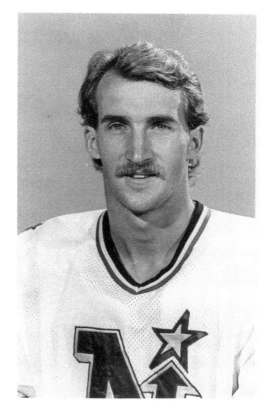

65. Steve Payne. Courtesy of the Dallas Stars

GOALTENDERS

Don Beaupre, Jon Casey, Roland Melanson, Kari Takko

1986 PLAYOFF RESULTS

Division Semifinals
April 9: St. Louis 2 at Minnesota 1
April 10: St. Louis 2 at Minnesota 6
April 12: Minnesota 3 at St. Louis 4
April 13: Minnesota 7 at St. Louis 4
April 15: St. Louis 6 at Minnesota 3

St. Louis wins best-of-five series, 3-2

1986–1987: 30-40-10, 70 Points (Fifth in Norris Division)

COACH

Lorne Henning (30-39-9), Glen Sonmor (0-1-1)

SKATERS

Keith Acton, Jim Archibald, Brian Bellows, Scott Bjugstad, Paul Boutilier, Bob Brooke, Neal Broten, Jack Carlson, Colin Chisholm, Dino Ciccarelli, Larry DePalma, Curt Giles, Dirk Graham, Jari Gronstrand, Marc Habscheid, Mats Hallin, Craig Hartsburg, Raimo Helminen, Paul Houck, Brian Lawton, Brian MacLellan, Dennis Maruk, Brad Maxwell, Tony McKegney, Frantisek Musil, Kent Nilsson, Mark Pavelich, Steve Payne, Willi Plett, Chris Pryor, Gordie Roberts, Bob Rouse, Randy Smith, Sean Toomey, Emanuel Viveiros, Ron Wilson

GOALTENDERS

Don Beaupre, Mike Sands, Kari Takko

1987 PLAYOFF RESULTS

Did not qualify

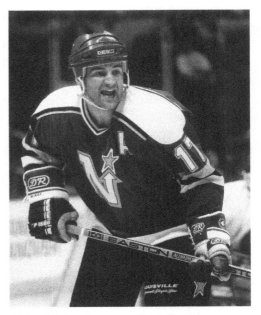

66. Basil McRae. Courtesy of the Dallas Stars

1987–1988: 19-48-13, 51 Points (Fifth in Norris Division)

COACH

Herb Brooks

SKATERS

Keith Acton, Dave Archibald, Warren Babe, Brian Bellows, Mike Berger, Scott Bjugstad, Rick Boh, Bob Brooke, Neal Broten, Jay Caufield, Shawn Chambers, Dino Ciccarelli, Larry DePalma, Gord Dineen, Ken Duggan, Curt Fraser, Dave Gagner, Curt Giles, Dirk Graham, Marc Habscheid, Craig Hartsburg, Tom Hirsch, Paul Houck, Brian Lawton, Brian MacLellan, Moe Mantha, Dennis Maruk, Basil McRae, Mitch Messier, Pat Micheletti, Frantisek Musil, Steve Payne, Pat Price, Chris Pryor, Gordie Roberts, Bob Rouse, Stephane Roy, Terry Ruskowski, Wally Schreiber, George Servinis, Bill Terry, Kirk Tomlinson, Allan Tuer, Emanuel Viveiros, Ron Wilson, Richard Zemlak

GOALTENDERS

Don Beaupre, Jon Casey, Kari Takko

1988 PLAYOFF RESULTS

Did not qualify

1988–1989: 27-37-16, 70 Points (Third in Norris Division)

COACH

Pierre Page

SKATERS

Dave Archibald, Warren Babe, Don Barber, Brian Bellows, Perry Berezan, Mike Berger, Bob Brooke, Neal Broten, Shawn Chambers, Shane Churla, Dino Ciccarelli, Larry DePalma, Gord Dineen, Curt Fraser, Link Gaetz, Dave Gagner, Mike Gartner, Stew Gavin, Curt Giles, Steve Gotaas, Marc Habscheid, Mark Hardy, Craig Hartsburg, Ken Hodge, Paul Jerrard, Kevin Kaminski, Dean Kolstad, Reed Larson, Brian MacLellan, Moe Mantha, Tom Martin, Dennis Maruk, Mike McHugh, Basil McRae, Mitch Messier, Larry Murphy, Frantisek Musil, Dusan Pasek, Bob Rouse, Terry Ruskowski, Wally Schreiber, Ville Siren, Mark Tinordi, Richard Zemlak, Rob Zettler

GOALTENDERS

Don Beaupre, Jon Casey, Jarmo Myllys, Kari Takko

1989 PLAYOFF RESULTS

Division Semifinals
April 5: Minnesota 3 at St. Louis 4 (OT)
April 6: Minnesota 3 at St. Louis 4 (OT)
April 8: St. Louis 5 at Minnesota 3
April 9: St. Louis 4 at Minnesota 5
April 11: Minnesota 1 at St. Louis 6

St. Louis wins best-of-seven series, 4-1.

1989–1990: 36-40-4, 76 Points (Fourth in Norris Division)

COACH

Pierre Page

SKATERS

Dave Archibald, Helmut Balderis, Don Barber, Brian Bellows, Perry Berezan, Bob Brooke, Aaron Broten, Neal Broten, Shawn Chambers, Shane Churla, Ulf Dahlen, Clark Donatelli, Gaetan Duchesne, Curt Fraser, Link Gaetz, Dave Gagner, Mike Gartner, Stew Gavin, Curt Giles, Peter Lappin, Ken Leiter, David Mackey, Mike McHugh, Basil McRae, Mitch Messier, Mike Modano, Jay More, Larry Murphy, Frantisek Musil, Scott Robinson, Ville Siren, Mario Thyer, Mark Tinordi, Neil Wilkinson, Rob Zettler

GOALTENDERS

Daniel Berthiaume, Jon Casey, Jarmo Myllys, Kari Takko

1990 PLAYOFF RESULTS

Division Semifinals
April 4: Minnesota 2 at Chicago 1
April 6: Minnesota 3 at Chicago 5
April 8: Chicago 2 at Minnesota 1
April 10: Chicago 0 at Minnesota 4
April 12: Minnesota 1 at Chicago 5
April 14: Chicago 3 at Minnesota 5
April 16: Minnesota 2 at Chicago 5

Chicago wins best-of-seven series, 4-3

67. Dave Gagner. Courtesy of the Dallas Stars

1990–1991: 27-39-14, 68 Points (Fourth in Norris Division)

COACH

Bob Gainey

SKATERS

Warren Babe, Don Barber, Brian Bellows, Perry Berezan, Neal Broten, Shawn Chambers, Shane Churla, Mike Craig, Ulf Dahlquist, Larry DePalma, Gaetan Duchesne, Kevin Evans, Dave Gagner, Stew Gavin, Curt Giles, Brian Glynn, Steve Gotaas, Jim Johnson, Dan Keczmer, Dean Kolstad, Pat MacLeod, Mike McHugh, Basil McRae, Mitch Messier, Mike Modano, Larry Murphy, Frantisek Musil, Brian Propp, Ilkka Sinisalo, Doug Smail, Bobby Smith, Peter Taglianetti, Mark Tinordi, Neil Wilkinson, Rob Zettler

GOALTENDERS

Jon Casey, Brian Hayward, Jarmo Myllys, Kari Takko

1991 PLAYOFF RESULTS

Division Semifinals
April 4: Minnesota 4 at Chicago 3 (OT)
April 6: Minnesota 2 at Chicago 5
April 8: Chicago 6 at Minnesota 5
April 10: Chicago 1 at Minnesota 3
April 12: Minnesota 6 at Chicago 0
April 14: Chicago 1 at Minnesota 3

Minnesota wins best-of-seven series, 4-2.

Division Finals

April 18: Minnesota 2 at St. Louis 1
April 20: Minnesota 2 at St. Louis 5
April 22: St. Louis 1 at Minnesota 5
April 24: St. Louis 4 at Minnesota 8
April 26: Minnesota 2 at St. Louis 4
April 28: St. Louis 2 at Minnesota 3

Minnesota wins best-of-seven series, 4-2.

Conference Finals

May 2: Minnesota 3 at Edmonton 1
May 4: Minnesota 2 at Edmonton 7
May 6: Edmonton 3 at Minnesota 7
May 8: Edmonton 1 at Minnesota 5
May 10: Minnesota 3 at Edmonton 2

Minnesota wins best-of-seven series, 4-1.

Stanley Cup Finals

May 15: Minnesota 5 at Pittsburgh 4
May 17: Minnesota 1 at Pittsburgh 4
May 19: Pittsburgh 1 at Minnesota 3
May 21: Pittsburgh 5 at Minnesota 3
May 23: Minnesota 4 at Pittsburgh 6
May 25: Pittsburgh 8 at Minnesota 0

Pittsburgh wins best-of-seven series, 4-2.

1991–1992: 32-42-6, 70 Points
(Fourth in Norris Division)

COACH
Bob Gainey

SKATERS
Brian Bellows, Brad Berry, Neal Broten, Marc Bureau, Shane Churla, Enrico Ciccone, Mike Craig, Ulf Dahlen, Chris Dahlquist, Gaetan Duchesne, Todd Elik, Dave Gagner, Stew Gavin, Brian Glynn, Derian Hatcher, Mark Janssens, Jim Johnson, Trent Klatt, Craig Ludwig, Steve Maltais, Steve Martinson, Basil McRae, Kip Miller, Mike Modano, Allan Pedersen, Brian Propp, Rob Ramage, Scott Sandelin, David Shaw, Bobby Smith, Derrick Smith, Mark Tinordi

GOALTENDERS
Jon Casey, Darcy Wakaluk

1991 PLAYOFF RESULTS

Division Semifinals
April 18: Minnesota 4 at Detroit 3
April 20: Minnesota 4 at Detroit 2
April 22: Detroit 5 at Minnesota 4 (OT)
April 24: Detroit 4 at Minnesota 5
April 26: Minnesota 0 at Detroit 3
April 28: Detroit 1 at Minnesota 0 (OT)
April 30: Minnesota 2 at Detroit 5

Detroit wins best-of-seven series, 4-3.

1992–1993: 36-38-10, 82 Points
(Fifth in Norris Division)

COACH
Bob Gainey

SKATERS
Doug Barrault, Brad Berry, James Black, Neal Broten, Shane Churla, Enrico Ciccone, Russ Courtnall, Mike Craig, Ulf Dahlen, Gaetan Duchesne, Todd Elik, Dave Gagner, Stew Gavin, Brent Gilchrist, Derian Hatcher, Jim Johnson, Trent Klatt, Craig Ludwig, Richard Matvichuk, Mike McPhee, Roy Mitchell, Mike Modano, Mark Osiecki, Brian Propp, Dan Quinn, Reid Simpson, Tommy Sjodin, Bobby Smith, Derrick Smith, Mark Tinordi

GOALTENDERS
Jon Casey, Darcy Wakaluk

1993 PLAYOFF RESULTS

Did not qualify

APPENDIX 2: All-Time Draft Picks

1992 NHL ENTRY DRAFT

The Forum, Montreal, Quebec (June 20)

NUMBER	ROUND	PLAYER	POSITION	FROM
34	2	Jarkko Varvio	RW	HPK Hameenlinna (Finland)
58	3	Jeff Bes	C	Guelph Storm (OHL)
88	4	Jere Lehtinen	RW	Kiekko-Espoo (Finland)
130	6	Mike Johnson	D	Ottawa 67's (OHL)
154	7	Kyle Peterson	LW	Thunder Bay Flyers (USHL)
178	8	Juha Lind	LW	Jokerit Helsinki (Finland)
202	9	Lars Edstrom	LW	Lulea HF (Sweden)
226	10	Jeff Romfo	RW	Blaine High School (Minnesota)
250	11	Jeff Moen	G	Roseville High School (Minnesota)

1991 NHL ENTRY DRAFT

Memorial Auditorium, Buffalo, New York (June 22)

NUMBER	ROUND	PLAYER	POSITION	FROM
8	1	Richard Matvichuk	D	Saskatoon Blades (WHL)
74	4	Mike Torchia	G	Kitchener Rangers (OHL)
97	5	Mike Kennedy	C	University of British Columbia
118	6	Mark Lawrence	RW	Detroit Compuware (OHL)
137	7	Geoff Finch	G	Brown University
174	8	Michael Burkett	LW	Michigan State University
184	9	Derek Herlofsky	G	St. Paul Vulcans (United States Hockey League)
206	10	Tom Nemeth	D	Cornwall Royals (OHL)
228	11	Shayne Green	C	Kamloops Blazers (WHL)
250	12	Jukka Suomalainen	D	Gr IFK (Finland)

1990 NHL ENTRY DRAFT

BC Place Stadium, Vancouver, British Columbia (June 16)

NUMBER	ROUND	PLAYER	POSITION	FROM
8	1	Derian Hatcher	D	North Bay Centennials (OHL)
50	3	Laurie Billeck	D	Prince Albert Raiders (WHL)
70	4	Cal McGowan	C	Kamloops Blazers (WHL)

71	4	Frank Kovacs	LW	Regina Pats (WHL)
92	5	Enrico Ciccone	D	Trois Rivieres (QMJHL)
113	6	Roman Turek	G	Plzen HC (Czech.)
134	7	Jeff Levy	G	Rochester Mustangs (USHL)
155	8	Doug Barrault	RW	Lethbridge Hurricanes (WHL)
176	9	Joe Biondi	C	University of Minnesota–Duluth
197	10	Troy Binnie	LW	Ottawa 67's (OHL)
218	11	Ole Dahlstrom	C	Furuset (Norway)
239	12	J. P. McKersie	G	Madison West High School (Wisconsin)

1989 NHL ENTRY DRAFT

Met Center, Bloomington, Minnesota (June 17)

NUMBER	ROUND	PLAYER	POSITION	FROM
7	1	Doug Zmolek	D	Rochester Marshall High School (Minnesota)
28	2	Mike Craig	RW	Oshawa Generals (OHL)
60	3	Murray Garbutt	C	Medicine Hat Tigers (WHL)
75	4	J. F. Quintin	LW	Shawinigan (QMJHL)
87	5	Pat MacLeod	D	Kamloops Blazers (WHL)
91	5	Bryan Schoen	G	Minnetonka High School (Minnesota)
97	5	Rhys Hollyman	D	Miami University (Ohio)
112	6	Scott Cashman	G	Kanata (Central Ontario Junior Hockey League)
154	8	Jon Pratt	LW	Pingree High School (Massachusetts)
175	9	Ken Blum	LW	St. Joseph's Prep (New Jersey)
196	10	Arturs Irbe	G	Dynamo Riga (Latvia)
217	11	Tom Pederson	D	University of Minnesota
238	12	Helmut Balderis	RW	Dynamo Riga (Latvia)

1988 NHL ENTRY DRAFT

The Forum, Montreal, Quebec (June 11)

NUMBER	ROUND	PLAYER	POSITION	FROM
1	1	Mike Modano	C	Prince Albert Raiders (WHL)
40	2	Link Gaetz	D	Spokane Chiefs (WHL)
43	3	Shaun Kane	D	Springfield Jr. B
64	4	Jeff Stolp	G	Greenway High School (Minnesota)
148	8	Ken MacArthur	D	University of Denver
169	9	Travis Richards	D	Armstrong High School (Minnesota)
190	10	Ari Matilainen	LW	Assat Pori (Finland)
211	11	Grant Bischoff	LW	University of Minnesota
232	12	Trent Andison	LW	Cornell University

NO SLAM-DUNK PICK

Life can take you on some circuitous paths. Just ask John Weisbrod, the North Stars' fourth-round pick in 1987. A center, Weisbrod suffered a shoulder injury in his senior year at Harvard that eventually forced him to quit hockey. He stayed in the game as a front-office executive in the minor leagues, first with the AHL's Albany River Rats and then with the IHL's Orlando Solar Bears.

When the IHL folded, the owner of the Solar Bears promoted Weisbrod to an administrative position with the NBA's Orlando Magic. He was soon promoted to general manager, a job for which he was ill-suited. Magic fans still haven't forgiven Weisbrod for engineering the 2004 trade of superstar Tracy McGrady to the Houston Rockets.

When he left the Magic to get back into hockey, Weisbrod confessed, "It's not in the best interest of the organization to have a GM that, in his heart, would trade three NBA championships for one Stanley Cup."

1987 NHL ENTRY DRAFT

Joe Louis Arena, Detroit, Michigan (June 13)

NUMBER	ROUND	PLAYER	POSITION	FROM
6	1	Dave Archibald	RW	Portland Winter Hawks (WHL)
35	2	Scott McCrady	D	Medicine Hat Tigers (WHL)
48	3	Kevin Kaminski	C	Saskatoon Blades (WHL)
73	4	John Weisbrod	C	Choate (Connecticut)
88	5	Teppo Kivela	C	HPK Hameenlinna (Finland)
109	6	Darcy Norton	LW	Kamloops Blazers (WHL)
130	7	Timo Kulonen	D	KalPa Kuopio (Finland)
151	8	Don Schmidt	D	Kamloops Blazers (WHL)
172	9	Jarmo Myllys	G	Lukko Rauma (Finland)
193	10	Larry Olimb	C	Warroad High School (Minnesota)
214	11	Marc Felicio	G	Northwood Prep (New York)
235	12	Dave Shields	C	University of Denver

1986 NHL ENTRY DRAFT

The Forum, Montreal, Quebec (June 21)

NUMBER	ROUND	PLAYER	POSITION	FROM
12	1	Warren Babe	LW	Lethbridge Broncos (WHL)
30	2	Neil Wilkinson	D	Selkirk Steelers (Manitoba Junior Hockey League)
33	2	Dean Kolstad	D	Prince Albert Raiders (WHL)
54	3	Rick Bennett	LW	Wilbraham & Monson (Massachusetts)
55	3	Rob Zettler	D	Sault Ste. Marie (OHL)
58	3	Brad Turner	D	Calgary Canucks (Albert Junior Hockey League)
75	4	Kirk Tomlinson	LW	Hamilton Steelhawks (OHL)

96	5	Jari Gronstrand	D	Tappara Tampere (Finland)
159	8	Scott Mathias	C	University of Denver
180	9	Lance Pitlick	D	Cooper High School (Minnesota)
201	10	Dan Keczmer	D	Detroit Little Caesars
222	11	Garth Joy	D	Hamilton Steelhawks (OHL)
243	12	Kurt Stahura	LW	Williston Academy (Massachusetts)

1985 NHL ENTRY DRAFT

Metro Toronto Convention Centre, Toronto, Ontario (June 15)

NUMBER	ROUND	PLAYER	POSITION	FROM
51	3	Stephane Roy	C	Granby Bisons (QMJHL)
69	4	Mike Berger	D	Lethbridge Broncos (WHL)
90	5	Dwight Mullins	RW	Lethbridge Broncos (WHL)
111	6	Mike Mullowney	D	Deerfield Academy (Massachusetts)
132	7	Mike Kelfer	C	St. John's Prep (Massachusetts)
153	8	Ross Johnson	LW	Rochester Mayo High School (Minnesota)
174	9	Tim Helmer	RW	Ottawa 67's (OHL)
195	10	Gordie Ernst	C	Cranston East High School (Rhode Island)
216	11	Ladislav Lubina	LW	Pardubice HC (Czechoslovakia)
237	12	Tommy Sjodin	D	Timra (Sweden)

1984 NHL ENTRY DRAFT

The Forum, Montreal, Quebec (June 9)

NUMBER	ROUND	PLAYER	POSITION	FROM
13	1	David Quinn	D	Kent High School (Connecticut)
46	3	Ken Hodge, Jr.	C	St. John's Prep (Massachusetts)
76	4	Miroslav Maly	D	Bayreuth ESV (Germany)
89	5	Jiri Poner	RW/C	Landshut EV (Germany)
97	5	Kari Takko	G	Assat Pori (Finland)
118	6	Gary McColgan	LW	Oshawa Generals (OHL)
139	7	Vladimir Kyhos	LW	Litvinov CHP HC (Czechoslovakia)
160	8	Darin McInnis	G	Kent High School (Connecticut)
181	9	Duane Wahlin	RW	St. Paul Johnson High School (Minnesota)
201	10	Mike Orn	RW	Stillwater High School (Minnesota)
222	11	Tom Terwilliger	D	Edina High School (Minnesota)
242	12	Mike Nightengale	D	St. Paul Simley High School (Minnesota)

DON'S BIGG BREAK

Don Biggs, Minnesota's eighth-round pick in 1983, played only one game as a North Star. But he achieved cinematic immortality (sort of) as the on-ice double for Patrick Swayze's skating scenes in the 1986 film *Youngblood*.

1983 NHL ENTRY DRAFT

The Forum, Montreal, Quebec (June 8)

NUMBER	ROUND	PLAYER	POSITION	FROM
1	1	Brian Lawton	C/LW	Mount St. Charles High School (Rhode Island)
36	2	Malcolm Parks	C/RW	St. Albert Saints (Alberta Junior Hockey League)
38	2	Frank Musil	D	Pardubice HC (Czechoslovakia)
56	3	Mitch Messier	RW	Notre Dame Academy (Saskatchewan)
76	4	Brian Durand	C	Cloquet High School (Minnesota)
96	5	Rich Geist	C	St. Paul Academy (Minnesota)
116	6	Tom McComb	D	Mount St. Charles High School (Rhode Island)
136	7	Sean Toomey	C	St. Paul Cretin High School (Minnesota)
156	8	Don Biggs	C	Oshawa Generals (OHL)
176	9	Paul Pulis	RW	Hibbing High School (Minnesota)
196	10	Milos Riha	LW	Czech National Team
212	11	Oldrich Valek	RW	Czech National Team
236	12	Paul Roff	RW	Edina High School (Minnesota)

1982 NHL ENTRY DRAFT

The Forum, Montreal, Quebec (June 9)

NUMBER	ROUND	PLAYER	POSITION	FROM
2	1	Brian Bellows	RW	Kitchener Rangers (OHL)
59	3	Wally Chapman	C	Edina High School (Minnesota)
80	4	Bob Rouse	D	Billings Bighorns (WHL)
81	4	Dusan Pasek	C	Bratislava (Czechoslovakia)
101	5	Marty Wiitala	C	Superior High School (Wisconsin)
122	6	Todd Carlile	D	North St. Paul High School (Minnesota)
143	7	Viktor Zhluktov	LW	CSKA Moscow (Russia)
164	8	Paul Miller	D	Crookston High School (Minnesota)
185	9	Pat Micheletti	C	Hibbing High School (Minnesota)
206	10	Arnold Kadlec	D	Litvinov CHP HC (Czechoslovakia)
227	11	Scott Knutson	LW	Warroad High School (Minnesota)

1981 NHL ENTRY DRAFT

The Forum, Montreal, Quebec (June 10)

NUMBER	ROUND	PLAYER	POSITION	FROM
13	1	Ron Meighan	D	Niagara Falls Flyers (OHL)
27	2	Dave Donnelly	C/LW	St. Albert Saints (Alberta Junior Hockey League)
31	2	Mike Sands	G	Sudbury Wolves (OHL)
33	2	Tom Hirsch	D	Patrick Henry High School (Minnesota)
34	2	Dave Preuss	RW	St. Thomas Academy (Minnesota)
41	2	Jali Wahlsten	C	TPS Turku (Finland)
69	4	Terry Tait	LW	Sault Ste. Marie (OHL)
76	4	Jim Malwitz	C	Grand Rapids High School (Minnesota)
97	5	Kelly Hubbard	D	Portland Winter Hawks (WHL)
118	6	Paul Guay	RW	Mount St. Charles High School (Rhode Island)
139	7	Jim Archibald	RW	Moose Jaw Canucks (Saskatchewan Junior Hockey League)
160	8	Kari Kanervo	C	TPS Turku (Finland)
181	9	Scott Bjugstad	C	University of Minnesota
202	10	Steve Kudebeh	G	Breck School (Minnesota)

1980 NHL ENTRY DRAFT

The Forum, Montreal, Quebec (June 11)

NUMBER	ROUND	PLAYER	POSITION	FROM
16	1	Brad Palmer	LW	Victoria Cougars (WHL)
37	2	Don Beaupre	G	Sudbury Wolves (OHA)
53	3	Randy Velischek	D	Providence College
79	4	Mark Huglen	D	Roseau High School (Minnesota)
100	5	David Jensen	D	University of Minnesota
121	6	Dan Zavarise	D	Cornwall Royals (QMJHL)
142	7	Bill Stewart	RW/LW	University of Denver
163	8	Jeff Walters	RW	Peterborough Petes (OHA)
184	9	Bob Lakso	LW	Aurora High School (Minnesota)
205	10	Dave Richter	D	University of Michigan

1979 NHL ENTRY DRAFT

Queen Elizabeth Hotel, Montreal, Quebec (August 9)

NUMBER	ROUND	PLAYER	POSITION	FROM
6	1	Craig Hartsburg	D	Sault Ste. Marie (OHA)
10	1	Tom McCarthy	LW/C	Oshawa Generals (OHA)
42	2	Neal Broten	C	University of Minnesota
63	3	Kevin Maxwell	C	University of North Dakota

NUMBER	ROUND	PLAYER	POSITION	FROM
90	5	Jim Dobson	RW	Portland (WHL)
111	6	Brian Gualazzi	C	Sault Ste. Marie (OHA)

1978 NHL AMATEUR DRAFT

Queen Elizabeth Hotel, Montreal, Quebec (June 5)

NUMBER	ROUND	PLAYER	POSITION	FROM
1	1	Bobby Smith	C	Ottawa 67's (OHA)
19	2	Steve Payne	LW	Ottawa 67's (OHA)
24	2	Steve Christoff	C	University of Minnesota
54	4	Curt Giles	D	University of Minnesota–Duluth
70	5	Roy Kerling	C	Cornell University
87	6	Bob Bergloff	D	University of Minnesota
104	7	Kim Spencer	D	Victoria Cougars (WCHL)
121	8	Mike Cotter	D	Bowling Green State
138	9	Brent Gogol	RW	Billings Bighorns (WCHL)
155	10	Mike Seide	D/LW	Bloomington Jr. Stars (USHL)

1977 NHL AMATEUR DRAFT

NHL Offices, Montreal, Quebec (June 14)

NUMBER	ROUND	PLAYER	POSITION	FROM
7	1	Brad Maxwell	D	New Westminster (WCHL)
25	2	Dave Semenko	LW	Brandon (WCHL)
61	4	Kevin McCloskey	D	Calgary Centennials (WCHL)
79	5	Bob Parent	D	Kingston Canadians (OHL)
97	6	Jamie Gallimore	RW	Kamloops Chiefs (WCHL)
115	7	Jean-Pierre Sanvido	G	Trois Rivieres (QMJHL)
130	8	Greg Tebbutt	D	Victoria Cougars (WCHL)
145	9	Keith Hanson	D	Austin Mavericks (MidJHL)

1976 NHL AMATEUR DRAFT

NHL Offices, Montreal, Quebec (June 1)

NUMBER	ROUND	PLAYER	POSITION	FROM
3	1	Glen Sharpley	C	Hull Festivals (QMJHL)
31	2	Jim Roberts	LW	Ottawa 67's (OHA)
39	3	Don Jackson	D	University of Notre Dame
51	3	Ron Zanussi	RW	London Knights (OHA)
57	4	Mike Fedorko	D	Hamilton Fincups (OHA)
75	5	Phil Verchota	LW	University of Minnesota
93	6	Dave Delich	C	Colorado College
110	7	Jeff Barr	D	Michigan State University

PIRUS THE PIOUS

After an impressive rookie season in which he netted twenty goals and displayed a willingness to hit and be hit, Alex Pirus (Minnesota's third pick in 1975) seemed to lose his scoring touch. Following a brief pro hockey career, he found religion. In the 1990s he joined Hockey Ministries International, an evangelical Christian organization supporting the spiritual needs of players, coaches, families, and fans. One of his responsibilities was serving as the chaplain for the Chicago Blackhawks (sacrilege!) and the AHL's Chicago Wolves.

1975 NHL AMATEUR DRAFT
NHL Offices, Montreal, Quebec (June 3)

NUMBER	ROUND	PLAYER	POSITION	FROM
4	1	Bryan Maxwell	D	Medicine Hat (WCHL)
40	3	Paul Harrison	G	Oshawa Generals (OHA)
41	3	Alex Pirus	C	University of Notre Dame
58	4	Steve Jensen	LW	Michigan Tech
76	5	Dave Norris	LW	Hamilton Fincups (OHA)
94	6	Greg Clause	RW	Hamilton Fincups (OHA)
112	7	Francois Robert	D	Sherbrooke (QMJHL)
130	8	Dean Magee	C	Colorado College
147	9	Terry Angel	RW	Oshawa Generals (OHA)
163	10	Michel Blais	D	Kingston Canadians (OHA)
177	11	Earl Sargent	RW	Fargo-Moorhead (MidJHL)
190	12	Gilles Cloutier	G	Shawinigan (QMJHL)

1974 NHL AMATEUR DRAFT
NHL Offices, Montreal, Quebec (May 28)

NUMBER	ROUND	PLAYER	POSITION	FROM
6	1	Doug Hicks	D	Flin Flon Bombers (WCHL)
24	2	Rich Nantais	LW	Quebec Remparts (QMJHL)
42	3	Pete LoPresti	G	University of Denver
78	5	Ron Ashton	LW	Saskatoon Blades (WCHL)
96	6	John Sheridan	C	University of Minnesota
114	7	Dave Heitz	G	Fargo-Moorhead (MidJHL)
131	8	Roland Eriksson	C	HC Tunabro (Sweden)
148	9	Dave Staffen	C/LW	Ottawa 67's (OHA)
164	10	Brian Andersen	D	New Westminster (WCHL)
179	11	Duane Bray	D	Flin Flon Bombers (WCHL)
193	12	Don Hay	RW	New Westminster (WCHL)
205	13	Brian Holderness	G	Saskatoon Blades (WCHL)
215	14	Frank Taylor	D	Brandon (WCHL)
222	15	Jeff Hymanson	D	St. Cloud Jr. Blues (MidJHL)

1973 NHL AMATEUR DRAFT

Mount Royal Hotel, Montreal, Quebec (May 15)

NUMBER	ROUND	PLAYER	POSITION	FROM
18	2	Blake Dunlop	C	Ottawa 67's (OHA)
25	2	John Rogers	RW	Edmonton Oil Kings (WCHL)
41	3	Rick Chinnick	RW	Peterborough Petes (OHA)
57	4	Tom Colley	C	Sudbury Wolves (OHA)
73	5	Lowell Ostlund	D	Saskatoon Blades (WCHL)
89	6	David Lee	LW	Ottawa 67's (OHA)
105	7	Lou Nistico	LW	London Knights (OHA)
121	8	George Beveridge	D	Kitchener Rangers (OHA)
136	9	Jim Johnston	C	Peterborough Petes (OHA)
152	10	Sam Clegg	G	Medicine Hat Tigers (WCHL)
161	11	Russ Wiechnik	C	Calgary Centennials (WCHL)
163	11	Max Hansen	LW	Sudbury Wolves (OHA)

1972 NHL AMATEUR DRAFT

Queen Elizabeth Hotel, Montreal, Quebec (June 8)

NUMBER	ROUND	PLAYER	POSITION	FROM
12	1	Jerry Byers	LW/C	Kitchener Rangers (OHA)
44	3	Terry Ryan	C	Hamilton Red Wings (OHA)
60	4	Tom Thomson	D	Toronto Marlboros (OHA)
76	5	Chris Ahrens	D	Kitchener Rangers (OHA)
92	6	Steve West	C	Oshawa Generals (OHA)
108	7	Chris Meloff	D	Kitchener Rangers (OHA)
116	8	Scott MacPhail	RW	Montreal Jr. Canadiens (OHA)
124	8	Bob Lundeen	RW	University of Wisconsin
140	9	Glen Mikkelson	RW	Brandon (WCHL)
145	10	Steve Lyon	RW	Peterborough Petes (OHA)
147	10	Juri Kudrasovs	C	Kitchener Rangers (OHA)
148	10	Marcel Comeau	C	Edmonton Oil Kings (WCHL)

1971 NHL AMATEUR DRAFT

Queen Elizabeth Hotel, Montreal, Quebec (June 10)

NUMBER	ROUND	PLAYER	POSITION	FROM
21	2	Rod Norrish	LW	Regina Pats (WCHL)
35	3	Ron Wilson	D	Flin Flon Bombers (WCHL)
49	4	Mike Legge	D	Winnipeg Jets (WCHL)
63	5	Brian McBratney	D	St. Catharines (OHA)
77	6	Alan Globensky	D	Montreal Jr. Canadiens (OHA)
91	7	Bruce Abbey	D	Peterborough Petes (OHA)
105	8	Russ Friesen	C/LW	Hamilton Red Wings (OHA)
113	9	Mike Antonovich	C	University of Minnesota
117	10	Rich Coutu	G	Rosemont National (QMJHL)

1970 NHL AMATEUR DRAFT

Queen Elizabeth Hotel, Montreal, Quebec (June 11)

NUMBER	ROUND	PLAYER	POSITION	FROM
17	2	Fred Harvey	RW	Hamilton Red Wings (OHA)
20	2	Fred Barrett	D	Toronto Marlboros (OHA)
34	3	Dennis Patterson	D	Peterborough Petes (OHA)
48	4	Dave Cressman	LW	Kitchener Rangers (OHA)
62	5	Hank Lehvonen	D	Kitchener Rangers (OHA)
76	6	Murray McNeil	LW	Calgary Centennials (WCHL)
89	7	Gary Geldart	D	London Knights (OHA)
101	8	Mickey Donaldson	LW	Peterborough Petes (OHA)

1969 NHL AMATEUR DRAFT

Queen Elizabeth Hotel, Montreal, Quebec (June 12)

NUMBER	ROUND	PLAYER	POSITION	FROM
5	1	Dick Redmond	D	St. Catharines (OHA)
14	2	Dennis O'Brien	D	St. Catharines (OHA)
25	3	Gilles Gilbert	G	London Nationals (OHA)
37	4	Fred O'Donnell	LW	Oshawa Generals (OHA)
49	5	Pierre Jutras	LW	Shawinigan Bruins (Quebec Junior A Hockey League)
61	6	Rob Walton	C	Niagara Falls Flyers (OHA)
72	7	Rick Thompson	D	Niagara Falls Flyers (OHA)
78	8	Cal Russell	RW	Hamilton Red Wings (OHA)

1968 NHL AMATEUR DRAFT

Queen Elizabeth Hotel, Montreal, Quebec (June 13)

NUMBER	ROUND	PLAYER	POSITION	FROM
5	1	Jim Benzelock	RW	Winnipeg Jets (WCHL)
15	2	Marc Rioux	C	Verdun Maple Leafs (Quebec Provincial Junior A Hockey League)
22	3	Glen Lindsay	G	Saskatoon Blades (WCHL)

1967 NHL AMATEUR DRAFT

Queen Elizabeth Hotel, Montreal, Quebec (June 7)

NUMBER	ROUND	PLAYER	POSITION	FROM
4	1	Wayne Cheesman	LW	Whitby Jr. B
13	2	Larry Mick	RW	Pembroke Jr. A

1967 NHL EXPANSION DRAFT

Queen Elizabeth Hotel, Montreal, Quebec (June 6)

NUMBER	ROUND	PLAYER	POSITION	FROM
4	1	Cesare Maniago	G	New York Rangers
8	2	Gary Bauman	G	Montreal Canadiens
14	3	Dave Balon	LW	Montreal Canadiens
20	4	Ray Cullen	C	Detroit Red Wings
26	5	Bob Woytowich	D	Boston Bruins
32	6	Jean-Guy Talbot	D	Montreal Canadiens
38	7	Wayne Connelly	RW	Boston Bruins
44	8	Ted Taylor	LW	Detroit Red Wings
50	9	Pete Goegan	D	Detroit Red Wings
56	10	Len Lunde	LW	Chicago Blackhawks
62	11	Bill Goldsworthy	RW	Boston Bruins
68	12	Andre Pronovost	LW	Detroit Red Wings
74	13	Elmer Vasko	D	Chicago Blackhawks
80	14	Murray Hall	RW	Chicago Blackhawks
86	15	Bryan Watson	D	Detroit Red Wings
92	16	Bill Collins	C	New York Rangers
98	17	Alex Fitzpatrick	C	New York Rangers
104	18	Parker MacDonald	LW	Detroit Red Wings
110	19	Billy Taylor	C	Chicago Blackhawks
116	20	Dave Richardson	LW	Chicago Blackhawks

APPENDIX 3: All-Time Trades

1993

March 20: North Stars acquire Mark Osiecki and a tenth-round pick in 1993 (No. 249, Bill Lang) from the Winnipeg Jets for a ninth-round pick in 1993 (No. 217, Vladimir Potapov).

March 4: North Stars acquire Brent Gilchrist from the Edmonton Oilers for Todd Elik.

1992

September 2: North Stars trade David Shaw to the Boston Bruins for future considerations.

September 2: North Stars acquire James Black from the Hartford Whalers for Mark Janssens.

August 31: North Stars acquire Russ Courtnall from the Montreal Canadiens for Brian Bellows.

August 14: North Stars acquire Mike McPhee from the Montreal Canadiens for a fifth-round pick in 1993 (No. 113, Jeff Lank).

August 4: North Stars acquire Collin Bauer from the Edmonton Oilers for future considerations.

July 16: North Stars acquire Mario Thyer from the New York Rangers for future considerations.

June 15: North Stars trade Allen Pedersen to the Hartford Whalers for a conditional draft pick in 1993 (No. 136, Rick Mrozik).

March 10: North Stars acquire Bobby Reynolds from the Washington Capitals for future considerations.

March 10: North Stars acquire Mark Janssens from the Rangers for Mario Thyer and a third-round pick in 1993 (No. 61, Maxim Galanov).

March 8: North Stars acquire Kip Miller from the Quebec Nordiques for Steve Maltais.

January 21: North Stars acquire David Shaw from the Edmonton Oilers for Brian Glynn.

1991

December 30: North Stars acquire Warren Rychel from the Winnipeg Jets for Tony Joseph and future considerations.

October 15: North Stars acquire Tony Joseph from the Winnipeg Jets for Tyler Larter.

August 9: North Stars acquire Jim Nesich from the Montreal Canadiens for future considerations.

June 22: North Stars acquire Todd Elik from the Los Angeles Kings for Randy Gilhen, Charlie Huddy, Jim Thomson, and a fourth-round pick in 1991 (No. 81, Alexei Zhitnik).

June 22: North Stars acquire Craig Ludwig from the New York Islanders for Tom Kurvers.

June 22: North Stars acquire Tom Kurvers from the Vancouver Canucks for Dave Babych.

June 22: North Stars acquire a fifth-round pick in 1991 (No. 97, Mike Kennedy) from Hartford for future considerations (Jukka Suomalainen).

June 21: North Stars acquire Trent Klatt and Steve Maltais from the Washington Capitals for Shawn Chambers.

June 3: North Stars acquire Shane Churla from the San Jose Sharks for Kelly Kisio.

May 31: North Stars acquire Alan Haworth from the Quebec Nordiques for Guy Lafleur.*

May 31: In exchange for the San Jose Sharks agreeing not to select Mike Craig in dispersal draft, the North Stars trade a second-round pick in 1991 (No. 30, Sandis Ozolinsh) and a first-round pick in 1992 (No. 10, Andrei Nazarov) to San Jose.

May 30: North Stars trade Rob Murray and future considerations to the Washington Capitals for a seventh-round pick in 1991 (No. 137, Geoff Finch).

May 30: North Stars acquire Steve Guenette from the Calgary Flames for a seventh-round pick in 1991 (No. 140, Matt Hoffman).

May 26: North Stars acquire Darcy Wakaluk from the Buffalo Sabres for an eighth-round pick in 1991 (No. 162, Jiri Kuntos) and a fifth-round pick in 1992 (No. 106, Chris DeRuiter).

March 5: North Stars trade Ilkka Sinisalo to the Los Angeles Kings for an eighth-round pick in 1991 (No. 174, Michael Burkett).

March 5: North Stars acquire Marc Bureau from the Calgary Flames for a third-round pick in 1991 (No. 52, Sandy McCarthy).

1990

December 11: North Stars acquire Chris Dahlquist and Jim Johnson from the Pittsburgh Penguins for Larry Murphy and Peter Taglianetti.

November 22: North Stars acquire Bruce Bell and future considerations from the Edmonton Oilers for Kari Takko.

---

* The Lafleur Trade: Although he had already announced that he was retiring for good and planning to take a front-office job with the Nordiques, Guy Lafleur was claimed by the North Stars in the 1991 expansion draft. However, because his retirement papers had not yet been filed with the league, NHL tampering bylaws prevented him from taking an office position with a team that didn't own his playing rights. To accommodate Lafleur the North Stars traded him back to Quebec for the rights to center Alan Haworth. Rather than play for Minnesota, Haworth chose to close out his career in Europe.

November 7: North Stars acquire Doug Smail and future considerations from the Winnipeg Jets for Don Barber and future considerations.

November 7: North Stars acquire Brian Hayward from the Montreal Canadiens for Jayson More.

October 26: North Stars acquire Brian Glynn from the Calgary Flames for Frantisek Musil.

September 30: North Stars acquire Peter Taglianetti from the Winnipeg Jets for future considerations.

September 7: North Stars trade James Mackey to the Vancouver Canucks for future considerations.

September 6: North Stars acquire Craig Duncanson from the Los Angeles Kings for Daniel Berthiaume.

September 6: North Stars acquire Brian Hunt from the Winnipeg Jets for Craig Duncanson.

August 21: North Stars trade Ken Hodge Jr. to the Boston Bruins for a fourth-round pick in 1992 (No. 88, Jere Lehtinen)

August 7: North Stars acquire Bobby Smith from the Montreal Canadiens for a fourth-round pick in 1992 (No. 82, Louis Bernard).

March 6: North Stars acquire Ulf Dahlen, a fourth-round pick in 1990 (No. 70, Cal McGowan) and future considerations (a fourth-round pick in 1991, No. 81, Alexei Zhitnik) from the New York Rangers for Mike Gartner.

January 22: North Stars acquire Daniel Berthiaume from the Winnipeg Jets for future considerations.

January 5: North Stars acquire Aaron Broten from the New Jersey Devils for Bob Brooke.

1989

November 1: North Stars acquire Jayson More from the New York Rangers for Dave Archibald.

October 7: North Stars acquire the rights to Keith Sullivan from the Hartford Whalers for Mike Berger.

September 5: North Stars acquire Peter Lappin from the Calgary Flames for a second-round pick in 1990 (No. 29, Chris Gotziaman).

June 19: North Stars acquire Gaetan Duchesne from the Quebec Nordiques for Kevin Kaminski.

March 7: North Stars acquire Reed Larson from the New York Islanders for a seventh-round pick in 1989 (No. 133, Brett Harkins) and future considerations (Mike Kelfer).

March 7: North Stars acquire Mike Gartner and Larry Murphy from the Washington Capitals for Dino Ciccarelli and Bob Rouse.

March 4: North Stars acquire Perry Berezan and Shane Churla from the Calgary Flames for Brian MacLellan and a fourth-round pick in 1989 (No. 70, Robert Reichel).

1988

December 17: North Stars acquire Steve Gotaas and Ville Siren from the Pittsburgh Penguins for Scott Bjugstad and Gord Dineen.

December 15: North Stars trade Stephane Roy to the Quebec Nordiques for future considerations.

December 9: North Stars acquire Larry Bernard and a fifth-round pick in 1989 (No. 97, Rhys Hollyman) from the New York Rangers for Mark Hardy.

December 8: North Stars trade Moe Mantha to the Philadelphia Flyers for a fifth-round pick in 1989 (No. 87, Pat MacLeod).

November 1: North Stars acquire the rights to Claudio Scremin from the Washington Capitals for Don Beaupre.

November 1: North Stars acquire the rights Rob Gaudreau from the Pittsburgh Penguins for Richard Zemlak.

October 11: North Stars acquire Paul Jerrard, Mike Sullivan, Mark Tinordi, a 1989 third-round pick (No. 60, Murray Garbutt), and the rights to Bret Barnett from the New York Rangers for Brian Lawton, Igor Liba, and the rights to Rick Bennett.

June 13: North Stars acquire Mark Hardy from the New York Rangers for future considerations (a third-round pick in 1989, No. 49, Louie DeBrusk).

May 20: North Stars acquire the rights to Igor Liba from the Calgary Flames for a fifth-round pick in 1988 (No. 85, Tomas Forslund).

March 8: North Stars acquire Gord Dineen from the New York Islanders for Chris Pryor and future considerations (a seventh-round pick in 1989, No. 133, Brett Harkins).

March 7: North Stars acquire the rights to John Blue from the Winnipeg Jets for a seventh-round pick in 1988 (No. 127, Markus Akerblom).

February 22: North Stars acquire John Barrett from the Washington Capitals for future considerations.

February 9: North Stars trade Gordie Roberts to the Philadelphia Flyers for a fourth-round pick in 1989 (No. 75, Jean-Francois Quinton).

January 22: North Stars acquire Moe Mantha from the Edmonton Oilers for Keith Acton.

January 4: North Stars acquire Curt Fraser from Chicago for Dirk Graham.

1987

November 20: North Stars acquire Curt Giles from the New York Rangers for Byron Lomow and future considerations.

October 13: North Stars acquire Andy Ristau from the Buffalo Sabres for a sixth-round pick in 1988 (No. 106, David DiVita).

October 8: North Stars acquire Jay Caufield and Dave Gagner from the New York Rangers for Paul Boutilier and Jari Gronstrand.

September 8: North Stars acquire Pat Price from the New York Rangers for Willi Plett.

June 13: North Stars trade their 1987 first-round pick (No. 4, Wayne McBean) to Los Angeles for the Kings' first-round pick (No. 6, Dave Archibald) and third-round pick (No. 48, Kevin Kaminski) in 1987.

March 10: North Stars acquire Paul Boutilier from the Boston Bruins for a fourth-round pick in 1987 (No. 67, Darwin McPherson).

March 10: North Stars acquire Raimo Helminen from the New York Rangers for future considerations.

March 2: North Stars trade Kent Nilsson to the Edmonton Oilers for a second-round pick in 1988 (No. 40, Link Gaetz) and cash.

February 21: North Stars acquire Brad Maxwell from the New York Rangers for cash.

1986

November 13: North Stars acquire Bob Brooke and a fourth-round pick in 1988 (No. 64, Jeffrey Stolp) from the New York Rangers for Curt Giles, Tony McKegney, and a second-round pick in 1988 (No. 22, Troy Mallette).

October 24: North Stars acquire the rights to Mark Pavelich from the New York Rangers for a second-round pick in 1988 (No. 22, Troy Mallette).

September 8: North Stars acquire Brian MacLellan from New York Rangers for a conditional pick in 1987.

May 16: North Stars trade Tom McCarthy to Boston for a third-round pick in 1986 (No. 55, Rob Zettler) and a second-round pick in 1987 (No. 35, Scott McGrady).

1985

December 20: North Stars acquire Don Barber, Marc Habscheid, and Emanuel Viveiros from the Edmonton Oilers for Don Biggs and Gord Sherven.

December 9: North Stars trade Roland Melanson to the New York Rangers for a second-round pick in 1986 (No. 30, Neil Wilkinson) and a fourth-round pick in 1987 (No. 73, John Weisbrod).

November 29: North Stars acquire Todd Bergen and Ed Hospodar from the Philadelphia Flyers for Bo Berglund and Dave Richter.

November 15: North Stars acquire Edward Lee from the Quebec Nordiques for a sixth-round pick in 1986 (No. 117, Scott White).

September 9: North Stars acquire Mats Hallin from the New York Islanders for a seventh-round pick in 1986 (No. 138, Will Anderson).

June 15: North Stars acquire Kent Nilsson and a third-round pick in 1986 *or* 1987 (1986, No. 58, Brad Turner) from the Calgary Flames for a second-round pick in 1985 (No. 27, Joe Nieuwendyk) and a second-round pick in 1987 (No. 25, Stephane Matteau).

May 31: North Stars acquire Paul Houck from the Edmonton Oilers for Gilles Meloche.

March 12: North Stars trade Lorne Molleken to the New York Islanders for cash.

January 24: North Stars acquire Terry Martin and Gord Sherven from the Edmonton Oilers for Mark Napier.

1984

December 14: North Stars acquire Bo Berglund and Tony McKegney from the Quebec Nordiques for Brent Ashton and Brad Maxwell.

November 19: North Stares acquire Roland Melanson from the New York Islanders for a first-round pick in 1985 *or* 1986 (1985, No. 6, Brad Dalgarno).

September 20: North Stars acquire Ken Solheim from the Detroit Red Wings for future considerations.

June 21: North Stars trade Al MacAdam to the Vancouver Canucks for future considerations (Harold Snepsts).

February 23: North Stars acquire Paul Holmgren from the Philadelphia Flyers for a third-round pick in 1985 (No. 48, Darryl Gilmour) and the rights to Paul Guay.

January 12: North Stars acquire Tim Trimper from the Winnipeg Jets for Jordy Douglas.

1983

October 28: North Stars acquire Keith Acton, Mark Napier, and third-round pick in 1984 (No. 46, Ken Hodge Jr.) from the Montreal Canadiens for Bobby Smith.

October 20: North Stars acquire Lars Lindgren from the Vancouver Canucks for a third-round pick in 1984 (No. 55, Landis Chaulk).

October 3: North Stars acquire Brent Ashton from the New Jersey Devils for Dave Lewis.

October 3: North Stars acquire Dave Lewis from the Los Angeles Kings for Fred Barrett and Steve Christoff.

August 3: North Stars acquire Craig Levie and the rights to Tom Ward from the Winnipeg Jets for Tim Young.

July 5: North Stars acquire Dennis Maruk from the Washington Capitals for a second-round pick in 1984 (No. 34, Stephen Leach).

June 29: North Stars acquire Steve Christoff and a second round pick in 1983 *or* 1984 (1983, No. 38, Frantisek Musil) from the Calgary Flames for Mike Eaves and Keith Hanson.

March 8: North Stars trade Ken Solheim to the Detroit Red Wings for future considerations.

February 1: North Stars trade Markus Mattsson to the Los Angeles Kings for future considerations (a third-round pick in 1985, No. 51, Stephane Roy).

January 10: North Stars acquire Dave Logan from the Toronto Maple Leafs for cash.

1982

October 28: North Stars acquire George Ferguson and a first-round pick in 1983 (No. 1, Brian Lawton) from the Pittsburgh Penguins for Anders Hakansson, Ron Meighan, and a first-round pick in 1983 (No. 15, Bob Errey).

October 1: North Stars trade Kent-Erik Andersson and Mark Johnson to the Hartford Whalers for a fifth-round pick in 1984 (No. 89, Jiri Poner) and future considerations (Jordy Douglas).

August 23: North Stars acquire Dan McCarthy from the New York Rangers for Shawn Dineen.

August 4: North Stars acquire Rollie Boutin and Wes Jarvis from the Washington Capitals for Robbie Moore and an eleventh-round pick in 1983 (No. 216, Anders Huss).

June 9: North Stars acquire an eleventh-round pick in 1983 (No. 212, Oldrich Valek) from the Quebec Nordiques for a twelfth-round pick in 1982 (No. 248, Jan Jasko).

June 9: North Stars trade Brad Palmer and the rights to Dave Donnelly to the Boston Bruins. In exchange the Bruins agree not to select Brian Bellows in the 1982 Entry Draft.

June 7: North Stars acquire Willi Plett and a fourth-round pick in 1982 (No. 81, Dusan Pasek) from the Calgary Flames for Steve Christoff, Bill Nyrop, and second-round pick in 1982 (No. 29, Dave Reierson).

March 2: North Stars acquire Mark Johnson from the Pittsburgh Penguins for a second-round pick in 1982 (No. 38, Tim Hrynewich).

1981

December 31: North Stars trade Kevin Maxwell and the rights to Jim Dobson to the Colorado Rockies for cash.

October 30: North Stars trade the rights to Tom Younghans to the New York Rangers for cash.

August 21: North Stars trade Greg Smith, a first-round pick in 1982 (No. 17, Murray Craven), and the rights to Don Murdoch to the Detroit Red Wings for a first-round pick in 1982 (No. 2, Brian Bellows).

August 21: North Stars acquire the rights to Don Murdoch from the Edmonton Oilers for Don Jackson and a third-round pick in 1982 (No. 59, Wally Chapman).

July 31: North Stars acquire Lindsay Middlebrook from the Winnipeg Jets for cash.

June 9: North Stars acquire Nelson Burton from the Quebec Nordiques for Dan Chicoine.

March 10: North Stars trade Ron Zanussi and a third-round pick in 1981 (No. 55, Ernie Godden) to the Toronto Maple Leafs for a second-round pick in 1981 (No. 27, Dave Donnelly).

February 2: North Stars trade Gary Edwards to the Edmonton Oilers for future considerations (a third-round pick in 1982, No. 59, Wally Chapman).

1980

December 29: North Stars acquire Ken Solheim and a second-round pick in 1981 (No. 33, Tom Hirsch) from the Chicago Blackhawks for Glen Sharpley.

December 16: North Stars acquire Gordie Roberts from the Hartford Whalers for Mike Fidler.

September 1: North Stars acquire Bill Nyrop from the Montreal Canadiens for future considerations.

July 4: North Stars trade Alex Pirus to the New York Islanders for future considerations.

June 6: North Stars acquire Alex Pirus from the Detroit Red Wings for cash.

March 11: North Stars acquire Jim Corsi from the Edmonton Oilers for future considerations.

January 4: North Stars trade Kris Manery to the Vancouver Canucks for a second-round pick in 1982 (No. 32, Kent Carlson).

January 3: North Stars trade Alex Pirus to the Detroit Red Wings for cash.

January 3: North Stars acquire Dave Hanson from the Detroit Red Wings for future considerations.

December 10: North Stars trade Per-Olov Brasar to the Vancouver Canucks for a second-round pick in 1981 (No. 31, Mike Sands).

August 9: North Stars trade Dave Semenko and a third-round pick in 1979 (No. 48, Mark Messier) to the Edmonton Oilers for a second-round pick (No. 42, Neal Broten) and a third-round pick (No. 63, Kevin Maxwell) in 1979.

August 8: North Stars acquire Bill Nyrop from the Montreal Canadiens for a second-round pick in 1979 (No. 27, Gaston Gingras) and a second-round pick in 1980, later changed to a second-round pick in 1982 (No. 32, Kent Carlson).

July 19: North Stars trade Chuck Arnason to the Vancouver Canucks for cash.

June 10: North Stars trade Ritchie Hansen and Bryan Maxwell to the St. Louis Blues for a second-round pick in 1982 (No. 29, Dave Reierson).

June 9: North Stars trade a fourth-round pick in 1979 (No. 69, Glenn Anderson) to the Edmonton Oilers. In exchange the Oilers agree not to make Paul Shmyr one of its priority selections in the 1979 NHL Expansion Draft.

April 24: North Stars acquire Chuck Arnason from the Washington Capitals for future considerations (cash).

March 12: North Stars trade Chuck Arnason to the Washington Capitals for future considerations.

1978

October 18: North Stars trade Dennis Maruk to the Washington Capitals for a first-round pick in 1979 (No. 10, Tom McCarthy).

October 9: North Stars trade Gerry O'Flaherty to the Calgary Flames for cash.

October 5: North Stars trade Walt McKechnie to the Toronto Maple Leafs for a third-round pick in 1980 (No. 53, Randy Velischek).

August 8: North Stars trade Bob Murdoch to the St. Louis Blues for cash.

July 27: North Stars acquire the rights to Jack Carlson from the Detroit Red Wings for future considerations.

June 15: North Stars trade Bob Stewart and future considerations (Harvey Bennett Jr.) to the St. Louis Blues for a second-round pick in 1981 (No. 41, Jali Wahlsten).

June 14: North Stars trade Paul Harrison to the Toronto Maple Leafs for a fourth-round pick in 1981 (No. 69, Terry Tait).

May 15: North Stars acquire Jim McKenny from the Toronto Maple Leafs for cash and future considerations (rights to Owen Lloyd).

March 14: North Stars acquire the rights to Ed Mio and future considerations (Pierre Plante) from the Chicago Blackhawks for Doug Hicks and a third-round pick in 1980 (No. 58, Marcel Frere).

February 19: North Stars acquire Gary Smith from the Washington Capitals for cash.

1977

October 28: North Stars acquire Harvey Bennett Jr. from the Philadelphia Flyers for Blake Dunlop and a third-round pick in 1978 (No. 37, Gord Salt).

1976

November 11: North Stars acquire Nick Beverley and Bill Fairbairn from the New York Rangers for Bill Goldsworthy.

August 23: North Stars acquire Gary Smith from the Vancouver Canucks for Cesare Maniago.

February 27: North Stars acquire Bill Hogaboam and a second-round pick in 1976 (No. 31, Jim Roberts) from the Detroit Red Wings for Dennis Hextall.

1975

December 9: North Stars trade the rights to Henry Boucha to the Kansas City Scouts for a second-round pick in 1978 (No. 24, Steve Christoff).

November 25: North Stars acquire Pierre Jarry from the Detroit Red Wings for Don Martineau.

November 21: North Stars acquire Bryan Hextall Jr. from the Detroit Red Wings for Rick Chinnick.

August 15: North Stars acquire Tim Young from the Los Angeles Kings for a second-round pick in in 1976 (No. 21, Steve Clippingdale).

July 9: North Stars acquire Glen Sather from the Montreal Canadiens for cash and future considerations (a third-round pick in 1977, No. 43, Alain Cote).

January 27: North Stars acquire Norm Gratton and a third-round pick in 1976 (No. 51, Ron Zanussi) from the Buffalo Sabres for Fred Stanfield.

January 7: North Stars acquire Craig Cameron from the New York Islanders for Jude Drouin.

January 5: North Stars acquire Bob Cook from the New York Islanders for cash.

January 5: North Stars acquire Ernie Hicke and Doug Rombough from the New York Islanders for J. P. Parise.

January 3: North Stars acquire Dwight Bialowas and Dean Talafous from the Calgary Flames for Barry Gibbs.

1974

October 1: North Stars trade Gary Bergman to the Detroit Red Wings a third-round pick in 1975 (No. 41, Alex Pirus).

August 27: North Stars acquire Henry Boucha from the Detroit Red Wings for Danny Grant.

May 27: North Stars acquire John Flesch and Don Martineau from the Calgary Flames for Jerry Byers and Fred Harvey.

March 1: North Stars trade Jim McElmury to the Los Angeles Kings for cash.

1973

November 7: North Stars acquire Gary Bergman from the Detroit Red Wings for Ted Harris.

September (exact date unknown): North Stars trade Gary Geldart to the Montreal Canadiens for cash.

May 29: North Stars acquire Murray Anderson and Tony Featherstone from the Montreal Canadiens for cash.

May 22: North Stars acquire Fred Stanfield from the Boston Bruins for Gilles Gilbert.

May 15: North Stars trade an eleventh-round pick in 1973 (No. 161, Russ Wiechnik) to the Toronto Maple Leafs for cash.

May 15: North Stars acquire an eleventh-round pick in 1973 (No. 163, Max Hansen) from the Los Angeles Kings for cash.

May 15: North Stars acquire a second-round pick in 1973 (No. 18, Blake Dunlop) from the Montreal Canadiens for a second-round pick in 1975 (No. 22, Brian Engblom).

March 1: North Stars acquire Don Blackburn from the New York Islanders for cash.

1972

June 8: North Stars acquire a tenth-round pick in 1972 (not exercised) from the Toronto Maple Leafs for cash.

June 8: North Stars acquire an eighth-round pick in 1972 (No. 116, Scott MacPhail) from the Los Angeles Kings for cash.

June 8: North Stars acquire a tenth-round pick in 1972 (No. 145, Steve Lyon) from the Los Angeles Kings for cash.

June 8: North Stars acquire a tenth-round pick in 1972 (No. 147, Juri Kudrasovs) from the California Golden Seals.

June 8: North Stars acquire a tenth-round pick in 1972 (No. 148, Marcel Comeau) from the Philadelphia Flyers for cash.

June 6: North Stars trade Gord Labossiere to the New York Islanders for future considerations (cash).

June 6: North Stars trade Bob Paradise to the Calgary Flames for cash.

January 7: North Stars acquire Craig Cameron from the New York Islanders for Jude Drouin.

1971

October 6: North Stars acquire Dean Prentice from the Pittsburgh Penguins for cash.

May 25: North Stars acquire Bob Nevin from the New York Rangers for a player to be named later (Bobby Rousseau).

May 25: North Stars trade Marshall Johnston to the Montreal Canadiens to complete the transaction that sent Danny Grant and Claude Larose to Minnesota in 1968. North Stars receive the rights to Bob Murdoch.

May 20: North Stars acquire Dennis Hextall from the California Golden Seals for Joe Johnston and Walt McKechnie.

May (exact date unknown): North Stars acquire Bob Paradise and the rights to Gary Gambucci from the Montreal Canadiens for cash.

March 7: North Stars acquire Ted Hampson and Wayne Muloin from the California Golden Seals for Dick Redmond and Tommy Williams.

March (exact date unknown): North Stars acquire Terry Holbrook from the Los Angeles Kings for Wayne Schultz and the rights to Steve Sutherland.

January 26: North Stars acquire Gord Labossiere from the Montreal Canadiens for Rey Comeau.

1970

August 10: North Stars trade Bob McCord to the St. Louis Blues for cash.

August (exact date unknown): North Stars acquire Bob McCord from the Montreal Canadiens for cash (McCord had previously been claimed by Montreal in the Intra-League Draft, June 9, 1970).

June 10: North Stars acquire Bobby Rousseau from the Montreal Canadiens for Claude Larose.

June 9: North Stars acquire Norm Beaudin from the Montreal Canadiens for cash.

May 22: North Stars acquire Murray Oliver from the Toronto Maple Leafs for Terry O'Malley and the rights to Brian Conacher.

May 22: North Stars acquire Jude Drouin from the Montreal Canadiens for a player to be named later (Bill Collins).

February 27: North Stars acquire Lorne (Gump) Worsley from the Montreal Canadiens for cash.

1969

June 10: North Stars acquire Bob Barlow from the Philadelphia Flyers for cash.

June (exact date unknown): North Stars acquire a first-round pick in 1969 (No. 5, Dick Redmond) from the Montreal Canadiens. In return the North Stars promise not to draft Dick Duff in the 1969 Intra-League Draft.

May 14: North Stars acquire John Miszuk from the Philadelphia Flyers for Wayne Hillman.

May 7: North Stars acquire Barry Gibbs and Tommy Williams from the Boston Bruins for a first-round pick in 1969 (No. 3, Don Tannahill) and future considerations (Fred O'Donnell).

February 15: North Stars acquire Danny Lawson and the rights to Brian Conacher from the Detroit Red Wings for Wayne Connelly.

February 14: North Stars acquire Bill Orban, Tom Reid and future considerations (Doug Shelton) from the Chicago Black Hawks Andre Boudrias and Mike McMahon Jr.

January 24: North Stars acquire Leo Boivin from the Pittsburgh Penguins for Duane Rupp.

1968

November 15: North Stars acquire Brian Smith from the Montreal Canadiens for cash.

October 1: North Stars trade Bob Woytowich to the Pittsburgh Penguins for a first-round pick in 1972 (No. 8, Dave Gardner).

June 12: North Stars acquire Wayne Hillman, Joe Johnston, and Dan Seguin from the New York Rangers for Dave Balon.

June 11: North Stars acquire Jim Paterson, the rights to Claude Piche, and the rights to Jack Rathwell from the Montreal Canadiens for cash.

June 10: North Stars acquire Danny Grant, Claude D. Larose, and future considerations (Bob Murdoch) from the Montreal Canadiens for a first-round pick in 1972 (No. 8, Dave Gardner), cash, and future considerations (Marshall Johnston).

June 6: North Stars acquire Jake Rathwell from the Montreal Canadiens for cash.

January 13: North Stars acquire Bronco Horvath from the Toronto Maple Leafs for cash.

1967

December 23: North Stars acquire Milan Marcetta and J. P. Parise from the Toronto Maple Leafs for Murray Hall, Duke Harris, Don Johns, Len Lunde, Ted Taylor, and the loan of Carl Wetzel.

October 19: North Stars acquire Duke Harris and Bob McCord from the Detroit Red Wings for Dave Richardson and Jean-Guy Talbot.

October 5: North Stars acquire Don Johns from the Montreal Canadiens for cash.

June 14: North Stars acquire Mike McMahon Jr.

June 14: North Stars acquire the rights to Danny O'Shea from the Montreal Canadiens for a first-round pick in 1970 (No. 6, Chuck Lefley).

June 8: North Stars acquire rights to Marshall Johnston from the New York Rangers for cash.

June 7: North Stars acquire the rights to Bill Masterton from the Montreal Canadiens for cash.

June 7: North Stars acquire Carl Wetzel from the Montreal Canadiens for cash.

June 6: North Stars acquire Ken Broderick, Barry MacKenzie and the rights to Gary Dineen from the Toronto Maple Leafs for cash.

June 6: North Stars acquire Andre Boudrias, Bob Charlebois and Bernard Cote from the Montreal Canadiens for a first-round pick in 1971 (No. 7, Chuck Arnason).

June 6: North Stars acquire Bill Plager, the rights to Barry Meissner and the rights to Leo Thiffault from the Montreal Canadiens for Bryan Watson.

APPENDIX 4: Statistics, Records, and Award Winners

The following is a register of the 353 players who appeared in a Minnesota North Stars uniform, along with their regular season statistics. Although some discrepancies exist between team and league statistical records, every effort has been made to resolve these inconsistencies by cross-referencing multiple sources.

ALL-TIME PLAYER REGISTER

	GP	G	A	PTS	PIM	SEASONS
Keith Acton	343	87	148	235	380	1983–88
Chris Ahrens	52	0	3	3	84	1972–78
Kent-Erik Andersson	322	59	68	127	56	1977–82
Mike Antonovich	14	0	2	2	8	1975–76, 81–82
Dave Archibald	162	28	44	72	46	1987–90
Jim Archibald	16	1	2	3	45	1984–87
Chuck Arnason	1	0	0	0	0	1978–79
Brent Ashton	97	11	17	28	69	1983–85
Warren Babe	21	2	5	7	23	1987–89, 90–91
John Baby	2	0	1	1	0	1978–79
Helmut Balderis	26	3	6	9	2	1989–90
Dave Balon	73	15	32	47	84	1967–68
Don Barber	74	23	24	47	44	1988–91
Bob Barlow	77	16	17	33	10	1969–71
Doug Barrault	2	0	0	0	2	1992–93
Fred Barrett	730	23	123	146	663	1970–83
John Barrett	1	0	1	1	2	1987–88
Gary Bauman	33	0	0	0	2	1967–69
Norm Beaudin	12	0	1	1	0	1970–71
Don Beaupre	316	0	3	3	128	1980–89
Brian Bellows	753	342	380	722	537	1982–92
Harvey Bennett	64	11	10	21	91	1977–78
Perry Berezan	132	15	22	37	65	1988–91
Mike Berger	30	3	1	4	67	1987–88
Bob Bergloff	2	0	0	0	5	1982–83
Bo Berglund	36	8	9	17	10	1984–86
Gary Bergman	57	3	23	26	66	1973–74
Brad Berry	70	0	3	3	115	1991–93
Daniel Berthiaume	5	0	0	0	2	1989–90

Nick Beverley	109	9	31	40	24	1976–78
Dwight Bialowas	116	8	37	45	24	1974–77
Don Biggs	1	0	0	0	0	1984–85
Scott Bjugstad	229	68	58	126	116	1983–88
James Black	10	2	1	3	4	1992–93
Don Blackburn	4	0	0	0	4	1972–73
Rick Boh	8	2	1	3	4	1987–88
Leo Boivin	97	4	18	22	46	1968–70
Jim Boo	6	0	0	0	22	1977–78
Henry Boucha	51	15	14	29	23	1974–75
Andre Boudrias	127	22	44	66	48	1967–69
Paul Boutilier	10	2	4	6	8	1986–87
Per-Olov Brasar	167	27	79	106	12	1977–80
Ken Broderick	7	0	0	0	0	1969–70
Bob Brooke	237	26	51	77	276	1986–90
Aaron Broten	35	9	9	18	22	1989–90
Neal Broten	876	249	547	796	459	1980–93
Murray Brumwell	22	0	3	3	18	1980–82
Marc Bureau	55	6	10	16	54	1990–92
Charlie Burns	268	27	53	80	60	1969–73
Bill Butters	72	1	4	5	77	1977–79
Jerry Byers	24	0	2	2	6	1972–74
Terry Caffery	8	0	0	0	0	1970–71
Craig Cameron	182	20	18	38	57	1971–72, 1974–76
Jack Carlson	124	18	6	24	264	1978–82, 1986–87
Jon Casey	325	0	11	11	106	1983–93
Jay Caufield	1	0	0	0	0	1987–88
Shawn Chambers	198	15	47	62	206	1987–91
Bob Charlebois	7	1	0	1	0	1967–68
Mike Chernoff	1	0	0	0	0	1968–69
Dan Chicoine	25	1	2	3	12	1978–80
Rick Chinnick	4	0	2	2	0	1973–75
Colin Chisholm	1	0	0	0	0	1986–87
Steve Christoff	145	60	49	109	91	1979–82
Shane Churla	236	14	22	36	1196	1988–93
Dino Ciccarelli	602	332	319	651	642	1980–89
Enrico Ciccone	42	0	1	1	163	1991–93
Tom Colley	1	0	0	0	2	1974–75
Bill Collins	220	47	30	77	113	1967–70
Wayne Connelly	129	49	37	86	51	1967–69
Joe Contini	1	0	0	0	0	1980–81
Bob Cook	2	0	1	1	0	1974–75
Tim Coulis	28	3	3	6	111	1983–86
Russ Courtnall	84	36	43	79	49	1992–93
Jim Craig	3	0	0	0	0	1983–84
Mike Craig	176	38	43	81	293	1990–93
Dave Cressman	85	6	8	14	37	1974–76
Ray Cullen	208	71	91	162	70	1967–70

Ulf Dahlen	241	94	91	185	22	1989–93
Chris Dahlquist	116	3	19	22	101	1990–92
Larry DePalma	121	18	14	32	362	1985–89, 1990–91
Gary Dineen	4	0	1	1	0	1968–69
Gord Dineen	15	1	2	3	23	1987–89
Jim Dobson	8	0	0	0	4	1979–82
Clark Donatelli	25	3	3	6	17	1989–90
Jordy Douglas	82	16	18	34	40	1982–84
Jude Drouin	319	79	183	262	187	1970–75
Gaetan Duchesne	297	45	45	90	185	1989–93
Ken Duggan	1	0	0	0	0	1987–88
Blake Dunlop	100	18	30	48	18	1973–77
Mike Eaves	207	55	78	133	50	1978–83
Gary Edwards	51	0	1	1	26	1978–80
Todd Elik	108	27	50	77	173	1991–93
Jerry Engele	100	2	13	15	162	1975–78
Grant Erickson	4	0	0	0	0	1969–70
Roland Eriksson	158	46	83	129	22	1976–78
Kevin Evans	4	0	0	0	19	1990–91
Bill Fairbairn	57	9	21	30	2	1976–78
Tony Featherstone	54	9	12	21	4	1973–74
George Ferguson	128	14	22	36	33	1982–84
Mike Fidler	103	33	42	75	61	1978–81
Sandy Fitzpatrick	18	3	6	9	6	1967–68
John Flesch	90	11	17	28	94	1974–76
Rob Flockhart	12	1	3	4	2	1979–81
Jon Fontas	2	0	0	0	0	1979–81
Curt Fraser	53	7	6	13	118	1987–90
Ron Friest	64	7	7	14	191	1980–83
Link Gaetz	17	0	2	2	86	1988–90
Dave Gagner	440	187	217	404	575	1987–93
Jamie Gallimore	2	0	0	0	0	1977–78
Gary Gambucci	51	2	7	9	9	1971–72, 1973–74
Mike Gartner	80	41	43	84	34	1988–90
Stewart Gavin	289	39	47	86	232	1988–93
Gary Geldart	4	0	0	0	5	1970–71
Barry Gibbs	375	35	121	156	600	1969–75
Gilles Gilbert	44	0	0	0	6	1969–73
Brent Gilchrist	8	0	1	1	2	1992–93
Curt Giles	760	40	177	217	625	1979–91
Brian Glynn	103	10	23	33	107	1990–92
Pete Goegan	46	1	2	3	30	1967–68
Bill Goldsworthy	670	267	239	506	711	1967–77
Steve Gotaas	13	1	3	4	8	1988–89, 1990–91
Dirk Graham	226	67	79	146	291	1983–88
Danny Grant	463	176	177	353	161	1968–74
Norm Gratton	66	21	15	36	22	1974–76
Jari Gronstrand	47	1	6	7	27	1986–87

Marc Habscheid	113	31	45	76	48	1985–89
Anders Hakansson	77	12	4	16	38	1981–83
Murray Hall	17	2	1	3	10	1967–68
Mats Hallin	44	3	2	5	90	1985–87
Ted Hampson	96	9	20	29	10	1970–72
Dave Hanson	22	1	1	2	39	1979–80
Mark Hardy	15	2	4	6	26	1988–89
Duke Harris	22	1	4	5	4	1967–68
Ted Harris	246	11	52	63	294	1970–74
Paul Harrison	35	0	0	0	12	1975–78
Craig Hartsburg	570	98	315	413	818	1979–89
Buster Harvey	199	49	59	108	66	1970–74
Derian Hatcher	110	12	19	31	266	1991–93
Peter Hayek	1	0	0	0	0	1981–82
Brian Hayward	26	0	0	0	2	1990–91
Bill Heindl	14	1	1	2	0	1970–72
Raimo Helminen	6	0	1	1	0	1986–87
Archie Henderson	1	0	0	0	0	1981–82
Bryan Hextall Jr.	58	8	20	28	84	1975–76
Dennis Hextall	328	84	216	300	567	1971–76
Ernie Hicke	199	68	52	120	169	1974–77
Doug Hicks	300	18	48	66	224	1974–78
Larry Hillman	12	1	5	6	0	1968–69
Wayne Hillman	50	0	8	8	32	1968–69
Tom Hirsch	31	1	7	8	30	1983–88
Ken Hodge	5	1	1	2	0	1988–89
Bill Hogaboam	109	19	25	44	26	1975–79
Terry Holbrook	43	3	6	9	4	1972–74
Paul Holmgren	27	6	8	14	84	1983–85
Bronco Horvath	14	1	6	7	4	1967–68
Ed Hospodar	43	0	2	2	91	1985–86
Paul Houck	16	1	2	3	2	1985–88
Don Jackson	27	0	7	7	41	1977–81
Steve Janaszak	1	0	0	0	0	1979–80
Mark Janssens	3	0	0	0	0	1991–92
Pierre Jarry	115	38	48	86	36	1975–78
Wes Jarvis	3	0	0	0	2	1982–83
David Jensen	18	0	2	2	11	1983–86
Steve Jensen	171	42	46	88	141	1975–78
Paul Jerrard	5	0	0	0	4	1988–89
Don Johns	4	0	0	0	6	1967–68
Jim Johnson	194	8	39	47	307	1990–93
Mark Johnson	10	2	2	4	10	1981–82
Joey Johnston	11	1	0	1	6	1968–69
Marshall Johnston	49	0	5	5	16	1967–71
Kevin Kaminski	1	0	0	0	0	1988–89
Dan Keczmer	9	0	1	1	6	1990–91
Udo Kiessling	1	0	0	0	2	1981–82

Trent Klatt	48	4	19	23	38	1991–93
Dean Kolstad	30	1	5	6	57	1988–89, 1990–91
Gord Labossiere	38	10	7	17	4	1970–72
Rob Laird	1	0	0	0	0	1979–80
Dave Langevin	80	0	8	8	58	1985–86
Alain Langlais	25	4	4	8	10	1973–75
Peter Lappin	6	0	0	0	2	1989–90
Claude Larose	142	49	60	109	215	1968–70
Reed Larson	11	0	9	9	18	1988–89
Danny Lawson	96	13	16	29	25	1968–71
Brian Lawton	303	71	91	162	250	1983–88
Ken Leiter	4	0	0	0	0	1989–90
Louis Levasseur	1	0	0	0	0	1979–80
Craig Levie	51	8	15	23	52	1983–84, 1985–86
Lars Lindgren	59	2	14	16	33	1983–84
Pete LoPresti	173	0	3	3	6	1974–79
Craig Ludwig	151	3	19	22	207	1991–93
Len Lunde	7	0	1	1	0	1967–68
Al MacAdam	459	138	202	340	268	1978–84
Parker MacDonald	104	21	32	53	22	1967–69
Kim MacDougall	1	0	0	0	0	1974–75
Barry MacKenzie	6	0	1	1	6	1968–69
David Mackey	16	2	0	2	28	1989–90
Brian MacLellan	211	64	86	150	247	1986–89
Pat MacLeod	1	0	1	1	0	1990–91
Dean Magee	7	0	0	0	4	1977–78
Steve Maltais	12	2	1	3	2	1991–92
Dan Mandich	111	5	11	16	303	1982–86
Kris Manery	88	20	23	43	32	1978–80
Cesare Maniago	420	0	1	1	47	1967–76
Moe Mantha	46	10	19	29	14	1987–89
Milan Marcetta	54	7	15	22	10	1967–69
John Markell	1	0	0	0	0	1984–85
Terry Martin	7	1	1	2	0	1984–85
Tom Martin	4	1	1	2	4	1988–89
Don Martineau	76	6	9	15	61	1974–75
Steve Martinson	1	0	0	0	9	1991–92
Dennis Maruk	309	80	156	236	236	1978–79, 1983–89
Bill Masterton	38	4	8	12	4	1967–68
Markus Mattsson	2	0	0	0	0	1982–83
Richard Matvichuk	53	2	3	5	26	1992–93
Brad Maxwell	471	82	217	299	1031	1977–85, 1986–87
Bryan Maxwell	43	3	11	14	87	1977–79
Kevin Maxwell	18	1	7	8	15	1980–82
Tom McCarthy	385	146	187	333	293	1979–86
Ted McCaskill	4	0	2	2	0	1967–68
Bob McCord	139	7	26	33	109	1967–69
Jim McElmury	7	0	1	1	2	1972–73

Mike McHugh	12	0	0	0	2	1988–91
Bruce McIntosh	2	0	0	0	0	1972–73
Walt McKechnie	112	9	13	22	77	1967–71
Tony McKegney	108	28	41	69	68	1984–87
Jim McKenny	10	1	1	2	2	1978–79
Mike McMahon	117	14	44	58	92	1967–69
Mike McPhee	84	18	22	40	44	1992–93
Basil McRae	323	32	58	90	1567	1987–92
Ron Meighan	7	1	1	2	2	1981–82
Barrie Meissner	6	0	1	1	4	1967–69
Rollie Melanson	26	0	0	0	9	1984–86
Roger Melin	3	0	0	0	0	1980–82
Gilles Meloche	327	0	5	5	41	1978–85
Mitch Messier	20	0	2	2	11	1987–91
Pat Micheletti	12	2	0	2	8	1987–88
Lindsay Middlebrook	3	0	0	0	0	1981–82
Kip Miller	3	1	2	3	2	1991–92
John Miszuk	50	0	6	6	51	1969–70
Roy Mitchell	3	0	0	0	0	1992–93
Mike Modano	317	123	186	309	257	1988–93
Doug Mohns	162	12	48	60	148	1970–73
Jayson More	5	0	0	0	16	1989–90
Wayne Muloin	7	0	0	0	6	1970–71
Larry Murphy	121	18	75	93	94	1988–91
Frank Musil	271	14	46	60	547	1986–91
Jarmo Myllys	12	0	0	0	2	1988–91
Lou Nanne	635	68	157	225	356	1967–78
Rich Nantais	63	5	4	9	79	1974–77
Mark Napier	97	23	46	69	19	1983–85
Bob Nevin	138	20	32	52	6	1971–73
Kent Nilsson	105	29	77	106	22	1985–87
Rod Norrish	21	3	3	6	2	1973–75
Bill Nyrop	42	4	8	12	35	1981–82
Dennis O'Brien	470	27	75	102	836	1970–78
Murray Oliver	371	83	118	201	62	1970–75
Bill Orban	30	1	7	8	17	1968–70
Danny O'Shea	208	39	70	109	186	1968–71
Mark Osiecki	5	0	0	0	5	1992–93
Brad Palmer	95	26	27	53	40	1980–82
Bob Paradise	6	0	0	0	6	1971–72
Jean-Paul Parise	588	154	242	396	509	1967–75, 1978–79
Dusan Pasek	48	4	10	14	30	1988–89
Mark Pavelich	12	4	6	10	10	1986–87
Steve Payne	613	228	238	466	435	1978–88
Allen Pedersen	29	0	1	1	10	1991–92
Alex Pirus	155	30	26	56	94	1976–79
Bill Plager	60	0	5	5	61	1967–68, 1973–76
Willi Plett	317	70	63	133	1137	1982–87

Tom Polanic	19	0	2	2	53	1969–71
Mike Polich	225	24	29	53	57	1978–81
Jean Potvin	64	5	16	21	65	1978–79
Dan Poulin	3	1	1	2	2	1981–82
Dean Prentice	168	48	46	94	40	1971–74
Pat Price	14	0	2	2	20	1987–88
Andre Pronovost	8	0	0	0	0	1967–68
Brian Propp	147	41	73	114	107	1990–93
Chris Pryor	64	1	4	5	71	1984–88
Dan Quinn	11	0	4	4	6	1992–93
Rob Ramage	34	4	5	9	69	1991–92
Dick Redmond	16	0	3	3	20	1969–71
Tom Reid	615	17	106	123	617	1968–78
Dave Richter	120	4	14	18	397	1981–86
Fern Rivard	55	0	0	0	10	1968–75
Gordie Roberts	555	33	224	257	832	1980–88
Jim Roberts	106	17	23	40	33	1976–79
Scott Robinson	1	0	0	0	2	1989–90
John Rogers	14	2	4	6	0	1973–75
Doug Rombough	59	8	11	19	39	1974–76
Bob Rouse	351	9	58	67	735	1983–89
Bobby Rousseau	63	4	20	24	12	1970–71
Stephane Roy	12	1	0	1	0	1987–88
Duane Rupp	29	2	1	3	8	1968–69
Terry Ruskowski	50	6	13	19	78	1987–89
Scott Sandelin	1	0	0	0	0	1991–92
Mike Sands	6	0	0	0	2	1984–87
Gary Sargent	187	32	71	103	120	1978–83
Glen Sather	72	9	10	19	94	1975–76
Wally Schreiber	41	8	10	18	12	1987–89
Danny Seguin	11	1	1	2	4	1970–71
George Servinis	5	0	0	0	0	1987–88
Glen Sharpley	318	98	138	236	176	1976–81
David Shaw	37	0	7	7	49	1991–92
Gord Sherven	45	2	14	16	19	1984–86
Paul Shmyr	124	4	24	28	163	1979–81
Reid Simpson	1	0	0	0	5	1992–93
Ilkka Sinisalo	46	5	12	17	24	1990–91
Ville Siren	91	3	23	26	118	1988–90
Tommy Sjodin	77	7	29	36	30	1992–93
Darryl Sly	29	1	0	1	6	1969–70
Doug Smail	57	7	13	20	38	1990–91
Bobby Smith	572	185	369	554	487	1978–84, 1990–93
Brian Smith	9	0	1	1	0	1968–69
Derrick Smith	42	2	5	7	35	1991–93
Gary Smith	39	0	0	0	18	1976–78
Greg Smith	209	15	61	76	376	1978–81
Randy Smith	3	0	0	0	0	1985–87

Harold Snepsts	71	0	7	7	232	1984–85
Ken Solheim	114	16	20	36	27	1980–83, 1984–85
George Standing	2	0	0	0	0	1967–68
Fred Stanfield	111	24	46	70	22	1973–75
Bill Stewart	8	0	2	2	13	1985–86
Peter Taglianetti	16	0	1	1	14	1990–91
Kari Takko	131	0	1	1	30	1985–91
Dean Talafous	277	61	90	151	59	1974–78
Jean-Guy Talbot	4	0	0	0	4	1967–68
Ted Taylor	31	3	5	8	34	1967–68
Bill Terry	5	0	0	0	0	1987–88
Leo Thiffault*	—	—	—	—	—	1967–68
Mario Thyer	5	0	0	0	0	1989–90
Mark Tinordi	314	29	88	117	872	1988–93
Kirk Tomlinson	1	0	0	0	0	1987–88
Sean Toomey	1	0	0	0	0	1986–87
Tim Trimper	20	1	4	5	15	1984–85
Al Tuer	6	1	0	1	29	1987–88
Elmer Vasko	145	2	13	15	113	1967–70
Randy Velischek	88	6	11	17	38	1982–85
Emanuel Viveiros	29	1	11	12	6	1985–88
Darcy Wakaluk	65	0	3	3	40	1991–93
Carl Wetzel	5	0	0	0	0	1967–68
Tony White	6	0	0	0	4	1979–80
Bob Whitlock	1	0	0	0	0	1969–70
Neil Wilkinson	86	2	14	16	217	1989–91
Tom Williams	116	25	65	90	34	1969–71
Ron Wilson	113	19	52	71	62	1984–88
Lorne Worsley	107	0	2	2	34	1969–74
Bob Woytowich	66	4	17	21	63	1967–68
Tim Young	564	178	316	494	401	1975–83
Warren Young	5	1	1	2	0	1981–83
Tom Younghans	382	41	36	77	356	1976–82
Ron Zanussi	244	49	75	124	353	1977–81
Richard Zemlak	57	1	4	5	320	1987–89
Rob Zettler	80	1	12	13	164	1988–91

*Denotes player who only appeared in playoffs.

GOALTENDER STATISTICS

	GP	W	L	T	SO	GAA
Gary Bauman	33	5	17	6	0	3.64
Don Beaupre	316	126	125	45	3	3.74
Daniel Berthiaume	5	1	3	0	0	3.50
Ken Broderick	7	2	4	0	0	4.33
Jon Casey	325	128	126	42	12	3.28
Jim Craig	3	1	1	0	0	4.91
Gary Edwards	51	15	18	15	0	3.44
Gilles Gilbert	44	16	22	5	2	3.39
Paul Harrison	35	6	22	3	1	4.18
Brian Hayward	26	6	15	3	2	3.14
Steve Janaszak	1	0	0	1	0	2.00
Jean-Louis Levasseur	1	0	1	0	0	7.00
Pete LoPresti	173	43	101	20	5	4.06
Cesare Maniago	420	144	190	70	26	3.17
Markus Mattsson	2	1	1	0	1	3.60
Roland Melanson	26	7	11	5	0	4.17
Gilles Meloche	327	141	117	52	9	3.51
Lindsay Middlebrook	3	0	0	2	0	3.00
Jarmo Myllys	12	1	9	0	0	5.85
Fern Rivard	55	9	26	11	2	3.98
Mike Sands	6	0	5	0	0	5.17
Gary Smith	39	10	19	9	1	3.92
Kari Takko	131	33	67	14	1	3.87
Darcy Wakaluk	65	23	31	6	2	3.44
Carl Wetzel	5	1	2	1	0	4.01
Lorne (Gump) Worsley	107	39	37	24	3	2.62

REGULAR SEASON LEADERS

SEASONS

Neal Broten	13
Fred Barrett	12
Curt Giles	12
Lou Nanne	11
Craig Hartsburg	10
Tom Reid	10
Steve Payne	10
Bill Goldsworthy	10
Brian Bellows	10

GAMES

Neal Broten	876
Curt Giles	760
Brian Bellows	753
Fred Barrett	730
Bill Goldsworthy	670

GOALS

Brian Bellows	342
Dino Ciccarelli	332
Bill Goldsworthy	267
Neal Broten	249
Steve Payne	228

ASSISTS

Neal Broten	547
Brian Bellows	380
Bobby Smith	369
Dino Ciccarelli	319
Tim Young	316

POINTS

Neal Broten	796
Brian Bellows	722
Dino Ciccarelli	651
Bobby Smith	554
Bill Goldsworthy	506

PENALTY MINUTES

Basil McRae	1,567
Shane Churla	1,196
Willi Plett	1,137
Brad Maxwell	1,031
Mark Tinordi	870

GOALTENDER WINS

Cesare Maniago	143
Gilles Meloche	141
Jon Casey	128
Don Beaupre	126
Pete LoPresti	43

SHUTOUTS

Cesare Maniago	26
Jon Casey	12
Gilles Meloche	9
Pete LoPresti	5
Don Beaupre	3
Gump Worsley	3

PLAYOFF LEADERS

GAMES

Neal Broten	104
Curt Giles	92
Brian Bellows	81
Bobby Smith	77
Steve Payne	71

POINTS

Brian Bellows	83
Bobby Smith	76
Neal Broten	75
Steve Payne	70
Dino Ciccarelli	51

GOALS

Steve Payne	35
Brian Bellows	34
Dino Ciccarelli	28
Bobby Smith	26
Neal Broten	26

PENALTY MINUTES

Willi Plett	201
Basil McRae	174
Shane Churla	134
Brad Maxwell	131
Brian Bellows	111

ASSISTS

Bobby Smith	50
Brian Bellows	49
Neal Broten	49
Brad Maxwell	39
Steve Payne	35

GOALTENDER WINS

Jon Casey	21
Gilles Meloche	21
Don Beaupre	15
Cesare Maniago	14

CAPTAINS

Bob Woytowich	1967–68	Paul Shmyr	1979–81
Elmer Vasko	1968–69	Tim Young	1981–82
Claude Larose	1969–70	Craig Hartsburg	1982–88
Ted Harris	1970–74	Brian Bellows (Interim)	1983–84
Bill Goldsworthy	1974–76	Curt Fraser	1988–89
Bill Hogaboam	1976–77	Bob Rouse	1988–89
Nick Beverley	1977–78	Curt Giles	1988–91
J. P. Parise	1978–79	Mark Tinordi	1991–93

COACHES

Wren Blair	June 6, 1967–November 4, 1968
John Muckler	November 4, 1968–January 19, 1969
Wren Blair	January 19–December 28, 1969
Charlie Burns	December 28, 1969–April 1970
Jack Gordon	April 1970–December 20, 1973
Parker MacDonald	December 20, 1973–April 1974
Jack Gordon	April 1974–January 5, 1975
Charlie Burns	January 5–April 1975
Ted Harris	April 1975–November 24, 1977
Andre Beaulieu	November 24, 1977–February 10, 1978
Lou Nanne	February 10–July 5, 1978
Harry Howell	July 5–November 7, 1978
Glen Sonmor	November 7, 1978–January 15, 1982

Murray Oliver	January 15–22, 1982
Glen Sonmor	January 22, 1982–January 13, 1983
Murray Oliver	January 13–June 3, 1983
Bill Mahoney	June 3, 1983–November 8, 1984
Glen Sonmor	November 8, 1984–June 21, 1985
Lorne Henning	June 21, 1985–March 31, 1987
Glen Sonmor	March 31–April 23, 1987
Herb Brooks	April 23, 1987–July 6, 1988
Pierre Page	July 6, 1988–May 4, 1990
Bob Gainey	June 19, 1990–May 1993

GENERAL MANAGERS

Wren Blair	1967–74
Jack Gordon	1974–78
Lou Nanne	1978–88
Jack Ferreira	1988–90
Bob Clarke	1990–92
Bob Gainey	1992–93

TEAM PRESIDENTS

Walter Bush	1967–76
Gordon Ritz	1976–78
John Karr	1978–88
Lou Nanne	1988–90
Norman Green	1990–93

STANLEY CUP FINALISTS

1981

Paul Shmyr (captain), Kent-Erik Andersson, Fred Barrett, Don Beaupre, Neal Broten, Jack Carlson, Steve Christoff, Dino Ciccarelli, Mike Eaves, Curt Giles, Craig Hartsburg, Don Jackson, Al MacAdam, Brad Maxwell, Kevin Maxwell, Tom McCarthy, Gilles Meloche, Brad Palmer, Steve Payne, Mike Polich, Gordie Roberts, Gary Sargent, Bobby Smith, Greg Smith, Ken Solheim, Tim Young, Tom Younghans, Ron Zanussi

1991

Curt Giles (captain), Brian Bellows, Perry Berezan, Neal Broten, Marc Bureau, Jon Casey, Shawn Chambers, Shane Churla, Mike Craig, Ulf Dahlen, Chris Dahlquist, Gaetan Duchesne, Dave Gagner, Stewart Gavin, Brian Glynn, Brian Hayward, Jim Johnson, Basil McRae, Mike Modano, Brian Propp, Doug Smail, Bobby Smith, Mark Tinordi, Neil Wilkinson, Rob Zettler

NHL AWARD WINNERS

BILL MASTERTON TROPHY

Named for the late Minnesota North Stars player, it is awarded by the Professional Hockey Writers' Association to the NHL player "who exemplifies the qualities of perseverance, sportsmanship, and dedication to hockey."

Al MacAdam	1980

CALDER MEMORIAL TROPHY

Awarded to the league's outstanding rookie, as selected by a vote of hockey writers and broadcasters in each NHL city.

Danny Grant	1969
Bobby Smith	1979

LESTER PATRICK TROPHY

An annual award "for outstanding service to hockey in the United States." Eligible recipients include players, coaches, and executives.

Walter Bush Jr.	1973
Lou Nanne	1989
George Gund	1996
Neal Broten	1998
Reed Larson	2006
Glen Sonmor	2006
Mark Johnson	2011

MISCELLANEOUS TROPHIES AND AWARDS (TEAM)

Clarence S. Campbell Bowl	1990–91
Norris Division Champions	1983–84
Norris Division Champions	1981–82

NORTH STARS CLUB AWARDS

THE BILL MASTERTON MEMORIAL CUP

Presented to the North Stars player voted by his teammates to be most valuable to the team during the season.

1992–93	Mike Modano
1991–92	Mike Modano
1990–91	Dave Gagner
1989–90	Brian Bellows
1988–89	Dave Gagner and Curt Giles
1987–88	Dino Ciccarelli
1986–87	Dino Ciccarelli
1985–86	Neal Broten
1984–85	Curt Giles
1983–84	Neal Broten
1982–83	Gordie Roberts
1981–82	Gilles Meloche
1980–81	Curt Giles
1979–80	Al MacAdam
1978–79	Gilles Meloche
1977–78	Per-Olov Brasar
1976–77	Tim Young
1975–76	Cesare Maniago
1974–75	Bill Goldsworthy
1973–74	Bill Goldsworthy
1972–73	Dennis Hextall
1971–72	Murray Oliver
1970–71	Cesare Maniago
1969–70	J. P. Parise
1968–69	Claude Larose
1967–68	Cesare Maniago

THE TOM DILL MEMORIAL CUP

Presented to the North Stars defenseman voted most proficient by a panel selected from members of the media who covered the team regularly.

1992–93	Mark Tinordi
1991–92	Chris Dahlquist
1990–91	Mark Tinordi
1989–90	Curt Giles
1988–89	Curt Giles
1987–88	Curt Giles
1986–87	Craig Hartsburg
1985–86	Curt Giles
1984–85	Curt Giles
1983–84	Gordie Roberts
1982–83	Gordie Roberts

1981–82	Craig Hartsburg
1980–81	Craig Hartsburg
1979–80	Fred Barrett
1978–79	Greg Smith
1977–78	Fred Barrett
1976–77	Nick Beverley
1975–76	Fred Barrett
1974–75	Fred Barrett
1973–74	Lou Nanne
1972–73	Ted Harris
1971–72	Barry Gibbs
1970–71	Ted Harris
1969–70	Leo Boivin
1968–69	Elmer Vasko

ROOKIE OF THE YEAR TROPHY

Awarded annually to the North Stars player selected by his teammates as most proficient in his first year.

1992–93	Trent Klatt
1991–92	Derian Hatcher
1990–91	Mike Craig
1989–90	Mike Modano
1988–89	Shawn Chambers
1987–88	Dave Archibald
1986–87	Kari Takko
1985–86	Jon Casey
1984–85	Bob Rouse
1983–84	Brian Lawton
1982–83	Brian Bellows
1981–82	Neal Broten
1980–81	Don Beaupre
1979–80	Mike Eaves
1978–79	Bobby Smith
1977–78	Per-Olov Brasar
1976–77	Roland Eriksson
1975–76	Tim Young
1974–75	Peter LoPresti
1973–74	Gary Gambucci
1972–73	Gilles Gilbert
1971–72	No award given
1970–71	Jude Drouin
1969–70	Barry Gibbs
1968–69	Danny Grant
1967–68	Andre Boudrias

LEADING SCORER TROPHY

Awarded annually to the North Stars player who led the team in scoring during the regular season.

1992–93	Mike Modano
1991–92	Mike Modano
1990–91	Dave Gagner
1989–90	Brian Bellows
1988–89	Dave Gagner
1987–88	Dino Ciccarelli
1986–87	Dino Ciccarelli
1985–86	Neal Broten
1984–85	Brian Bellows
1983–84	Neal Broten
1982–83	Neal Broten and Bobby Smith
1981–82	Bobby Smith
1980–81	Bobby Smith
1979–80	Al MacAdam
1978–79	Bobby Smith
1977–78	Roland Eriksson
1976–77	Tim Young
1975–76	Tim Young
1974–75	Dennis Hextall
1973–74	Dennis Hextall
1972–73	Dennis Hextall
1971–72	Bill Goldsworthy
1970–71	Jude Drouin
1969–70	J. P. Parise
1968–69	Danny Grant

MOST IMPROVED PLAYER TROPHY

Awarded annually to the North Stars player deemed most improved over the previous season by a panel of sportswriters and broadcasters.

1992–93	Russ Courtnall
1991–92	Ulf Dahlen
1990–91	Mark Tinordi
1989–90	Jon Casey
1988–89	Dave Gagner
1987–88	Brian Bellows
1986–87	Brian Lawton
1985–86	Scott Bjugstad
1984–85	Randy Velischek
1983–84	Brian Bellows
1982–83	Gordie Roberts
1981–82	Gordie Roberts
1980–81	Kent-Erik Andersson
1979–80	Steve Payne
1978–79	Brad Maxwell

MOST POPULAR PLAYER AWARD

Presented each season to the North Stars player named most popular in a vote conducted during the year among spectators at home games.

1992–93	Mike Modano
1991–92	Ulf Dahlen and Mike Modano
1990–91	Jon Casey and Mike Modano
1989–90	Mike Modano
1988–89	Neal Broten
1987–88	Dino Ciccarelli
1986–87	Dino Ciccarelli
1985–86	Neal Broten
1984–85	Willi Plett
1983–84	Neal Broten
1982–83	Neal Broten
1981–82	Neal Broten and Dino Ciccarelli
1980–81	Steve Christoff
1979–80	Al MacAdam
1978–79	Bobby Smith
1977–78	Per-Olov Brasar
1976–77	Roland Eriksson
1975–76	Pierre Jary
1974–75	Peter LoPresti
1973–74	Bill Goldsworthy
1972–73	Dennis Hextall
1971–72	Lou Nanne
1970–71	Jude Drouin
1969–70	Bill Goldsworthy
1968–69	Danny Grant
1967–68	J. P. Parise and Cesare Maniago

STAR OF THE GAME AWARD

Presented to the North Stars player selected most often as the Star of the Game in the season-long selection for each home game.

1992–93	Russ Courtnall
1991–92	Mike Modano
1990–91	Dave Gagner
1989–90	Jon Casey
1988–89	Dave Gagner
1987–88	Dino Ciccarelli
1986–87	Dino Ciccarelli
1985–86	Don Beaupre
1984–85	Steve Payne
1983–84	Neal Broten
1982–83	Brian Bellows
1981–82	Neal Broten
1980–81	Bobby Smith
1979–80	Al MacAdam
1978–79	Bobby Smith
1977–78	Per-Olov Brasar

COMMUNITY SERVICE AWARD

Awarded annually to a member of the North Stars organization for showing a strong commitment to community and service.

1992–93	Dave Gagner
1991–92	Mark Tinordi
1990–91	Curt Giles
1989–90	Curt Giles
1988–89	Frantisek Musil
1987–88	Basil McRae
1986–87	Dennis Maruk and Brian Bellows
1985–86	Brian Bellows
1984–85	Dennis Maruk
1983–84	Dennis Maruk
1982–83	John Mariucci
1981–82	Walter Bush Jr.

HOCKEY HALL OF FAME

Lorne (Gump) Worsley	1980
John Mariucci	1985
Leo Boivin	1986
Al Shaver	1993
Mike Gartner	2001
Larry Murphy	2004
Dino Ciccarelli	2010
Mike Modano	2014

UNITED STATES HOCKEY HALL OF FAME

John Mariucci	1973
Robert B. Ridder Sr.	1976
Robert (Bob) Dill	1979
Walter Bush Jr.	1980
Thomas (Tommy) Williams	1981
Bob Paradise	1989
Herb Brooks	1990
Dave Langevin	1993
Henry Boucha	1995
Reed Larson	1996
Bill Nyrop	1997
Gordie Roberts	1999
Lou Nanne	1998
Neal Broten	2000
Mark Johnson	2004
Murray Williamson	2005
Gary Gambucci	2006
Aaron Broten	2007
Derian Hatcher	2010
Dr. V. George Nagobads	2010
Mike Modano	2012
Ron Wilson	2017
Paul Holmgren	2021

Note: Both Hall of Fame lists include former North Stars players as well as club executives, hockey operations staff, team physicians, and broadcasters.

NORTH STARS IN THE NHL ALL-STAR GAME

1967–68	Dave Balon
1968–69	Danny Grant, Claude Larose, Danny O'Shea, Elmer Vasko
1969–70	Bill Goldsworthy, Danny Grant, Claude Larose, Danny O'Shea, J. P. Parise.
1970–71	Danny Grant, Ted Harris
1971–72	Bill Goldsworthy, Ted Harris, Doug Mohns, Gump Worsley
1972–73	Barry Gibbs, J. P. Parise
1973–74	Bill Goldsworthy, Dennis Hextall
1974–75	Bill Goldsworthy (did not play, injured), Dennis Hextall
1975–76	Bill Goldsworthy
1976–77	Tim Young
1977–78	Roland Eriksson
1978–79	No All-Star Game (Challenge Cup)
1979–80	Craig Hartsburg, Gilles Meloche, Steve Payne, Gary Sargent (did not play, injured)
1980–81	Don Beaupre, Bobby Smith
1981–82	Dino Ciccarelli, Craig Hartsburg, Gilles Meloche, Bobby Smith
1982–83	Neal Broten, Dino Ciccarelli, Craig Hartsburg, Tom McCarthy
1983–84	Brian Bellows, Brad Maxwell
1984–85	Tony McKegney (did not play, injured), Steve Payne
1985–86	Neal Broten
1986–87	No All-Star Game (Rendez-Vous '87)
1987–88	Brian Bellows
1988–89	Dino Ciccarelli
1989–90	Mike Gartner
1990–91	Dave Gagner
1991–92	Brian Bellows, Mark Tinordi
1992–93	Jon Casey, Mike Modano

RETIRED NUMBERS

No. 19	Bill Masterton (Retired on January 17, 1987)
No. 8	Bill Goldsworthy (Retired on February 15, 1992)

ANNUAL AVERAGE ATTENDANCE

1967–68	11,861	1980–81	14,180
1968–69	12,919	1981–82	15,220
1969–70	14,317	1982–83	14,485
1970–71	14,503	1983–84	14,355
1971–72	15,319	1984–85	13,480
1972–73	15,264	1985–86	13,215
1973–74	15,251	1986–87	13,512
1974–75	13,587	1987–88	11,440
1975–76	9,655	1988–89	9,795
1976–77	9,083	1989–90	11,354
1977–78	8,666	1990–91	7,838
1978–79	10,722	1991–92	13,447
1979–80	13,094	1992–93	13,910

PRIMARY MINOR LEAGUE AFFILIATES

1967–68	Memphis South Stars (CHL)
1968–69	Memphis South Stars (CHL)
1969–70	Iowa Stars (CHL)
1970–71	Cleveland Barons (AHL)
1971–72	Cleveland Barons (AHL)
1972–73	Cleveland/Jacksonville Barons (AHL)
1973–74	New Haven Nighthawks (AHL)
1974–75	New Haven Nighthawks (AHL)
1975–76	New Haven Nighthawks (AHL)
1976–77	New Haven Nighthawks (AHL)
1977–78	Oklahoma City Stars (CHL)
1978–79	Oklahoma City Stars (CHL)
1979–80	Oklahoma City Stars (CHL)
1980–81	Oklahoma City Stars (CHL)
1981–82	Nashville South Stars (CHL)
1982–83	Birmingham South Stars (CHL)
1983–84	Salt Lake Golden Eagles (CHL)
1984–85	Springfield Indians (AHL)
1985–86	Springfield Indians (AHL)
1986–87	Springfield Indians (AHL)
1987–88	Kalamazoo Wings (IHL)
1988–89	Kalamazoo Wings (IHL)
1989–90	Kalamazoo Wings (IHL)
1990–91	Kalamazoo Wings (IHL)
1991–92	Kalamazoo Wings (IHL)
1992–93	Kalamazoo Wings (IHL)

BIBLIOGRAPHY

Beddoes, Richard, Ira Gitler, and Stan Fischler. *Hockey: The Story of the World's Fastest Sport*. New York: Macmillan, 1971.

Blair, Wren. *The Bird*. Etobicoke ON: Quarry Press, 2002.

Brown, Frank, and Sherry Ross. *Hockey Scouting Report 1991-92*. Vancouver BC: Douglas & McIntyre, 1991.

Diamond, Dan. *National Hockey League Official Guide & Record Book*. Chicago: Triumph Books, 2003.

———. *Total Hockey: The Official Encyclopedia of the National Hockey League*. New York: Total Sports, 1998.

———. *Total NHL*. Toronto: Dan Diamond & Associates, 2003.

Duff, Bob. *The Bruise Brothers: Hockey's Heavyweight Champions*. Wayne IL: Immortal Investments, 2008.

Duhatschek, Erik, Trent Fayne, Lance Hornby, and Gord Miller. *Hockey Chronicles: An Insider History of National Hockey League Teams*. New York: Checkmark Books, 2001.

Farrington, S. Kip, Jr. *Skates, Sticks and Men: The Story of Amateur Hockey in the United States*. New York: David Mackay, 1972.

Fischler, Stan. *Hockey Stars Speak*. Toronto: Warwick, 1996.

Gilbert, John. *Herb Brooks: The Inside Story of a Hockey Mastermind*. Minneapolis: MVP Books, 2008.

Hollander, Zander. *The Complete Handbook of Pro Hockey*. New York: Signet Books, 1981, 1985.

Hunter, Douglas. *A Breed Apart*. Toronto: Penguin Books, 1998.

Irvin, Dick. *In the Crease*. Toronto: McClelland & Stewart, 1996.

Libby, Bill. *Pro Hockey Heroes of Today*. New York: Random House, 1974.

Lowe, Kevin, with Stan and Shirley Fischler. *Champions: The Making of the Edmonton Oilers*. Scarborough ON: Prentice-Hall, 1988.

McDonell, Chris. *Hockey All-Stars: The NHL Honor Roll*. Buffalo NY: Firefly Books, 2000.

McFarlane, Brian. *Fifty Years of Hockey: An Intimate History of the National Hockey League*. Toronto: Pagurian Press, 1970.

Nelson, Kevin. *Slap Shots*. New York: Fireside Books, 1995.

Proudfoot, Jim. *Pro Hockey '72-'73*. New York: Pocket Books, 1972.

Ronberg, Gary. *The Ice Men*. New York: Crown, 1973.

Ross, Sherry. *Hockey Scouting Report 2000*. Vancouver BC: Greystone Books, 1999.

Schofield, Mary Halverson. *Henry Boucha: Star of the North*. Edina MN: Snow-
  shoe Press, 1999.
Sonmor, Glen, with Ross Bernstein. *Old Time Hockey*. Egan MN: Bernstein
  Books, 2007.
Stein, Gil. *Power Plays: An Inside Look at the Big Business of the National Hockey
  League*. Seacaucus NJ: Birch Lane Press, 1997.
Townsend, Murray, and Dan Hamilton. Fearless: *Pro Hockey's Most Fearless
  (and Feared) Players*. New York: Universe, 2000.
Weir, Glenn, Jeff Chapman, and Travis Weir. *Ultimate Hockey*. Toronto: Stod-
  dart, 1999.

NEWSPAPERS AND MAGAZINES

Boston Herald
Calgary Herald
Chicago Sun-Times
Chicago Tribune
Dallas Morning News
Detroit Free Press
ESPN *The Magazine*
Fort Worth Star-Telegram
Hartford Courant
Hockey Digest
Hockey News
Hockey Stars
Minneapolis Star-Tribune
Montreal Gazette
New York Daily News
New York Post
New York Times
Ottawa Sun
People
Pittsburgh Post-Gazette
Providence Journal
Rochester Democrat & Chronicle
Rocky Mountain News
San Francisco Chronicle
San Jose Mercury News
Sporting News
Sports Illustrated
St. Louis Post-Dispatch
St. Paul Pioneer Press
Toronto Globe & Mail
Toronto Star
USA *Today*
Vancouver Sun
Washington Post
Washington Times

WEBSITES

Internet Hockey Database (hockeydb.com)
Hockey Draft Central (hockeydraftcentral.com)
Legends of Hockey (legendsofhockey.net)
NHL.com
NHL Trade Tracker (nhltradetracker.com)